Profile of a Nation

Profile of a Nation: Trump's Mind, America's Soul

By Bandy X. Lee, MD, MDiv

World Mental Health Coalition, Inc.
New York, NY

A World Mental Health Coalition Book

Profile of a Nation: Trump's Mind, America's Soul

www.worldmhc.org
www.bandylee.com

Cover Design by Stacey L. Pritchett
Special consultant Mark A. Bruzonsky

Library of Congress Cataloging-in-Publication Data available upon request.

ISBN 978-1-7355537-4-0 (softcover)
ISBN 978-1-7355537-5-7 (ebook)

To my fellow Americans, yearning to be free

CONTENTS

PREFACE

This is an unprecedented report meant for unprecedented times. It seeks to keep with the principles and standards of psychiatry over format of typical presentation, since, for an extraordinary situation, trying to keep with appearances can also lead to distortion. It is written because, if not for dealing with a global mental health emergency, wherein at stake could be nothing less than humanity's survival, I do not know what psychiatry is good for. The public will understand this, as it has from the moment it made the request....

So how did a clinician consultant and academic psychiatrist with no background or interest in politics come to speak up nationally about the president? I often say politics invaded my area of expertise, and that would be true. I was in forensic psychiatry, with an almost twenty-year career working with violent offenders. I consulted widely on prison reform and collaborated with governments and international organizations on public health approaches to violence prevention.

In the context of my work increasingly turning global, with an eye on preventing genocides, gender-based violence, and civil wars, domestic U.S. politics was the last on my mind. Yet I was unexpectedly summoned the morning after the 2016 presidential election, starting at 8:00 a.m., when my phone was ringing off the hook and emails were flooding in from civil society organizations, patient advocacy groups, lawyers, students, activists, civil servants, and documentary filmmakers—mostly because of my work with a high-profile prison reform project in New York City. They were contacting me because they were afraid of the violence that was to come, and they were right. In the midst of answering those calls, I had to ask myself: If I have devoted my career to studying, predicting, and preventing violence, could I turn away now, in the face of potentially the greatest risk of violence we could ever confront?

It was the morning Donald Trump was elected to the presidency. Growing up in New York City, I knew of him as a libertine tabloid personality, a failed businessman, and somewhat a crook, but I did not consider him necessarily dangerous. He came to a Broadway producer friend of mine while in his early twenties, trying to get into show business, but as he was only interested in the credits and the showcasing of his name, my Tony Award-winning friend told him off: "Go back to real estate!" (My friend regrets this advice to this day, for he believes his words may not have been without influence at a pivotal point.) A handful of other friends, all women, had direct encounters with him and, despite being from higher society than he, experienced uniformly hurtful, degrading treatment with gratuitous humiliation mixed into their otherwise simple, passing interactions. Still, I may have considered him an odious personality but not dangerous.

Then, in 2015 I saw him televised during one of his direct interactions with followers, and by now a seasoned psychiatrist who saw things differently, I recognized the personality patterns and the interpersonal dynamic I specialize in treating among offenders of violence—and this was very dangerous. Still, I was too preoccupied with personal affairs at the time, taking care of my mother who had gone from a seeming perfect state of health to passing away in less than a year. Glioblastoma is what Senator John McCain and Vice President Joseph Biden's son, Beau Biden, also had, and its course is swift. While my mother had followed politics, it was never my area, and I had just returned from another trip abroad after her departure—until the citizen calls came on the morning after the election. Still, things seemed remote, even otherworldly. My mother had been far more socially conscious than I, and my public role was about to coincide with my determination to take on her legacy.

At that time, a former colleague from Harvard, Dr. Judith Herman, had written to President Barack Obama, along with two other psychiatrists, Drs. Nanette Gartrell and Dee Mosbacher, asking that the president-elect undergo a neuropsychiatric evaluation. Delighted to find like minds, I reconnected with Dr. Herman after more than a dozen years and became acquainted with her colleagues, with whom I formed invaluable friendships. I started composing letters myself, but those around me, while unanimously agreeing that the situation was dangerous, would not put their names to any letter. They were essentially afraid that they would spend the rest of their careers fighting for their licenses in light of the litigious and vindictive president, or that they may have to fear for their and their family's safety in light of his violence-prone followers. I thought to myself all the more that a breaking of ice was necessary and decided to organize a conference at my institution, the Yale School of Medicine.

Foremost on my mind was ethics—how can we meet our societal

responsibility, while speaking ethically and responsibly? I wished to give consideration to an ethical guideline we informally call "the Goldwater rule," which encourages activities that improve the community and better public health by educating the public when asked about public figures—only without diagnosing. It was simply a repetition of good standards of practice. But what was alarming was the fact that, shortly after Donald Trump's inauguration, the American Psychiatric Association expanded the caution not to diagnose without a personal examination and not to publicize a diagnosis without authorization—to cover far beyond just diagnosis. From now on, restrictions would apply to any comment on any objective observation—even in an emergency, without exception. No other ethical guideline held such absolute status. In other words, it was turned into a prohibition, a gag order, that now abandoned the affirmative obligation of "the Goldwater rule," which included educating the public and improving community health, not to mention all other core medical obligations such as placing safety first—all in subordination to privileging a public figure!

Never mind what history has shown us regarding what silencing relevant voices does under dangerous regimes. This change was shocking enough for me to drop everything in order to speak up. The question I wished to address was, if there were a restriction on our speech about a public figure, like a patient (since a public figure isn't a patient), then shouldn't there be situations where there is a positive duty to speak, as with a patient (since even confidentiality, as sacrosanct as it is in psychiatry, has exceptions)? To answer this question, I invited top members of my field, each of whom I had known for at least fifteen years and could attest to their exemplary ethical stances from other dark times: Dr. Judith Herman, certainly, and also Drs. Robert Jay Lifton and James Gilligan, and Dr. Charles Dike, a colleague from my division currently on the American Psychiatric Association's ethics committee, whom I invited to speak first.

At the end of the conference, our conclusion was that we had a duty to warn and that the dangers were too great: the public was in the process of believing that the new president was finally settling in and about to "pivot" to normalcy. We, however, knew too much about human behavior for any conclusion other than that Donald Trump's disturbances would place the country and the world in existential danger—not to mention be a threat to governmental institutions, social norms, and, ultimately, the fabric of the country. In other words, that psychological dangerousness in the most powerful office on the planet would translate into social, cultural, and geopolitical dangerousness was only a matter of time.

Even though we had held the conference in the largest auditorium of the School, the audience did not exceed two dozen. This "failure" soon turned into the realization that hundreds had tuned in online, confirming that there was great interest but also considerable fear—and as the meeting received national and international attention, eventually thousands of mental health professionals from all over the country as well as from multiple continents got in touch. I quickly realized that this was historic, that we had a medical consensus, and from that arose the National Coalition of Concerned Mental Health Experts, now the World Mental Health Coalition.

Immediately after the conference, an editor of Macmillan Publishers contacted me, as we were just putting together the proceedings of the conference into a public-service book. When it was released in early October, it became an instant *New York Times* bestseller—unusual for a multi-authored book of specialized knowledge. We could see that it spoke to the public's hunger for understanding. The book was *The Dangerous Case of Donald Trump: 27 Psychiatrists and Mental Health Experts Assess a President*, intended for the sharing of expertise as a public service and donation of all revenues to the public good. In it, we warned that his condition was more serious than people assumed, that it would grow worse with actual power, and that he would eventually become uncontainable. By the end, it was on the bestseller list for seven weeks and the *Washington Post* dubbed it "the Most Courageous Book of the Year."

Meanwhile, various Congress members who heard of the conference began reaching out. Initially, I consulted with them privately over the phone. One influential former Majority and Minority House Leader said he would like to arrange for me to testify before the whole Congress and proposed early September, when the Congress would have just returned for session. For various political and other reasons, this did not happen, and both September and October passed.

By November, Special Counsel Robert Mueller, who had been appointed to investigate Russia's role in influencing the 2016 presidential election, released his first indictments, and the president began showing signs of deterioration. Two White House officials got in touch with me about their concerns over his "unraveling," but with so few mental health professionals speaking up, I did not wish to compromise my educative role by taking him on as a "patient". Hence, I elicited only limited information and referred them to the emergency room, hoping that this might lead to the recruitment of another psychiatrist. When I called the on-call psychiatrist after the referral, however, he was hostile and made clear he did not wish to get involved; no matter the condition of the president, his main concern was to be left alone. This is another regret I have: I underestimated the reluctance to apply standard psychiatric procedures, simply because it concerns a president. Why, is a president not a human being who deserves care like everyone else? Is he not an equal citizen within a republic?

If I had been more experienced in the media world at that time—in other words, knew what I do now—I would have requested a public statement from the two gentlemen, or an appearance in the media with me to spell out our concerns to the public. I was still thinking in terms of choosing between the roles of provider and educator. Of note, people have asked me if either of them seemed to be the famous "anonymous" White House official who wrote a *New York Times* opinion piece and later a book; I have said no, since the anonymous official was initially confident in his and other insiders' ability to handle the situation, whereas the two gentlemen who got in touch with me were more correct in their estimation that they could not.

In early December 2017, impatient of hearing about no movement regarding my congressional testimony, former Assistant U.S. Attorney Sheila Nielsen arranged for me to meet with a dozen Democratic Congress members of her own contacts. I asked Dr. James Gilligan, a foremost violence expert, to join me, and we found that the lawmakers were eager beyond expectation: one senator even stated that it was his most awaited meeting in eleven years! Overall, I was impressed that our country had such seemingly capable, informed, and concerned leaders; I was immensely humbled when one of them called me his "hero". Nevertheless, they said that, while they shared our concerns, they did not feel they could do anything, being in the minority party. Surprisingly, they looked to us! They stated that they had little power, but if we continued to educate the public as we had been, from a professional point of view, then they might be able to garner the public's support to do something. They confided that they knew of Republican lawmakers who were also very concerned about the president but doubted they would act on those concerns, and so this would be the only way. They turned out to be right: even fears that the president would trigger "World War III," as one Republican senator put it, did not prevent Republican lawmakers from rallying behind him when it became time to pass tax legislation.

Therefore, in January 2018, when the president tweeted that his "Nuclear Button ... is a much bigger & more powerful one" than North Korean leader Kim Jong-Un's, I gave up waiting for Republican Congress members to consult with me and went to the press. For several days, I was interviewing for fifteen hours a day without a break, and invitations came in from all the most prominent prime time programs on CNN, MSNBC, network television, and even Fox News. I put aside all other tasks to attend to this national need, while the president's mental health was the number one national conversation and in the news every day. I declined the biggest shows that could only promise five to ten minutes of discussion, however, to allow for a slower, more serious buildup of discussion that did not sensationalize—another decision I would regret later. I regretted this because, just as it seemed we were getting somewhere, the American Psychiatric Association (APA) stepped in and made public accusations I thought I would never encounter: claiming we were practicing "armchair psychiatry," using psychiatry as a "political tool," and doing for "self-aggrandizing purposes." The irony of these attributions was that it was violating its own, stricter version of "the Goldwater rule" that it adopted with the Trump presidency, prohibiting not just diagnosis but making any comment of any kind on public figures, without a personal examination and without authorization—and I was a public figure at this point! What was puzzling apart from its claim to know my innermost intentions was that its arguments did not make any sense from an ethical or scientific point of view. The highly acerbic, seemingly unprofessional attacks also seemed unbecoming of a professional organization. Later, I would come to learn that this is characteristic of institutions that choose to side with power over principle. By this time, numerous chairs of psychiatry departments and other prominent psychiatrists from around the country had reached out to me with compliments and gratitude, but the APA's position halted their ability to come forth publicly. Is this how it goes, no matter how wrong the leadership of the professional establishment is? I wondered to myself. And I wonder to this day what might have happened if all these figures in power positions felt free to come out in unison; it was a much riskier proposition now.

By the fall of 2018, the nation was reeling after the deadliest anti-Semitic attack in U.S. history and an extraordinary "pipe bomber" sending sixteen explosives to prominent Democrats, including the former president, former vice president, and former presidential candidate, as well as critics of the president. The obvious immediate source? The incendiary rhetoric of a president who would do anything to sway mid-term elections. By then, white supremacist killings had already more than doubled, hate crimes jumped 226 percent in counties that hosted his rallies, mass shootings rose to an all-time high, and gun deaths more generally rose to their highest in twenty-five years, not to mention widespread schoolyard bullying in his name, a more hostile civic life, and a more divided country with common threats of a civil war to defend the president. This is all without mentioning the creation of thousands of young orphans and bereaved families at the U.S.-Mexico border, the emboldening of despots around the world as they committed human rights abuses and murders of journalists with impunity, the heightened risk of war in many unstable regions, and a renewed nuclear arms race.

Crises only deepened through 2019, which began with the longest government shutdown in U.S. history, because of the president's insistence on funding for a wall on the southern border, creating needless hardship for 800,000 federal employee families. Public pleas for us to speak more never ceased to pour into our web site despite the drying up of media inquiries. Meanwhile, the World Mental Health Coalition had grown multifold in size, with membership from four continents, and it incorporated into a nonprofit organization with officers and a full board of directors.

The new Democratic-majority House of Representatives was sworn in in January 2019, but it did not proceed immediately with impeachment as expected. In March 2019, with the release of the second edition of *The Dangerous Case of Donald Trump*, now updated with ten more mental health experts to make thirty-seven, we held an interdisciplinary conference to bring attention to the need. Thirteen top experts from the fields of psychiatry, law, history, political science, economics, social psychology, journalism, propaganda studies, nuclear science, and climate science came together in unprecedented ways to explain how the president was unfit from each of their perspectives. Renowned economist Jeffrey Sachs moderated the event, which was held in the National Press Club Grand Ballroom, and C-SPAN broadcast it. Attendees, stunned at the caliber and sheer number of illustrious experts on a single panel, stated that the lack of news coverage was "shocking." Some asked: "What does it say about our country that a monumental, unparalleled event such as this is attracting no attention?"

With only political pundits commenting on a matter requiring of expert-level knowledge, a malignant normality set in, providing fertile ground for pathology to spread. What ensued was psychological conditioning for the continual gutting of institutions, the replacement of career personnel with unqualified flatterers, and the catering to a president's emotional needs at the expense of public good, until presidential powers were used only to expand personal power. The lack of media coverage did not match the flood of public inquiries to our web site.

We tried our best to perform our professional societal duty. When Special Counsel Robert Mueller released his report on a two-year investigation into the Russian government's interference in the 2016 elections and the role of Mr. Trump's campaign in it, we issued our own "report on the Mueller report." Attorney General William Barr had preempted its public release with his own summary of the report, falsely interpreting as it an exoneration of both conspiracy and obstruction of justice. An alarmed special counsel issued a letter that attempted to correct the interpretation, requesting that his own summary be released, but the psychological conditioning for dismissal was already complete. Mr. Mueller's report, when released a month later, revealed an alarming pattern of numerous attempts at or requests for cooperation from the Russians, regardless of whether or not there was a formally agreed-upon conspiracy, and a dozen counts of obstruction that merely could not be prosecuted while the president was in office, but it did not matter. The attorney general had paved the way for the president's ability to claim: "total exoneration." If Mr. Mueller's report was not usable for prosecution, it allowed us the perfect information to perform a mental capacity evaluation, which we did as a public service: it contained within it abundant, high-quality reports from coworkers and close associates of direct interactions with the president, under sworn testimony. Drs. Edwin Fisher, Leonard Glass, James Merikangas, James Gilligan, and I formed a panel to prepare the report: "Mental Health Analysis of the Special Counsel's Report on the Investigation into Russian Interference in the 2016 Presidential Election." This assessment showed, definitively, that the president did not meet any of the standard criteria for rational decision-making, and therefore lacked the basic mental capacity to discharge the duties of his office. We offered a chance for the president to interview with us if he believed himself fit, but while we learned that he received our communication, he did not respond within our timeframe. We therefore went ahead and published our recommendations that: (a) the president be removed from access to the nuclear codes; and (2) his war-making powers be curtailed.

However, without inroads into a public conversation, our report went ignored. We had planned a town hall with several Congress members the day before Mr. Mueller's Congressional testimony in July 2019, but his last-minute postponement of it gave us only the option to hold it online. We organized a conference at Yale Law School in September 2019, with former Chief White House Ethics Counsel Richard Painter as speaker, only to learn that the Law School, having gradually changed from a public interest focus to power-centeredness over the sixteen years I had been teaching there, was quite hostile. It may not even have been possible without the sponsorship of former Dean Robert Post, a champion of free speech and academic freedom. Then, everything changed later that month. A whistleblower revealed that the president had allegedly abused his powers and the governmental purse by pressuring Ukrainian President Volodymyr Zelensky to investigate the front-running Democratic presidential candidate's son, Hunter Biden, so that it could be used for campaigning advantage. In response, Speaker of the

House Nancy Pelosi, who had long resisted calls for impeachment, finally announced an impeachment inquiry.

Upon this news, we had to get to work. While we had long encouraged early impeachment for behavioral management reasons, proceeding now after a protracted delay, after having allowed the president to balloon in his false sense of omnipotence and impunity, was dangerous. In early October 2019, Drs. Stephen Soldz, Fisher, and I, along with more than 250 mental health professionals, sent in an urgent letter to the Congress warning of the president's psychological dangers. Three days later, he ordered the withdrawal of troops from northern Syria, without warning and catching our European allies by surprise, that caused the massacre of our Kurdish allies and destabilized the region. In early December 2019, Drs. John Zinner, Jerrold Post, and I, along with over 800 mental health professionals, sent in another warning against proceeding with impeachment without guardrails. One month later, the president ordered the assassination of a top Iranian general, Qassim Soleimani, without justification, taking us to the brink of war with Iran. We still tried, issuing a final warning from the World Mental Health Coalition of the need urgently to contain his psychological dangers, but the House proceeded to the end without consulting with us, voting to impeach and then handing over the articles of impeachment, which we had already advised were too few and should be held onto. As a result, the House's hesitations only enraged him and failed to contain him when the Senate acquitted him through a sham trial without witnesses or evidence. Once he was clear, the president went on a revenge spree against those who lawfully testified against him, while pardoning and hiring war criminals before declaring himself the law of the land.

Our final warning came less than two weeks before the first case of the novel coronavirus was to be detected within the United States. Now, the same danger we were warning against turned into a domestic threat: a president who fights facts and reality for psychopathological reasons was now in charge of leading the nation through a deadly pandemic. Not only had he defunded the Centers for Disease Control and Prevention (CDC) and dismantled the pandemic response teams that had been lauded throughout the world, out of pathological envy of his predecessor, he had fired the CDC team in China whose job it was to detect and prevent the very kind of respiratory infectious disease as was to arise in China just months later. While China began its response similarly as the United States—stifling expert voices, spreading misinformation, and helping the virus to gain a tenacious hold—it quickly changed course when the rapid spread of the virus threatened both its international standing and its control over the population at home. The

United States, on the under hand, showed no such versatility and, with the pandemic occurring at a moment of peak perception of impunity and fewest moderating forces against the person in charge, quickly superseded China in infections and deaths.

Donald Trump went as far as to call the pandemic a Democrats' "hoax", resisting widespread testing, and pushing for policies that would artificially prop up the economy while putting lives at greater risk—until the United States became the world's pandemic epicenter. Once he made this misstep, there was no going back, for he could never admit an error and never take responsibility. He did everything possible to refuse providing personal protective equipment, to delay invoking the Defense Production Act, and to resist the testing, tracing, and isolating that was the only means for control in the absence of a vaccine or a cure. No amount of medical, financial, or military resources would halt the avoidable loss of hundreds of thousands of lives, tens of millions of jobs, and one of the greatest economies in the world. At the time of this writing, deaths from the pandemic are approaching 200,000 in the United States—an overwhelming majority of which public health experts say was avoidable—with no sign of waning. All the countries surrounding China, with far less notice and fewer resources, have managed to contain it, and almost all European countries have done better than the United States. None of this has been surprising but is the exact result we expected from the evidence we outlined in *The Dangerous Case of Donald Trump* and a result that was essentially inevitable based on our mental capacity evaluation of the Mueller report.

Equally unsurprising is his response to one of the largest people's movements in Black Lives Matter. His psychological need for "total authority" and inability to tolerate criticism or even differing opinion has made him quick to portray largely peaceful protesters as "professional anarchists, violent mobs, arsonists, looters, criminals, rioters, Antifa, and others." Even as there has been no proof of what he calls "Antifa-led" violence, but rather only of opportunists and his own followers, he has used the occasion for unleashing federal forceson several cities—even as local authorities implore Congress to make it illegal to send them where they are unwelcome. Even the police force has been a shocking instigator of violence, responsible for 125 documented violent acts against protesters throughout the country over an 11-day period. And as the president calls journalists "truly bad people with a sick agenda," the U.S. Press Freedom Tracker documented over 400 direct police harassment and attacks of reporters at protests, many of whom have suffered permanent injuries, over the span of two weeks. All this is consistent with the multiple ways in which Donald Trump has directly inspired, incited, fueled, and laid down a culture of violence, in line with his paranoia and violence-proneness under stress.

As a psychiatrist, I believe there is no greater oppression than the hijacking of the mind, and critical information at a critical time is necessary to empower the public to be able to protect itself and to act while it is still possible. It is always easier to prevent than to try to limit losses after a problem has become barely containable. This is the reason for the current volume. Some have questioned my ethical basis for speaking up, but professionals are supposed to act on the principles of their field as their own moral agents, not as technicians who follow fiats. The latter, a form of ceding one's autonomy, is a formula for becoming an instrument of authoritarianism if not careful. I maintain that the humanitarian goals of medicine and our practice of giving precedence to human lives and safety above all else override any etiquette I owe a public figure. This is why the Declaration of Geneva was established, and what the Nuremberg trials were for; we were never supposed to privilege a powerful political figure who is a not a patient above the foremost principles of medical ethics to which we have pledged. The mind is considered tyranny's battleground because thought reform occurs through "milieu control," or the control of information in the environment. Most of this has been done through the spread of false information, but we have the chance to change it through a better understanding of truth.

INTRODUCTION

On February 7, 2020, during a taped interview with Bob Woodward, Donald Trump said: "This is deadly stuff.… You just breathe the air, and that's how it's passed."

Over the next month, in five cities around the country, Mr. Trump held large indoor rallies with thousands of attendees.

On March 19, 2020, Mr. Trump told Mr. Woodward: "I wanted to always play it down. I still like playing it down, because I don't want to create a panic" (New York Times Editorial Board, 2020).

On the same day he said in public: "I would view it as something that just surprised the whole world.… Nobody knew there would be a pandemic or epidemic of this proportion."

In the wake of the 2016 Ebola outbreak, the national security council had drawn up a playbook on tracking, testing, and stockpiling for a new virus. As late as in October 2019, an internal federal government report warned how underprepared the U.S. would be if it needed to tackle a new virus.

In January 2020, the president said the situation was "totally under control." Just six weeks later the U.S. emerged as the new global center of the pandemic (Milman, 2020).

What does mental health have to do with it?

During Donald Trump's presidency, the importance of mental health has risen to the forefront of the public mind. "What is wrong with him?" was a common question people asked since the beginning of his campaign, but they were not referring to his physical health, nor his political ideologies. The public was, in fact, far ahead of pundits, journalists, and even some psychiatrists in their assessment of Donald Trump. So what does mental health have to do with a presidency?

Mental health is fundamental to a well-functioning social and political life, but it is something we often take for granted, and we seldom stop to consider the mental health of our leaders. Yet, mental health issues do not stop at the highest office of the land, and the president is not immune from problems. Rather, the stakes are substantially higher if the same problems affect someone with great influence and power, and the mental health of a president is an especially important matter that affects everyone in the public domain. The nuclear age, dramatically raised the stakes, with the president of the United States able to decide within minutes how to respond to a dire emergency. In the aftermath of the assassination of President John F. Kennedy, Congress proposed the Twenty-Fifth Amendment to the U.S. Constitution, which the states ratified to outline the procedures for replacing the president or vice-president in the event of death, removal, resignation, or incapacitation.

That a president's ability to exercise good judgment could be compromised became apparent when President T. Woodrow Wilson suffered several "small strokes" while at the Paris Peace Conference in early1919. He was under physician care but continued to represent the United States during a time when his thinking was impaired. Much worse, the stroke he suffered in October 1919 completely paralyzed his left side and impaired him until his death in 1924. These months of inability became some of the most significant in American history. When the Treaty of Versailles between Germany and the Allied Powers was brought before the Senate, the compromised president could not defend ratification that would have brought the United States into membership in the new League of Nations.

A similar situation occurred in the latter years of Franklin D. Roosevelt's presidency. Stricken by poliomyelitis in 1921, which left him unable to walk, Roosevelt was impaired but able to serve in office. Whereas he had met the challenges of the dictators of Germany, Italy, and the Japanese militarists as commander-in-chief, he had the responsibility of leading America through a global war while suffering from uncontrolled severe hypertension. By his fourth election in 1944, he was in the late stages of heart failure and cerebral vascular disease. The degree to which these disorders contributed to his reluctance to "stand up" to Stalin at the Yalta Conference of February 1945 is unknown. However, there is general agreement that dementia led to his refusal to join British Prime Minister Winston Churchill in a military operation to occupy Berlin, Germany, and Czechoslovakia in advance of the Russians during the last months of the war in Europe. Roosevelt died of hypertensive stroke soon after in April 1945 (Toole et al., 1997).

With the global deployment of nuclear weapons following World War II, the possibility that impulsive misjudgment could precipitate a catastrophic disaster increased exponentially. While Harry S. Truman was in the pink of health during his presidency, from 1945 to 1953, his successor, Dwight D. Eisenhower, suffered a heart attack in 1955, intestinal blockage and surgery in 1956, and a stroke in 1957, prompting him to make "specific arrangements for the Vice President to succeed to my office if I should incur a disability that precluded proper performance of duty" (Eisenhower, 1965).

Acknowledging that even the briefest lapse in the president's ability to exercise executive power would be dangerous to the nation, Lyndon B. Johnson said in a special message to Congress in January 1965:

> A nation bearing the responsibilities we are privileged to bear for our own security, and the security of the free world, cannot justify the appalling gamble of entrusting its security to the immobilized hands or uncomprehending mind of a Commander in Chief to command (Johnson, 1965).

Senator Birch Bayh was soon thereafter able to achieve Congressional approval of the Twenty-Fifth Amendment in 1965 and ratification by the necessary thirty-eight state legislatures in 1967. While Sections One and Two of the Amendment deal with succession, Sections Three and Four are designed to maintain an active and empowered chief executive office if the president is so physically or mentally impaired that his or her advisers judge him or her to be unable to discharge its duties.

During Ronald Reagan's term of office, there were occasions when the provisions of the Twenty-Fifth Amendment might have been used. Following an assassination attempt in March 1981, Reagan underwent surgery under general anesthesia and, thereafter, was severely incapacitated during parts of his recovery. Apparently, nobody suggested that the president invoke Section Three when he reasonably could have done so, and suggestions that the appropriate decision-makers invoke Section Four were dismissed. When Reagan underwent cancer surgery in 1985, he transferred powers to then-Vice President George Bush but reclaimed his powers some nine hours later. Unfortunately, it now appears that Reagan, while recuperating in the hospital, gave "final approval" to the devastating Iran-Contra scandal that ended in humiliation for the president and his entire administration. Section Four of the Twenty-Fifth Amendment is the only section that has never been utilized, possibly because of the unpleasant nature of involuntary separating the president from the powers and duties of the office, by the cooperative action of the vice president and a majority of the cabinet. Apparently, Reagan's chief of staff briefly considered invoking it late in Reagan's second term when the president appeared at times to be disengaged from the work of his administration (Gilbert, 2015).

What is mental health?

For human beings, our physical, mental, and social health are closely interwoven and vital necessities. In recent decades, significant investments have been made in education, screening, and treatment to manage physical health conditions. Health education campaigns have focused on the links between sun exposure and skin cancer, the importance of diet and exercise in reducing the risk of cardiovascular disease, and the role of safe sex in preventing the transmission of the human immunodeficiency virus (HIV). Many people know the appropriate sources of professional help that are available for physical health conditions, some of the treatments they might receive, and the likely benefits of those treatments. They may also be familiar with available complementary treatments and lifestyle changes they might make. This knowledge can also be beneficial to those around them; someone who has taken a first aid course to learn how to apply cardiopulmonary resuscitation in an emergency may save a life.

We can contrast this situation with that for mental health conditions. Many people do not recognize the signs and symptoms of mental disorders, have beliefs about prevention and treatment that differ from those of health professionals, and are not sure how to help themselves or someone else with a mental disorder. Yet, mental disorders are very common. In any one year, up to one-fifth of the population experience a mental disorder, and over a lifetime, that number rises to one in three (Kessler et al. 2009). Depression, anxiety, and other related disorders are among the leading causes of disability (World Health Organization, 2008).

Mental health as a medical specialty field deals with the diagnosis, treatment, and prevention of mental disease, to promote psychological wellbeing, emotional balance, and resilience. It treats maladaptive behaviors because of mood, thinking process, or perception. According to the World Health Organization, mental health includes: "subjective well-being, perceived self-efficacy, autonomy, competence, inter-generational dependence, and self-actualization of one's intellectual and emotional potential, among others" (World Health Organization, 2001).

Disorders of the mind are just as serious and can be just as debilitating as those that affect the body. They can also vary greatly: most cause greater suffering inwardly, but others do outwardly. Some show obvious symptoms, while others are more hidden. But because it affects the mind, even though mental disorder prevalence rates are high, many people either do not see the need or delay seeking help, often for many years. As a result, mental health problems are not given anywhere near the same level of importance as physical ailments, despite the growing awareness that mental health is critical to the wellbeing of individuals and societies.

This lack of awareness has led to numerous misconceptions about mental health problems, with many people being victimized for their illness and becoming targets of stigma and discrimination. However, scientific developments have shown that most illnesses are a combination of biological, psychological, and social factors and that mental illnesses are not set apart. Individuals should not be identified by their illnesses and should not be accused of any moral failing because of their mental affliction, as even the most severely impaired individual retains significant free will and should be held accountable where appropriate.

Approaching mental health issues can be intimidating, but there is perhaps no greater reward than the restoration of mental health—or at least that is what patients in recovery say. Because of the unique characteristics of that mental illnesses can exhibit, professionals in the area spend much of their time educating, or, in the case of need for care, convincing patients that they need it.

Forensic mental health

In addition to mental health, there is forensic mental health. This just means that the mental health professional works at the intersection of mental health and the law. Forensic psychiatry (one area of forensic mental health), for example:

> is a subspecialty of psychiatry in which scientific and clinical expertise is applied in legal ... or legislative matters, and in specialized clinical consultations in areas such as risk assessment for employment" (American Academy of Psychiatry and the Law, 2005).

A psychiatrist in this setting uses psychiatric expertise to help inform legal, criminal justice, and governmental systems. The word "forensic" derives from the Latin word for "the forum" or the court system of Ancient Rome. The forum was also where public speeches, gladiatorial matches, and commercial affairs happened. Most importantly, it was a place where ideas were exchanged, and different disciplines could meet and work together to solve problems.

The modern-day justice system is not very different. Legal professionals and mental health professionals—psychiatrists, psychologists, and social workers—often work closely together. Mental health expert witnesses especially play a large role in the judicial process. For example, a trial lawyer may invite an expert witness to evaluate if there is psychological damage to an injured party; an immigration lawyer may consult an expert to see if trauma can explain inconsistencies in a story, or a public defender may solicit an expert into whether mental health issues were involved in a crime. Additionally, an employer may call upon an expert consultant to perform a risk assessment or fitness-for-duty evaluation if an employee were posing a threat to the safety of himself or herself and others at work.

Expert witnesses, like fact witnesses, provide evidence that is admissible in court. This is because expert or professional opinion—unlike personal opinion, which is not admissible in court—is based on the expert's scientific, technical, or other specialized knowledge, applied to the facts of a case using reliable principles and methods. Expert witnesses have a responsibility to provide documentation, to educate about their area of expertise, and to make the information accessible. This way, lawyers, judges, or public and private governing bodies can obtain information in areas that are outside their own knowledge base. The public was looking to mental health professionals for similar information when it reached out to me in large numbers, as both a psychiatrist and as an expert on violence, the morning after the 2016 presidential election. Mental health experts may, in turn, influence law and policy through teaching in law schools, public education, and public health methods.

Mental health in the public domain

What happens when a mental health problem afflicts a president? First, it is important to distinguish between mental incapacity and mental illness. Mental illness per se does not make a person unfit for duty, just as one can be unfit for a job without having a diagnosis of mental disorder. Abraham Lincoln famously suffered from debilitating depression, which may even have helped him to be a better, more empathic leader. Similarly, Theodore Roosevelt's hypomanic moods made him an exuberant and influential personality. In fact, a study of U.S. presidents between 1776 and 1974 shows that almost half of U.S. presidents suffered from some kind of mental disorder (Davidson et al, 2006). It is reasonable, therefore, to assert that mental illness is a president's private business, as long as it does not impact on their ability to discharge the duties of their office.

Mental capacity, however, is a different matter. It is a requirement for fitness, and it does not require a diagnosis. Forensic mental health professionals conduct mental capacity evaluations all the time: capacity to stand trial, capacity to sign a will, and capacity to perform the duties of one's office are all very common. Capacity evaluations for employment, in particular, are routinely required for law enforcement or military personnel, and even doctor and lawyer groups are beginning to mandate capacity evaluations, necessitated by the rising average age of practitioners. Anyone who exhibits signs of incapacity can be referred for an evaluation by the employers or the courts, which in turn call upon an independent forensic mental health professional. Dangerousness to self or others, or risk assessment, is another evaluation that mental health professionals carry out, and a positive result usually means automatic disqualification from employment. If the mental capacity of a president is in question, the first order should be to consult an independent forensic mental health professional like any other situation. This seldom happens, however, and the White House physician is often the reason why. A White House-employed physician, often also a military officer subordinate to the commander-in-chief, is not eligible to perform fitness-for-duty examinations on one's employer or superior. Capacity evaluations are done for the benefit of employers—which, in the case of a president, would be the people—not the patient. Dangerousness assessments, similarly, are done for potential victims or authorities protecting them and not those posing danger. Yet, outside referrals are rare, and public confusion about diagnosis versus functional assessment leaves much in the hands of the president's personal physician, who has historically done much to cover up any signs of incapacity, and very little to serve the public.

Mental health, like every other medical discipline, involves clinical and public health practice. While clinical practice involves diagnosing and treating one patient at a time after individuals have already become ill, public health and preventive medicine involve population-level interventions that help keep people healthy and prevent them from falling ill in the first place. While both approaches are necessary, prevention is increasingly emphasized as we enhance our understanding and accumulate more information on how to stop illness, injury, and suffering before they occur. For this reason, our code of medical ethics states: "a physician must recognize responsibility to patients ⊠ as well as to society" (AMA, 2016). Our responsibility to society takes the form of preventing illness and injury in a healthy population, stopping illness from spreading if contagious, and lessening their progression if already pervasive. From this perspective, mental health professionals have a positive obligation to protect the public if we have reason to believe, based on our experience and research of the most dangerous individuals in society, that a public figure, through his words, actions, and influence, represents a danger to public health and safety.

Suffering from a lack of mental health alone may not be a problem for a presidency. However, a lack of mental capacity is very dangerous, for it means that the president and commander-in-chief, whatever the reasons, cannot properly conduct their duties. This would be problematic for any job, but for the most powerful office on the planet, on which millions, if not billions of lives depend, it is a catastrophic emergency. Psychological dangerousness is also a serious problem. While many presidents have been dangerous because of "warlike" dispositions or faulty policies, dangerousness for psychological reasons means that dangers could be produced for reasons that are not only erratic but completely irrelevant to politics. Having both mental incapacity and psychological dangerousness, furthermore, means that attempts to cover up one's incapacity could spark unnecessary conflict and cause society to descend into violent chaos.

"The Goldwater rule"

"The Goldwater rule" was an obscure guideline before the Trump presidency—so obscure in fact, that few scholars studied it and many psychiatrists had not even heard of it. Having been considered outdated since the day it entered the books, and its premise invalid since 1980, when diagnostic practices changed, it would not be an exaggeration to say that it was not abolished only because of it was too obscure to be bothered with. Then, everything changed with the Trump presidency.

Through massive public campaigns, the American Psychiatric Association made "the Goldwater rule" a household phrase, and it became the unfortunate barrier to not just APA members, but all mental health professionals' ability to contribute. What is it? The "Goldwater scandal," as some have described it, arose following a survey by *Fact* magazine in 1964. After Republicans nominated Barry Goldwater for president, Ralph Ginzburg, the editor of the magazine, sent a questionnaire to 12,356 psychiatrists, asking: "Do you believe Barry Goldwater is psychologically fit to serve as President?" His questionnaire included some information about Goldwater's personal history, which included a statement about "nervous breakdowns." With this prejudicial framing, 2,417 psychiatrists responded, and while more than half said they did not know enough or thought Goldwater was fit, 1,189 opined poorly or irresponsibly, stating he was "schizophrenic" and "severely paranoid." With less than 10 percent commenting irresponsibly, it should not really have been news, but the magazine sensationalized it in a special issue with the headline: "1,189 Psychiatrists Say Goldwater is Psychologically Unfit to be President!" After a landslide loss, unsurprisingly, Goldwater was furious. He successfully sued Ginzburg and his magazine for defamation. The jury awarded him $1 in compensation, $25,000 in punitive damages against Ginzburg, $50,000 in punitive damages against Fact magazine, and the magazine went out of business.

Although it was not directly implicated in the lawsuit, the APA was also embarrassed by the situation, and under pressure from the American Medical Association (AMA), a powerful lobbying force in Washington at the time that had long supported Republicans, including Goldwater, it made a move to discipline its members. The result was what is now informally called "the Goldwater rule." In the years that followed, it became clear to everyone who knew Goldwater that he was neither mentally ill nor unfit. However, if the concern were over science or standard of practice, the problem should have been irresponsible diagnosis, not the act of commenting. But, because the circumstances leading to the adoption of the rule had more to do with political compromise and preserving the profession's public image, the focus remained on keeping members of the profession quiet (Stone, 2018). Although not commenting on matters of real concern should be of equal professional irresponsibility as commenting on matters of unconcern, scientific or ethical rigor was not the focus. The awkward placement in the code of ethics is revealing: it is stated as an encouragement to educate the public regarding public figures for the purpose of public health—just without diagnosing. But an "ethics" guideline arising out of a political compromise was perhaps bound to be politically abused: with the current presidency, the part that discourages diagnosis was expanded to prohibit all comment on any aspect of a public figure under *any* circumstance, including national emergencies.

This alarming act, occurring two months after Donald Trump's inauguration, caused many of us to revolt and name it a "gag rule" (Glass, 2017). First, the "rule" is a misnomer to start, since the preamble of the profession's ethical code makes it clear that its guidelines are principles, not rules, to which the individual professional must apply moral agency to circumstance, as all ethical decision making requires. However, alarmed at the number of mental health professionals speaking up about the new president, the APA decided to reinterpret the guideline. Two important changes happened:

first, the expansion of "professional opinion" to cover not just diagnosis but any observation of any kind that one can make as a professional. Second, it eliminated the profession's public health responsibility in relation to public figures. These were significant changes, since not just any opinion counts as "professional opinion" for the courts, and there are plenty of useful insights professionals can provide outside of making a diagnosis—which is not even necessary outside a treatment relationship. By eliminating any public health responsibility, under all circumstances—even a national emergency (APA, 2017a)—it was requiring its members to go against the core principles of medical ethics, not to mention the "rule" itself. "The Goldwater rule" falls under the guideline that psychiatrists "recognize a responsibility to participate in activities contributing to the improvement of the community and the betterment of public health" (APA, 2013b). By creating a "gag order," it was requiring psychiatrists to violate the purpose of "the Goldwater rule," the profession's primary responsibility to society, and the modern Hippocratic oath called the Declaration of Geneva (World Medical Association, 2020). This universal pledge by every health professional in the world since 1948 was instituted in response to the experience of Nazism, clarifying that the humanitarian goals of medicine are contrary to *either* silence *or* active cooperation with a destructive regime. And as an absolute prohibition without the possibility of moral agency, the gag order was arguably no longer an ethical principle, but an edict.

The duty to warn and to protect

Like every other ethical guideline since Ancient Greek times, ethical deliberation involves weighing two or more competing obligations. Therefore, one of the problems with "the Goldwater rule" is that it has no countervailing rule. Before we go into this, there are other problems that have to do with messaging. Whereas it is perfectly acceptable for a private trade association to have its own rules, it is not acceptable to overreach with a campaign of misimpression, if not misinformation, that "the Goldwater rule" applies universally. The APA is the only known mental health association in the country, if not the world, to have this rule, and its membership is just 6 percent of practicing mental health professionals in the United States, according to the Department of Labor's Bureau of Labor Statistics (Bureau of Labor Statistics, 2019). Many, including myself, resigned from the APA in 2007 upon the revelation that it was taking about 30 percent of its income from the pharmaceutical industry—and its policies reflected this through an increase in support of pharmacotherapy over patient rights, which it had previously advocated more strongly. Now, the association was potentially harming public health through the spread of misconceptions about its "Goldwater rule," causing the public to confuse it with the Health Insurance Portability and Accountability Act (HIPAA), or patient confidentiality laws. Meanwhile, it used the public figure's non-patient status to make this rule more stringent than patient confidentiality, stating that a "duty to warn" does not apply, based on the narrow Tarasoff doctrine of a doctor-patient relationship.

Society is one of our primary responsibilities, and we not only have a duty to warn and to protect it in the case of potential victimization, but a duty to enhance public health and well-being more generally even in the absence of immediate danger (Kroll and Pouncey, 2016). The independence of the APA has also come into question, for it receives federal funding, and admitted to changing "the Goldwater rule" to protect federal funding (Gersen, 2017). The federal government has rewarded it substantially since its public campaign (Kendall, 2020). It is not unreasonable to believe, therefore, that its acceptance of federal funding has to do with its odd policy of privileging governmental figures over the public's health, and the sidelining of the professions best suited to answer the public's questions about mental problems that are quite clearly of national consequence (Grohol, 2019).

The duty to warn and to protect patients and society is built into our professional responsibility, but this responsibility was expanded to non-patients with the case of *Tarasoff v. Regents of the University of California,* which was decided in 1976. In 1967, Prosenjit Poddar, a graduate student from Bengal, India, came to the University of California at Berkeley. In the fall of 1968, he met Tatiana Tarasoff at folk dance lessons in the International House where he resided. They saw each other about once a week until New Year's Eve when Tarasoff kissed him. Poddar interpreted the kiss as a symbol of the seriousness of their relationship. When he explained this to Tarasoff, she replied that he was wrong and that she was interested in dating others. This rejection caused Poddar to undergo a severe emotional crisis during which he became withdrawn, ignored his studies, often stayed alone, and wept frequently. His condition continued to deteriorate until he began to visit a campus psychologist. Sometime later in the summer, when Tarasoff was apparently on vacation to Brazil, he confided to the psychologist that he was planning to kill her when she returned.

The psychologist believed Poddar and notified the campus police, requesting that they have him committed. They briefly detained him, but he was released because he appeared rational and promised to stay away from Tarasoff. The patient terminated therapy because of attempts to hospitalize him. At the order of the psychologist's superior, a psychiatrist, no further steps were taken to commit Poddar or to warn Tarasoff. In late October, Poddar went to Tarasoff's home with a pellet gun and a butcher knife. He shot her with the pellet gun, and as Tarasoff ran from the house, Poddar followed, catching her and stabbing her repeatedly and fatally with the butcher knife. Tarasoff's parents brought suit against the psychologist, his superior, the campus police, and their employer, the University of California, for failure to warn them, Tatiana, or anyone who could have reasonably been expected to notify Tatiana of the dangers and for negligently failing to confine Poddar.

A ruling by the California Supreme Court of California in 1974 stated that mental health professionals have a "duty to warn" non-patients if they are potential victims of threats their patients made, or if their patients otherwise displayed behaviors that could pose a "serious danger of violence to another." A rehearing of the case in 1976 expanded it with the provision of a "duty to protect." In other words, if a therapist should have made the prediction that his or her patient posed a danger to another person, on the basis of professional standards, he or she "bears a duty to exercise reasonable care to protect the foreseeable victim of that danger" (Tarasoff v. Regents of the University of California, 1976).

It is important to emphasize the three clarifications that the Tarasoff ruling made: (a) that a duty to protect (and to warn in the case of danger) that already exists with patients and society expands to include non-patients in the case of danger; (b) that a therapist cannot claim "no responsibility" toward a non-patient; and (c) that patient confidentiality is not absolute, especially in situations of a threat to safety or survival. In contrast to the Goldwater rule, which is based on one litigation against a third party fifty-six years ago, the Tarasoff doctrine has been relitigated about one hundred times, directly involving treaters, and has been codified in forty-four U.S. states, as well as increasingly across the world as a standard of care. While U.S. states are not permitted to adopt the Goldwater rule as it would violate the First Amendment, the Tarasoff doctrine, with each litigation, has expanded beyond the patient-provider relationship (Johnson et al., 2014). In other words: "the victim was not my patient," "the information did not come from my patient," or, in the case of universities, "the perpetrator was not a direct patient," are arguments that no longer hold (Regents of the University of California v. Superior Court of Los Angeles County, 1970). In this context, if "the Goldwater rule" were (even if less strict) an analogy to patient confidentiality and consent, the Tarasoff doctrine would have to serve as an analogy to a duty to warn and to protect society—even if society were not our direct, primary responsibility, which it is.

Mental health in politics versus politicization of mental health

We need to make a distinction between using our mental health credentials for political purposes and applying mental health principles in the political realm where relevant. Under Nazism, the former was encouraged, and the latter discouraged. As a result, not only psychiatrists, but most German clergy, professors, lawyers, doctors, and other leading thinkers became passive if not active enablers of some of the worst atrocities in their nation's history. In the short run, it may have ensured their personal safety or political expediency, but not their collective wellbeing as a society. Not meeting their obligations, in the end, served no one. Because of this experience, the World Medical Association (1948) issued its Declaration of Geneva to clarify that silence in collusion with a destructive regime was just as incompatible with the humanitarian goals of medicine as active collusion. Infamous Nazi, Soviet, and Chinese abuses of psychiatry, whereby psychiatry falsely diagnosed in order to imprison dissidents in hospitals, or otherwise served a destructive state over patients and society, are instances of active collusion that we must distinguish and avoid.

The American Psychiatric Association's turning the obsolete "Goldwater rule" into an absolute decree of silence, apparently to be in good graces with the present administration, is an unfortunate instance of passive collusion. Its public misinformation campaigns, defying science and evolving practice, and attacking independent professionals, or groups of professionals who would speak up, even when they are not members and oppose its new interpretation of "the Goldwater rule," is arguably active collusion. While in the beginning there were scores of member protests, resignations, and demands for a vote, with time many professionals fell in line, fearful of possible negative impacts on their careers if they spoke out against the official policy.

The media took to heart what should have been a voluntary guideline for only 6 percent of mental health professionals, not adopted by any licensing board, and on which the APA itself has not dared discipline any members through official channels: dozens of lawyers stood ready to challenge the APA if it had done so. They colluded in the silencing of professionals by canceling all invitations (one network did so over fifty times), preventing fully completed interviews from going to print, and editing out of dozens of articles only the words of experts—such that almost none would reach the public through major sources in two-and-a-half years. As with the conflict between membership and leadership of the APA, reporters, and editors often seemed to be in conflict. No doubt the fact that "the Goldwater rule" began with a lawsuit against a magazine, not against practitioners, and the fact that we were dealing with a very litigious president, played a role. Even though defamation lawsuits are intended to be for cases where the allegations are false, truth no longer mattered. The misconception of mental health as a nebulous, subjective area, instead of the scientific field that it is, persisted. Hence began a "malignant normality," as Dr. Robert Jay Lifton describes in his foreword to *The Dangerous Case of Donald Trump* (Lee, 2019b), where those who are best positioned to comment on the greatest threat to public health and safety are silenced and darkness descends upon a nation, initiated by the very association that is supposed to enlighten the public on mental health.

We are now at a very dangerous point. Just as we predicted with *The Dangerous Case of Donald Trump*, the president has turned out to be more dangerous than the public ever could have known on its own, has grown more dangerous with time, and is about to become uncontainable. Just as we alerted would be the case, the APA's distortion of ethics has turned out to be worse than the change of ethics its psychological counterpart, the American Psychological Association effectuated during the Iraq War in order to facilitate governmental plans of torture. At the time of this writing, the United States has lost almost 200,000 lives as a direct result of the president's dangerous mental state, which was entirely predictable—and predicted—and therefore preventable. Without insight into mental health principles and interventions, an enabling and spreading of pathology was inevitable. Mental health adheres to medical neutrality, which means that the description of a situation must be commensurate with the actual need, not attenuated or withheld because of political pressures. In medical assessments, there is no room for politics. Yet because of the APA's politicization of psychiatry, a mental health issue in a dangerous political figure was allowed to be "normalized" into social, cultural, civic, and geopolitical dangers. This document is to counter some of those adverse effects so that the public might protect itself. Whereas I had not laid down any detailed analysis when I compiled The Dangerous Case of Donald Trump, I do so here to help this very end.

Criterion for commenting on a president

To justify this profile analysis, I will first prove dangerousness. Dangerous risk assessment and management have become central to the current mental health practice of almost all areas. It has also become among the most important activities defining professional responsibility. Mental health professionals may diagnose rarely, but dangerous risk assessment must occur with every encounter. Once assessed, it is the basis for limiting a person's freedom in our civil liberties-favoring society, which allows exceptional latitude for behavioral variation. When one is dangerous, that behavior impinges on the freedom and safety of others. When law permits, even require, that mental health professionals and physicians detain people against their will, they must demonstrate that those people are a danger to themselves or others for mental health reasons, or are gravely disabled and unable to care for themselves. The same goes for revealing confidential information — professionals must be ready to present evidence and solid reasoning on the risk of danger, which is a medical emergency.

What does it mean to be a danger to others for mental health reasons? It is important to separate mental symptoms from things such as poor judgment or opinions and points of view that differ from one's own, which the law clearly permits. In the United States, it must be a disturbance of cognition, emotional regulation, or behavior that is driving the pattern of dangerousness. Additionally, the magnitude of the perceived harm must be considerable. Is it that feelings are being hurt? Or is there actual injury being perpetrated? Are there patterns of behavior and statements of intent that reasonably indicate that harm is imminent? Does the person carry weapons or any other instruments of harm?

Stipulating here the high standard of imminent danger to self or others as a condition for speaking up about a public figure—even though the actual threshold for speaking about a non-patient public figure should be lower and even protected speech—we will adopt this as the minimum standard. Any standard that goes higher risks unduly endangering the public, which has vastly greater priority than a public figure, to whom we do not have a primary professional responsibility. It is arguably more important to point out if the leader of the United States is not mentally or emotionally stable, the threshold for assessing the risk of violence should be lower than that of the average citizen.

The president, in a position of great power and making critical decisions, should theoretically meet higher standards of mental stability. Despite these greater requirements, our response is the opposite, hampered by common misperception: the president is supposed to be the nation's protector; how can he be unwell and harmful? In an extreme case scenario, he would be unwilling to admit of any disturbance—which is a feature of grave disability—what do we do then? If we did not act, would we continue to deny until we were at a point of no return? Those who dare apply these mental health principles to the First Citizen may find themselves at risk of losing their jobs, their livelihoods, or even their personal safety—because of

26

either the president, or the segment of the population currently empowered by the very symptoms that make him so dangerous. If successful, these actions would drive the latter around the emotional bend. As president, Donald Trump has control over the executive branch and its agencies; is commander-in-chief of the military; has unilateral authority to launch nuclear weapons capable of destroying the world many times over (which the secretary of defense authenticates but cannot veto). For the leader of the free world, inappropriate words alone may create a snowball effect that ultimately results in devastating harm to others (Jhueck, 2017). A complex web of factors requires consideration, which is why public education is essential, in collaboration with other professionals, such as politicians, lawyers, and social psychologists.

The MacArthur Violence Risk Assessment Study has a number of indicators for whether an individual will commit future violence. Examples include a past history of violence, a criminal or substance-abusing father, personal substance abuse, having a generally suspicious nature, and a high score on the Novaco Anger Scale. We look at "actuarial" data, as outlined in the Violence Risk Appraisal Guide: did the person live with both biological parents to age 16? Did the person have discipline problems in elementary school? Does the person lead a parasitic lifestyle, exploiting others for financial gain? Personality traits such as glibness with superficial charm, a grandiose sense of self, seeking stimulation in constant activity, and pathological lying, conning, and manipulation all factor in. Lack of remorse, shallow affect, and lack of empathy are additional warning signs, as are poor behavioral controls, irritability, verbal abuse, and sexual promiscuity. Juvenile delinquency between the ages of thirteen and eighteen, and signs of carelessness and criminal versatility, are also things we look for. With respect to categories of mental disorder, perhaps counterintuitively, major illnesses such as schizophrenia have a lower rate of harm to others than personality disorders. Sociopathy or psychopathy, as measured by a screening version of the Hare Psychopathy Checklist, is the most strongly associated with violence among risk factors studied (Monahan et al., 2001). Psychopathy is a constellation of personality traits that may manifest with emotional detachment, interpersonal manipulation, social deviance, impulsive lifestyle, and antisocial behavior (Cleckley, 1941; Hare, 2003).

The ensuing list includes just a sample of incidents in the public record before and since his presidency. It is only a small fraction taken from a vast body of data, but all that is needed for dangerousness is a preponderance of evidence. Since no one can predict future dangerousness with absolute certainty, the identification of factors associated with potentially dangerous behavior is sufficient, and this creates an overabundance of information for one book; each topic could become the potential theme for an entire book in its own right, and the number of topics would easily fill a library. But this much information is not necessary; it suffices that we have enough to demonstrate dangerousness, which triggers the next step: a mandatory evaluation and a complete assessment with recommendations for further management. Until then, we err on the side of safety. The intent here is to show that there are sufficient indicators of acceptable quality and reliable records to reach a reasonable conclusion of Donald Trump's pattern of "danger to others."

Of note, dangerousness is not the same as a psychiatric diagnosis, but it is an evaluation mental health professionals perform more often than diagnosis. Most people with "mental illness" are not dangerous, and most dangerous people are not diagnosable with mental illness. Only about one percent of the perpetrators of homicide in this country are found to be "not guilty by reason of insanity." The rest are declared by our courts to be subject to "criminal responsibility" for whatever act they committed. Donald Trump may or may not meet the criteria for any number of diagnoses of mental disorders defined in the Diagnostic and Statistical Manual of the American Psychiatric Association (2013a), but that is irrelevant here. Even the presence of "insanity" seldom leads to an insanity defense, given the considerable free will people retain, even in cases of debilitating mental affliction. Dangerousness assessments do not require and are often not obtainable from a personal interview, for dangerous individuals are likely to deny, minimize, or attempt to conceal the facts that identify them as dangerous. The most reliable data usually come from the person's family and friends, police reports, criminal histories, medical, prison, or judicial records, and other publicly available information from third parties. In Donald Trump's case, we have many opportunities for direct observation in real situations in real-time, including his public speeches, interviews, and constant "tweets," which express his numerous threats of violence, incitements to violence, and boasts of violence that he himself has acknowledged committing repeatedly and habitually, in addition to the collateral reports of others who have directly interacted with him (Gilligan, 2017). The evaluation of dangerousness is what is most relevant to public health, which mental health professionals assess precisely through the kind information presented here.

Documenting dangerousness

During a rally in Wilmington, North Carolina, Donald Trump stated, "Hillary wants to abolish, essentially abolish the Second Amendment⊠. And by the way, if she gets to pick her judges, nothing you can do, folks. Although [for] the Second Amendment people, maybe there is, I don't know." A reporter covering this incident was moved to say: "While the remark was characteristically glib, it finds Trump again encouraging violence⊠ suggesting either an armed revolt or the assassination of a president" (Blistein, 2016). Former Head of the Central Intelligence Agency (CIA) General Michael Hayden told CNN's Jake Tapper: "If someone else had said that outside the hall, he'd be in the back of a police wagon now with the Secret Service questioning him" (Diamond and Collinson, 2016). It is true also for medical and mental health professionals: if a patient had said that, an emergency certificate would have been signed, and the person taken to the nearest emergency room for further evaluation. A common explanation by defenders of his aggressive remarks in public settings is that what he said was a joke. This does not change the dangerousness of the remark but rather flags as a concern his deeming the remark so lightly as to consider it as a joke, which could be indicative of an even greater pathological risk that requires evaluation.

Donald Trump has on other occasions asked why we have nuclear weapons if we cannot use them. In an interview with Chris Matthews on MSNBC, he said: "Somebody hits us within ISIS, you wouldn't fight back with a nuke?" When Matthews remarked: "the whole world [is] hearing a guy running for President of the United States talking of maybe using nuclear weapons. No one wants to hear that about an American president," Trump replied, "Then why are we making them?" Another MSNBC host, Joe Scarborough, reported that Trump asked a foreign policy advisor three times: "If we have them, why can't we use them?" (Fisher, 2016).

Donald Trump also urged that five innocent African-American youths be given the death penalty, years after it had been proven beyond a reasonable doubt to have been committed by someone else. In 1989, he spent 85,000 dollars placing ads in New York's four daily newspapers calling for the return of the death penalty so that the youths who had been wrongfully convicted of raping a woman in Central Park could be given the death penalty. He was still advocating the same penalty in 2016, fourteen years after DNA evidence and a detailed confession had proved that a serial rapist had actually committed the crime (Burns, 2016).

At political rallies, Donald Trump urged his followers to beat up protestors so badly that they would have to be taken out on stretchers. An editorial in the *New York Times* quotes the following: "I'd like to punch him in the face, I'll tell you." "In the good old days this doesn't happen, because they used to treat them very, very rough." "I love the old days. You know what they used to do to guys like that when they were in a place like this? They'd be carried out on a stretcher, folks." "If you see somebody getting ready to throw a tomato, knock the crap out of them, would ya? Seriously. Just knock the hell out of them. I will pay for the legal fees, I promise you." He even complained that his supporters were not being violent enough (even though many had assaulted protesters severely enough to be arrested and tried for assault and battery): "Part of the problem and part of the reason it takes so long [to remove protesters], is because nobody wants to hurt each other anymore" (*New York Times* Editorial Board, 2016). He even seemed to sense that his followers did not mind or may even be attracted to his violence: "I could stand in the middle of Fifth Avenue and shoot somebody, and I wouldn't lose voters" (Diamond, 2016).

The infamous "Grab 'em by the pussy" video, which Access Hollywood's Billy Bush recorded in September 2005, includes comments from the newly-married Donald Trump when he sees actress Arianne Zucker outside the bus where he is being recorded: "I better use some Tic Tacs, just in case I start kissing her.... You know I'm automatically attracted to beautiful—I just start kissing them. It's like a magnet. Just kiss. I don't even wait" (Fahrenthold, 2016). During the course of the video, he boasts of even more disturbing and assaultive things he has done to women. Therapists of mental health across the country reported having to expand their practices "with women who experienced sexual abuse when younger ... being re-wounded, re-traumatized" (LaMotte, 2016).

A great danger to vulnerable groups as well as the potential for human rights abuses arise from an inability to tolerate criticism and perceived threats to his ego. Claims of unearned superiority and delusional levels of grandiosity were present since the start of his campaign (Gamboa, 2015). The flip side of that is often paranoia, a sense of entitlement, and the potential for dangerous outbursts of rage if one's inflated self-image were challenged in any way. The compulsive need to shift blame can lead to scapegoating and persecution. As anticipated, reports of hate crimes with racial or ethnic bias jumped the day after Donald Trump won the election, with greater reports of hate crimes on November 9 than any other day in 2016 (Williams, 2018). Derrick Johnson, president of the National Association for the Advancement of Colored People (NAACP), noted: "The acceptance of intolerance that has been condoned by President Trump and many others across the country has simply emboldened individuals to be more open and notorious with their racial hatred" (Eligon, 2018).

Social psychologists at the University of Kansas conducted a study on prejudice that surveyed almost four hundred Donald Trump and Hillary Clinton supporters. They measured perceptions of social norms and people's own levels of prejudice toward nineteen social groups, shortly before and after the election. Some groups were targeted by the Trump campaign (such as Muslims and immigrants) and some were not (such as atheists and alcoholics). There was an increase in the acceptability of prejudice against groups Donald Trump targeted but little shift against untargeted groups, which meant that the Trump presidency produced a new normative climate favoring several prejudices that the authors label, "the Trump effect." Research suggests that individual expressions of prejudice and potential violence depend highly on perceived social norms, and Donald Trump had changed those norms (Crandall et al., 2018).

Assessment of dangerousness since the Trump presidency must therefore take into consideration these changes of norms. In other words, a dangerous presidency is bound to normalize and institutionalize many dangers, making them seem acceptable precisely because a president is an authority figure who sets norms and not just meets or breaks them. This fact makes him dangerous beyond what can immediately be studied or be directly observed.

Dangerous new norms

Over the three-and-a-half years of Donald Trump's presidency, we have watched white supremacist terrorism become much more mainstream. As of 2019, white nationalist hate groups in the U.S. had surged 55 percent since the Trump presidency, according to the Southern Poverty Law Center (2020). The perpetrator of a massacre in August 2019 in El Paso, Texas, where twenty-six were killed, much like the man who plowed his car into a crowd of protesters after a white supremacist rally in Charlottesville, Virginia, in 2017, the 46-year-old who attacked a Pittsburgh synagogue in 2018, and the Australian man who killed 51 people at two mosques in Christchurch, New Zealand, in 2019, drew inspiration from violent white supremacist ideas, if not from Donald Trump himself (Beckett and Wilson 2019). While the Federal Bureau of Investigation (FBI) and the Department of Homeland Security (DHS) made attempts to give the threat of deadly white supremacism priority and to shift strategies, senior members of the Trump administration such as Stephen Miller, long allied with anti-immigrant hate groups, have hampered efforts. Perhaps one of the more shocking, related legacies of this administration is the traumatic separation of small children from their migrant families at the U.S.-Mexico border (Associated Press, 2019).

Mass shootings and other forms of violence have increased to unprecedented levels. In 2019, there were 417 mass shootings in the U.S., according to data from the nonprofit Gun Violence Archive (GVA, 2020), which tracks every mass shooting in the country. GVA defines a mass shooting as any incident in which at least four people are shot, excluding the shooter. The group also tracks mass murders as defined by the FBI—incidents in which at least four people are killed; 31 of the mass shootings were mass murders. The year 2019 had the highest number of mass shootings in any year since 2014, when the GVA started its count, with a progressive increase each year. Individual violence has also seen a rise: a nationwide review by ABC News has identified at least 54 criminal cases where Donald Trump was invoked in direct connection with violent acts, threats of violence, or allegations of assault (Levine, 2020). A review of police reports and court records found that perpetrators in at least twelve cases hailed Donald Trump in the midst, or the immediate aftermath of physically assaulting innocent victims, in another eighteen cases cheered or defended him while taunting or threatening others, and in another ten cases cited him and his rhetoric in court to explain their violent or threatening behavior. By contrast, ABC News could not find a single criminal case filed in federal or state court where an act of violence or threat was made in the name of President Barack Obama or President George W. Bush. There has also been a 226 percent spike in hate crimes in counties that hosted his rallies (Feinberg et al., 2019). Violent behavior is known to be especially susceptible to shifts in culture and to spread by contagion (Slutkin, 2017).

At the time of this writing, the U.S. announced that it was pulling out of the Open Skies Treaty, the third withdrawal from an arms control agreement under the Trump presidency. The Trump administration also debated conducting the first U.S. nuclear test explosion since 1992, which would reverse a decades-long moratorium on such actions (Hudson and Sonne, 2020). In this manner, regardless of stated intentions, and as expected of his long-standing, expressed attraction to violence and aggressive posturing, he has made the world a much more volatile and unsafe place. The destructive power of the U.S. arsenal apparently thrills him, as he has boasted about the size of his nuclear "button" (Baker and Tackett, 2018), a mystery "super-duper" missile he claims he has (Lye, 2020), and "the mother of all bombs" that once "dazzled" him (Wright, 2017). His flamboyant summitry with Kim Jong-un notwithstanding, analysts believe that North Korea poses an even greater threat, such that we may need to abandon the decades-long insistence that North Korea drops its nuclear program, entirely for lack of options (Bierman, 2020). His abandonment in 2018 of the historic nuclear deal with Iran, against international uproar, has escalated animosity as well as the possibility that Iran will begin production of nuclear weapons. And his withdrawal from the Intermediate-range Nuclear Forces (INF) treaty in 2019 has the potential to trigger an unlimited nuclear arms race with Russia.

The U.S. did not sign the United Nations treaty on the Prohibition of Nuclear Weapons, which 122 nations adopted in July 2017 (Associated Press, 2017), the Senate never ratified the 1996 Comprehensive Test Ban Treaty, and the 2010 New Start Treaty is due to expire in February 2021, but there is no indication of an intention to reinforce any of them (Borger, 2020). In addition, the Trump administration has proposed to develop new low-yield nuclear capabilities and pushed forward on a 1.7 trillion-dollar plan to maintain and upgrade the U.S. nuclear arsenal. In May 2020, the American Nuclear Policy Initiative (ANPI), a task force of former government and non-governmental experts, released a detailed, objective analysis by the title: "Blundering toward Nuclear Chaos: The Trump Administration after Three Years" (Wolfsthal, 2020). Overall, after bringing the world to the verge of various crises in South America, the Middle East, Europe, and Asia and alienating traditional allies, the world is closer than ever closer to the possibility of devastating wars and a nuclear war. The abrupt withdrawal of U.S. troops in northern Syria that incurred a massacre of Kurdish allies and the unprovoked, illegal assassination of top Iranian General Qassim Soleimani during his impeachment proceedings are perfect examples of the reckless decision-making that demonstrate Donald Trump's extreme dangerousness to society (Sonne et al., 2020).

Finally, the utterly disastrous handling of the novel coronavirus pandemic illustrates Donald Trump's psychological dangerousness, not just through commissions but through deadly omissions, repeatedly, brazenly, and recklessly. In addition to depleting or disbanding every aspect of pandemic preparedness, he ignored ominous, classified warnings about the danger through the first critical months, allowing the disease to spread freely throughout the U.S. by actively downplaying the threat, falsely stating: "we have it totally under control," calling it the Democrats' "new hoax," and "like a miracle, it will disappear" (Qiu et al., 2020). He caused the need for extreme lockdown measures and the subsequent economic collapse, and at the time of this writing, the death toll is nearly 200,000. Despite only having 4 percent of the world's population, the U.S. has maintained a quarter of the world's coronavirus deaths with no policy change that would allow for abatement. Rather, evidence has emerged that he deliberately lied about the deadliness of the virus, while knowing full well the risks posed to the public (Costa and Rucker, 2020). The death toll will undoubtedly be far greater because he pulled out of the World Health Organization, in his attempt to shift blame for his failures, undermining critical global cooperation and defunding the world's pandemic response capability (Peters 2020). His devaluation of science, fight with reality, reckless disregard for human life, and neutering of the Centers for Disease Control (CDC) are responsible for depleting pandemic preparedness, ignoring intelligence and sidelining the experts, and politicizing a public health issue in ways that have vastly worsened a deadly pandemic (Saletan, 2020). As a result, the United States has become the world's epicenter of a pandemic, isolated through widespread travel bans and unique among advanced economies to be so stricken with a plague. With accompanying economic devastation, "deaths of despair," and growing violence, the Trump presidency is now entering what may well be the most dangerous period of all.

Dangerous weapons and power

Access to weapons is a crucial part of a dangerousness assessment. The president of the United States has 1750 nuclear warheads at his or her disposal and has the authority to order these weapons to be launched even if our country has not yet been attacked (Kristensen and Korda, 2020). Weapons fired against the United States from a submarine would take about twelve minutes to hit Washington, DC. Missiles fired from most continents would reach the U.S mainland in around thirty minutes. For these reasons, the president of the United States has the unfettered authority to launch nuclear weapons at any time for any reason. There is no formalized way of preventing this unless the commander of the U.S. Strategic Command, who has been given the order to launch, explicitly disobeys that order. The nightmare scenario of an unstable, impulsive, blame-shifting, and revenge-obsessed individual having mere minutes to make the kind of monumental decision is of the gravest possible concern and is a risk that defies rationality.

All this is on top of outsized war-making powers that the president has at his disposal. Despite the isolationist rhetoric and the stated aim to end "endless wars," Donald Trump has ramped up warfare on many fronts. Strikes in Somalia have increased eightfold since his presidency (Turse, 2020), loosened rules of engagement have killed even more civilians, and thousands have died in needlessly brutal operations in Iraq and Syria as a result of slackened targeting standards (Cooper, 2017). As commander-in-chief, he has gone out of his way to encourage war crimes and even to celebrate those who commit them (Cole, 2019). Recently, we learned that a direct clash between U.S. and Russian troops in northern Syria had been ongoing for months without congressional authorization. This is the same president who continued U.S. participation in Saudi Arabia's war in Yemen even after Congress voted to stop it and affirmed that it was unconstitutional (Hueval, 2020). In May 2020, after bringing the nation to the brink of war with Iran just months earlier, he vetoed the Iran War Powers resolution, a bipartisan effort to rein in presidential authority to use military force against Iran without congressional approval (Carvajal, 2020).

The ability to make policy is as important a consideration as access to weapons in dangerousness assessments, where applicable. Because dangerousness is more situational than person-oriented, various factors need to be considered, such as the individual's ability to cause harm through secondary influence or authority, such as policies that are well-established to stimulate violence or cause direct harm. Whereas these aspects have been more nebulous in the past, three decades of scholarly research in violence prevention allow for rigorous prediction. In many ways, violence prediction has become much more precise with policy changes (Ouimet, 2012) than with individual behavior, as the latter is largely circumstantial, dependent on the setting and social contacts of the moment Some of the greatest harm can be inflicted through policy: the climate is a perfect example. Experts have warned that another decade on our present course, we will have likely passed a point beyond which catastrophic harm is unavoidable (Harvey, 2019). In addition to leading the nation out of the Paris climate accord, Donald Trump and the former industry executives and lobbyists placed in control of the Environmental Protection Agency and the Department of the Interior, spent four years rolling back auto emissions standards, opening the Arctic National Wildlife Refuge to drilling, rejecting stronger air pollution standards, and weakening the National Environmental Policy Act, which has served as the foundation of environmental protection in the United States for a half-century. Having opened the pathway to everything from pipelines to the destruction of natural habitats, he is said to have done more to damage the environment than any president in history (Loeb et al, 2020). Every increase in global temperatures already translates into death and misery for millions around the world, but we are now speaking of the potential extinction of the human species, as well as many others. This would not be possible without access to policymaking by a dangerous individual.

Whenever danger is suspected in an individual, the first thing we do before the involuntary assessment is to remove the individual from access to weapons or other means of inflicting grave harm. An individual in a powerful office can be dangerous not only through access to destructive powers but through absence, such as the lack of mental capacity.

Mental incapacity

Verbal, behavioral, and policy-based violence are not the only forms of danger; whether a president has the mental capacity to serve in his office is also a critical question that needs answering. Special Counsel Robert Mueller's Report on the Investigation into *Russian Interference in the 2016 Presidential Election* (2019), which was released to the public in redacted form on April 18, 2019, provided a wealth of relevant information regarding the president's mental capacity, or his ability to function in office. It was also unique for other reasons. Until then, all the information that was available, regardless of abundant quantity or sophisticated quality—real-time, often candid video and audio recordings of responses to real events in real-time, over decades; thorough investigative reporting by some of the most respected journalists of the most trusted newspapers; books, interviews, and tell-all accounts by a range of those who have closely interacted with him; and persistent, unfiltered and undisciplined stream-of-consciousness Twitter comments—could still be dismissed as unorganized, unvetted public information. Information in the Mueller report, however, was verified with the accuracy and expertise of the highest-order criminal investigations, and represented the most relevant information for a capacity evaluation, being of reports by his close associates and coworkers who directly interacted with him. And unlike a diagnostic exam, a functional exam depends most heavily on a person's colleagues' reports on his actual performance at his job, not on a personal interview.

Mental capacity is about possessing the mental soundness that is necessary to fulfill a task. It is deemed that the office of president requires, at minimum, the ability to make sound, rational decisions based on reality and the ability not to place the nation in grave danger. The final determination of "competency" is a judicial decision usually made by the courts, while capacity is a medical assessment that forensic psychiatrists and other mental health professionals make as expert witnesses to present to the courts to aid them in making their legal decisions. Similarly, presidential fitness is a political decision, but just as the courts routinely rely on mental health professionals' assessments for fitness for duty, political bodies should not be denied access to the same medical and professional information and expertise from which the judicial system benefits. A panel of top psychiatrists and psychologists joined me in assembling our analysis as a public service, and what follows is just a sampling of illustrations, which can be read in full elsewhere (Lee et al., 2019).

A capacity evaluation involves the test of three main components: (a) comprehension, or the ability to take in information and advice without undue influence from delusions or excessive emotional needs; (b) information processing, or the ability to appreciate and make flexible use of information and advice; and (c) sound decision making, or the ability to weigh different options and to consider consequences based on rational, reality-based, and reliable thinking without undue influence from impulsivity, delusions, magical thinking, or fluctuating consistency and self-contradiction. When it comes to serving in a high governmental office, constantly repeating demonstrable untruths despite a consensus that these violate easily verified, objective, factual reality, and often following by denying that those statements were made in the first place, even when they were made in public and have been recorded on tape and video, would obviously be disqualifying. Other important standards may be added, such as capacity for trust, discipline and self-control, judgment and critical thinking, self-awareness, and empathy (Gourguechon, 2019), but we decide here to deal only with the bare minimum.

1.   Compromises in comprehension

The Mueller report (2019) outlines how the Russians systematically and sweepingly attacked America before and during the 2016 election. The president's refusal to acknowledge the severity of these attacks, his investment in a certain "reality"—that the Russian attack was insignificant—and his resistance against advice that challenges his established notions, show a compromise in his ability to comprehend and to absorb important information. When the highly-respected White House lawyer, Don McGahn, failed to meet the president's demands that he tell Acting Attorney General Rod Rosenstein to fire Special Counsel Mueller, and then to "put out a statement denying that he had been asked to fire the Special Counsel" (Mueller, 2019), he became the object of ridicule ("Lawyers don't take notes") and headed for the exit. His advisors similarly and repeatedly blocked the president from acting impulsively and self-destructively, preventing him from committing a crime. These reports illustrate a president who is: (a) predisposed to rash, short-sighted, and dangerous acts, without consideration of consequences, motivated by self-protection to the degree that shows him incapable of considering national interest; and (b) surrounded only by the most informal and personal resistance around him to curtail those acts, until the pressure of his predisposition pushes out the advisors.

2.   Faulty information processing

The report sheds light on the extent to which Donald Trump lies to his staff and his colleagues. This trend is so obvious, and yet also so unusual among public servants that it raises a question of serious mental pathology: namely, does he actually believe the obvious untruths that he utters (in which case we would need to ask whether he is suffering from delusions), or, does he know that they are untrue but utters them anyway (in which case he is deliberately and consciously lying in an attempt to manipulate others into advancing his financial, political, or psychological interests and needs, which in severe form can be manifestations of an antisocial or sociopathic/psychopathic disorder). Either instance constitutes faulty information processing.

His combative style of ridiculing his opponents, or a "hit first and ask questions later" approach—as in, "low-energy Jeb," "little Marco," or "crooked Hillary"—enabled the candidate Donald Trump to avoid rational and evidence-based debates over actual policy positions. He has also shown predatory skills, being remarkably talented at deciphering his opponents' vulnerabilities and brazenly talking down challenges. He lures and "hypnotizes" his followers through factually untrue assertions that he may make up one day and then deny the next, through a primitive form of cognition that is called "magical thinking" or "wishful thinking." It is a form of cognition that follows "the pleasure principle" (adhering to whatever makes one feel good, or at least less distressed, and appears to gratify one's wishes), rather than "the reality principle" (which will often frustrate or be incompatible with one's wishes). This kind of brashness is often a reaction to one's own vulnerability, and the reality of human weakness and uncertainty, also shown in the president's intolerance for investigative reporting, which he calls, "fake news" and "the enemy of the people." Our deepest concern is that when reality smothers his accusations and neutralizes his assaults, he will then resort to his most dangerous and violent strategies.

3.   Interferences to sound decision making

Angry outbursts in the president are documented with an alarming frequency, intensity, and lack of control. Former White House Chief Strategist Steve Bannon described the President's anger upon learning of Attorney General Jeff Sessions' recusal, "as mad as I've ever seen him," and he "screamed at McGahn." In response to Comey's confidential briefing to congressional leaders on the existence of the Russia probe in March 2017, notes taken by Annie Donaldson, then McGahn's chief of staff, state: "POTUS in panic/chaos." Others reported that the president was "beside himself," "became very upset and directed his anger at Sessions." Hicks described the President as "extremely upset by the Special Counsel's appointment⊠ she had only seen the president like that one other time, when the Access Hollywood tape came out during the campaign." And when he hears of the appointment of the special counsel, he exclaims: "Oh my God. This is terrible. This is the end of my Presidency. I'm fucked" (Mueller, 2019). It is notable that the nature of the provocation is always threats to self, not because he is furious that a staff member or cabinet secretary had bungled an important legislative or foreign policy initiative. There is no, "What are we going to do? This will undermine all our plans and policies," but his responses are a virtual admission of guilt, remarkable for the extent to which the president is preoccupied with himself without room to consider the welfare of the nation.

Recklessness can be seen in the instances in which the president acted against the advice of others, including the White House lawyer, McGahn. Following Comey's March 2017 meeting with congressional leaders, at which he disclosed the existence of the Russia probe, the president twice called Comey directly, notwithstanding guidance from McGahn to avoid direct contacts with the Department of Justice. The president initiated several efforts to have him removed or at least to limit his powers. In the first instance, he raised issues about Mueller's supposed conflicts of interest. These were generally dismissed by McGahn, Bannon, and others. McGahn pointed out that advancing these arguments could add evidence of an attempt to obstruct the special counsel. In spite of this, the president's personal attorney contacted the special counsel's office asserting the alleged conflicts. Four days later, the president called McGahn and directed him to have Rosenstein fire Mueller, something that McGahn had no intention of doing. In a second call the same evening, the president told McGahn: "Call Rod, tell Rod that Mueller has conflicts and can't be the Special Counsel" (Mueller, 2019). McGahn prepared to resign before the president backed down.

In parallel sequence, the president directed Lewandowski to contact Sessions and to have him assert that the president had done nothing wrong and that the special counsel's authority would be limited to "investigating election meddling for future elections" (Mueller, 2019). Scheduling conflicts delayed Lewandowski's opportunity to meet with Sessions. A month later, when the president asked Lewandowski about progress, Lewandowski asked

Rick Dearborn, a senior White House official, to serve as an intermediary and gave Dearborn a typed version of the statement the president had dictated for Sessions, but Dearborn never acted on it.

In both instances, the president directed actions to be taken, the dismissal of Mueller as special counsel, and the limitation of the special counsel's role by an unrecused Sessions, which were avoided only by the passive resistance of those he directed. The combination of reckless decisions, false denials, and threatened vengeance against those who kept his recklessness in check, illustrate a dangerous pattern of impulsive harm-doing which, when challenged, is only redirected in more threatened harm. Above all, in a post-Richard Nixon era, knowing that that former president was forced to resign because of his firing of law-enforcement officials who were facilitating or even just permitting the investigation into his behavior to proceed, constituted an obstruction of justice, a rational person presumably would have considered the consequences of such actions. The president himself discovered that the firing of "nut job" Comey did not "take the pressure off," (Smith, 2017) but only brought on a new special counsel with new investigations into him that did not work to his advantage. Ousting moderating forces that he would have done well to listen to, only a few capable staff now remain in spite of the president.

Conclusion

Mental capacity, especially decisional capacity, is the most important mental health evaluation for assessing a president's ability to discharge the duties of his or her office. Like dangerousness, it is a separate evaluation from the diagnosis of mental disorder and does not mean one has a mental illness. It means that should a crisis arise—from a pandemic to nuclear war—the person would not be able to make the necessary decisions to handle the situation. It does not preclude criminal-mindedness; rather, the combination of mental incapacity and criminal-mindedness can create some of the *most dangerous* kind of leadership possible. The special counsel's abundant documentation of clear and pervasive, cumulative *patterns,* under sworn testimony, allowed for a top-quality assessment of the president's impaired capacity, in which he failed every criterion. In other words, he was found *incapable* of making responsible decisions free of impulsivity, recklessness, suspiciousness, or absorption in self-interest that precludes attention to the national interest. He was found incapable of weighing consequences before taking action, without detachment from reality, creation of chaos and danger, and cognitive and memory problems. In addition, the counsel recorded extensively and in detail criminal intent (a "guilty mind") in the presence of wrongful action (a "guilty act") in relation to obstruction of justice, which demonstrates criminal responsibility and indictability. We added in our report "proneness to place himself and others in danger," as an additional criterion to determine fitness for duty—since dangerousness alone disqualifies—and this returns us to the assessment earlier in the chapter. Thus, having proven Donald Trump's dangerousness from multiple angles, I have exceeded my most rigorous threshold for proceeding with more detailed analysis, so as to help the public better understand, and protect itself from the very real threat that Donald Trump poses.

A PROFILE OF DONALD TRUMP

Commenting on a president

While it is unethical to speak about matters one has insufficient information about, it is also unethical to withhold an assessment on which one has more than enough information—especially when societal safety is at stake. Particularly disturbing is the total absence of a request for assessment on the part of the authorities, despite the severity of the president's disturbances, the obviousness to which he presents a danger, and the degree to which the public has been clamoring for expert input. Bringing attention to mildly significant mental problems in a high office could be detrimental and should be carefully considered. However, failure to disclose serious mental problems in such an office, especially in a democracy, where the electorate must be informed to make the right choices, could have catastrophic consequences. Whatever the reason for this gap, to fill this void is one of the purposes of this study. First, we must establish a level of knowledge. In April 2019, when presenting Grand Rounds to a group of Harvard psychiatrists and other mental health professionals, they stated during the discussion: "We know more about this president than we do about any patient we have ever treated." I would agree. And if we have a duty to report, to inform, to warn, and to protect society against any knowledge of danger we have about a patient, how much greater is it for a nonpatient, toward whom we have no confidentiality requirements?

What we have to offer in this case is not the information we have access to but the perspective we bring, given our years of training, decades of clinical observations and interest, and more than a century of scientific research investment and evidence. I bring training from Bellevue and Massachusetts General Hospitals in New York City and Boston respectively, two decades of practice in maximum-security prisons in various parts of the country, and over one hundred peer-reviewed publications, including a textbook on public health approaches to violence prevention. The profile I present here is not political but grounded in applying these perspectives to the individual in the context of society. In addition, I have had in-depth personal conversations with Donald Trump's ghostwriter and his niece, to gauge the reliability of the public information that they provide, as well as draw upon further intimate information. At the same time, throwing out labels such as "narcissistic personality disorder" or "antisocial personality disorder" is marginally helpful at best, since diagnosis is not so much about inclusion as it is exclusion. In other words, there is a greater likelihood that attempts to diagnose will simplify and minimize the situation by closing off inquiry into the actual scope and true complexity of the problem. Using phrases that mean very little to the general public does not achieve much. Instead, we must encourage a nuanced discussion aimed at establishing and understanding the true danger to public health. This is the ultimate litmus test: how will this discussion help to improve public health and safety? Will it enhance understanding and empower the public with knowledge, and will it help steer the course in a positive and life-affirming direction? Study is important to achieve the desired outcome since a leader's behavior is not just dependent on personal characteristics but on how the people respond to and interact with him.

Donald Trump as he sees himself

In late 2018, Donald Trump made an extraordinary suggestion after a dispute with his hand-picked Federal Reserve chairman for raising interest rates:

> *I have a gut, and my gut tells me more sometimes than anybody else's brain can ever tell me (Sullivan, 2018).*

It was not only an unusual statement for the leader of the Free World to make but a strikingly precarious approach to take when engaging in high-stakes negotiations as with North Korea over nuclear disarmament. Donald Trump seemed to believe that following his "gut" would serve him better than any preparation, deliberation, or listening to the wisdom of his career advisers. Without any experience, underlying knowledge, or even curiosity, he walked into conversations with potentially hostile world leaders, stating: "We will see what happens. Whatever it is—it is" (Guild, 2018). He took the same approach with the crisis of the coronavirus pandemic: "One day—it's like a miracle—it will disappear. We'll see what happens," he said in February 2020, as the virus raged through communities (Bump, 2020). When confronted six months later with the fact that a thousand Americans were dying a day, he said: "They are dying. That's true…. it is what it is" (Cole and Subramaniam, 2020).

Later, we learned his motivations through journalist Bob Woodward's recordings in March 2020: "I wanted to always play it down. I still like playing it down because I don't want to create a panic." In public, just three weeks earlier, he went as far as to say that Democrats were using the coronavirus outbreak as a "new hoax" to damage him. And yet on another occasion in March 2020, he said: "This is a pandemic…. I've felt that it was a pandemic long before it was called a pandemic" (Rogers, 2020). This is not the pattern of someone trying to solve a problem behind the scenes and attempting to calm the public; it is the pattern of someone who wishes to minimize a problem even as others are worried about it, and then justifies to himself that he, too, was worried all along and denies the decisive role he played in impeding efforts to stop it. He later stated: "I don't take responsibility at all" (Oprysko, 2020).

It makes little difference to public health whether he consciously understood the seriousness of the pandemic and was lying, or was trying to impress the journalist with the rational-sounding explanation that he did not "want to create a panic," when in reality he cared little for the consequences. His actions remain the same, leading the country into a vast underestimation of a deadly problem, while he not only refused to act but actively undermined the efforts of others. Central to his persuasion of his followers is that he "knows more about anything" and "understands better than anybody," regardless of the topic, the proof of this being that he is he is president (Britzky, 2019). "When somebody's the president of the United States, the authority is total. And that's the way it's got to be," he said in a press briefing (Sheth, 2020).

His self-aggrandizement had shown through in remarks once made while praising his own "trade war" against China: "Somebody had to do it." Then, while looking to the heavens, he said: "I am the Chosen One." Earlier the same day, he had retweeted a right-wing pundit's flattering, messiah-flavored comments: "The Jewish people in Israel love him like he's the King of Israel. They love him like he is the second coming of God" (Breuninger, 2019). Suggestions that he was sent by God, and that he has a particular mission to perform flatter him as he feeds into the world view of evangelical Christians (Kobes Du Mez, 2020). Just what he has to offer, other than a feeling of ascendency and power, is rather vague, but this does not concern him greatly because the praise he receives satisfies his "gut". And it does not seem to matter where the flattery is coming from. More recently, he endorsed QAnon, a virtual cult and a potential domestic terrorist threat that, according to the FBI, reveres him: "I don't know much about the movement other than I understand they like me very much, which I appreciate," he said in a press briefing (Liptak, 2020).

Such personal statements abound. "No one knows the system better than me," he said on his first campaign trail. "That's why only I can fix it." He painted a dire state of affairs in the United States and the world—instability abroad and crumbling infrastructure at home—and blamed these problems on career politicians. "This is [their] legacy.... Death, destruction, terrorism, and weakness." To Americans shaken by violence at home and around the world, he promised: "Safety will be restored." He would replace Obama-era health care with the kind that is "affordable and accessible for all." He would overhaul tax laws and get rid of regulations that would "make our country rich again" (Jalonick and Daly, 2016). These were some examples of the sweeping ways in which, without experience or a plan, he would "make America great again." His belief in his power bordered on feelings of omnipotence and delusions of grandeur.

He prides himself on being tough, stating: "The world is laughing at us, at our stupidity," something he mentioned more than fifty times between 2011 and 2016 when he was elected. In 2014, he tweeted: "We need a President who isn't a laughing stock to the entire World. We need a truly great leader, a genius at strategy and winning. Respect!" His primary theme as a candidate whenever he discussed foreign affairs or international trade was that China was laughing at us, Europe was laughing at us, the Taliban was laughing at us, OPEC was laughing at us, and the world was laughing at us. Once he became president, he promised, the laughter would stop. "We don't want other leaders and other countries laughing at us anymore, and they won't be," he said. Yet, two years later, the Washington Post remarked: "literally not a single person on Earth gets laughed at more than Donald Trump"—and a video captured Canadian Prime Minister Justin Trudeau, French President Emmanuel Macron, British Prime Minister Boris Johnson, and others doing just that at the NATO summit (Waldman, 2019).

Nevertheless, there can be little room for doubt over Donald Trump's belief in his greatness. What are the sources of this belief? Some have attributed his confidence to the fact that he believes in his superior "gut" to guide him through a course of action. He said there was no need to prepare for trade negotiations with the Chinese president because: "I know it better than anybody knows it, and my gut has always been right." He said on another occasion that his decisions about which candidates to endorse were based on: "very much my gut instinct." He claimed his 2016 campaign strategy came from multiple sources, including: "Yeah, gut," but also "from my heart." He said in 2011, "my gut tells me" President Barack Obama's birth certificate may have been forged. His gut also told him to do "The Apprentice." He has over the years touted the primacy of the gut: "Go with your gut.... You have to follow your gut.... Develop your gut instincts and act on them.... I've seen people that are super genius, but they don't have that gut feeling" (Milbank, 2018).

Consequently, Donald Trump does not attribute his abilities to any real knowledge or intellectual capacity. "I love the poorly educated," he once said during a victory speech (Hafner, 2016). He has long belittled science, except when there is an opportunity to boast about himself. During a visit with doctors and researchers at the Centers for Disease Control and Prevention (CDC) at the onset of the coronavirus pandemic, he announced: "Every one of these doctors said, 'How do you know so much about this?' Maybe I have a natural ability." Before winning the presidency, he had publicly questioned science by expressing skepticism about vaccines, and by suggesting that climate change was a hoax fabricated by China. Once in office, he systematically downplayed or ignored science to weaken environmental health and global warming regulations. He disbanded expert advisory boards and either suppressed or altered findings that warned of the dangers of pollution and global warming. As the new viral outbreak engulfed the nation, he repeatedly muzzled, sidelined, and pushed aside his public health experts (Friedman and Plumer, 2020). Those who contradicted his preferred narrative were either removed from their positions or had their funding withdrawn (Goldberg, 2020a).

It may indeed seem as though Donald Trump acts under some secret guidance that gives himself and others the feeling of magical infallibility: his ability to sense the needs of a crowd and to spellbind them, his Harry Houdini-like escapes from troubles that would have sunk anyone else, or his ability to build a Teflon presidency centered around what can only be described as obvious criminality. Armed with bravado, bluster, boundless audacity, and ruthlessness, thriving in the tumult of his creation, he has until now, exhibited an extraordinary knack for recasting obvious losses into strange wins, accustomed to the prodigious safety net of his wealthy father or of the bankers and lenders of New York City. His supporters allow him to live large on their dime until the point at which letting him die would mortally wound themselves, and he effectively occupied and used his hosts to grow bigger until he was not only "too big to fail" but "too big to jail" (Kruse, 2019). This is, in a sense, how he has scrounged the U.S. presidency and has held onto it to escape any prosecution or accountability.

He sees his approach as a binary choice. He told *New York* magazine in 1994:

> Hey, look, I had a cold spell from 1990 to '91. I was beat up in business and in my personal life…. But you learn that you're either the toughest, meanest piece of shit in the world, or you just crawl into a corner, put your finger in your mouth, and say, "I want to go home" (Horowitz, 1994).

Mary Trump, his niece, and a clinical psychologist told me:

> Even though my grandfather died twenty years ago, whenever Donald is talking about he is the best, he is the greatest, whenever he is starved for attention and compliments and the rally crowds, what he is really doing is speaking to his audience of one, which was my grandfather, and saying, "You know, Dad, I am the best, I am the winner, do not kill me" (Lee, 2020b).

In other words, you need to be the toughest killer on the block or die.

A staggeringly fragile ego lurks behind the façade. Many trace his bid for the presidency itself to the 2011 White House Correspondents' Association dinner when he became the butt of jokes by President Barack Obama and "Saturday Night Live" comedian Seth Meyers. Humiliated by the experience, he swiftly left the dinner in a dour mood, and many who observed him said it seemed to trigger some deep yearning for revenge. "That evening of public abasement … accelerated his ferocious efforts to gain stature in the political world," the *New York Times* wrote (Roberts, 2016). He has spent his entire adult life plastering his name on skyscrapers and casinos, obsessed with his image, and spending perhaps the greatest amount of time as president monitoring television coverage of him, angrily accusing, "Fake news!" or "Enemy of the people!" simply for accurate, unflattering reporting (Sullivan, 2020). Perhaps most shockingly, when the coronavirus pandemic hit, governors had to grovel to him to receive medical equipment, and those who he refused had their entire states "going through hell as a result" (McCarthy, 2020).

Donald Trump as the public sees him

When we try to paint a portrait of Donald Trump as the public sees him, we must not forget that propaganda distorts a large part of their view. Millions of people have seen him in staged rallies and press conferences, but most of their information comes from media sources, which have diverged with time into highly conflicting narratives, divided into two camps: whether they support him or not. Reporting has also become split, dependent on whether they believe him or not. In other words, his awkwardness, belligerence, and even antisocial tendencies have come to be experienced as endearing, reassuring, and alternately sympathy-evoking and awe-inspiring, depending on the framing.

He is, at first glance, an alert and oriented, tall but mildly obese Caucasian man who appears his stated age or perhaps slightly younger. He is well-groomed with an elaborate hairdo and bulky, ill-fitting suit with an exceptionally long red tie. His posture is forward-leaning, whether sitting or standing. His eye contact is often uneasy and fleeting when around others in a room, where he can oscillate between the attitude of a scolded child (especially around other world leaders) or a belligerent commander (especially around reporters). He gesticulates often as if playing an invisible accordion and, unlike most people, appears most comfortable when addressing large crowds, especially stadiums full of them. His speech is often loud and voluminous, rarely letting others speak in his presence, but otherwise normal in rate and rhythm. His expressed emotion is often labile if not volatile, able to transition from being charming to being aggressive on a moment's notice, but is highly dependent on his audience. His thought process is often loose, jumping from one topic to another through free association, which others have described as "bumbling, tangential, and bordering on the nonsensical" (Shpancer, 2020). His thought content is often detached from reality, bordering on delusion, but we will delve further into this in the analysis.

Physical descriptions of him in the media hardly fail to notice his hair, as far back as in 1984: "His sandy hair is probably a bit long by standards of the corporate world," a newspaper profile stated politely of the then-38-year-old. "With the sides slicked back just a bit." Three decades later, the hairdo of the leading Republican presidential candidate became a topic of conversation in its own right: "Is it swirled or swooped? Animal or vegetable? (Mineral?) Burnt sienna or orange Creamsicle? Recently, Gawker published an extensive investigation asserting that the whole concoction might actually be a $60,000 weave" (Hesse, 2016). *The Chicago*

Tribune called him:

> The braggart with the ducktail who would be president…. It is the most famous ducktail in America today, the hairdo of wayward youth of a bygone era, and it's astonishing to imagine it under the spotlight in Cleveland, being cheered by Republican dignitaries. The class hood, the bully and braggart… is the C-minus guy who sat behind you in history and poked you with his pencil and smirked when you asked him to stop. That smirk is now on every front page in America. It is not what anybody—left, right or center—looks for in a president. There's no philosophy here, just an attitude (Keillor, 2016).

Early remarks on his dress were not flattering, either. "He's known for a swaggering businessman's style that offers little in the way of a statement on personal aesthetics or even rarefied taste," one article said.

> His suits … are cut from conservative but quality fabric yet lack an attention to fit. They are always a little too roomy, the sleeves a tad too long. So much so that they look cheap—or more diplomatically, they look a lot like the mass-market suits that bore his name and were once sold at Macy's until the department store shuttered the line after his derogatory remarks about Mexicans. Trump's tie always seems to hang just a little too far below his belt, which makes a perfectly fine four-in-hand look not quite right. He makes ties look sloppy (Givhan, 2015).

Not looking fastidiously tailored is possibly how he aims to appeals to the average voter, not as a man with his name plastered on assorted buildings who touts his wealth, but as an ordinary, angry middle-management guy. He lacks the confidence or subtlety to settle with a discreet elegance without a searing, fire-engine red tie, for instance. People have asked: "Why does Trump wear suit jackets that are (literally) two sizes too big?" And an article has answered: "It might have something to do with his attempts to look bigger and therefore more powerful" (Croffey, 2016).

Indeed, his electoral success owes a great deal to a large portion of the population placing importance on having a strong leader and to their perception that he looked the part. Morning Consult/Politico exit polls showed the importance of the presidential candidate appearing to be strong.

It was twice as salient a factor in the 2016 election, with 36 percent, against 18 percent in 2012, saying that having a strong leader was particularly important. The image Donald Trump projected was of a nationalist strongman, which resonated with those whom globalization had marginalized. The notion of a "strong leader" has been interpreted as "one who maximizes his (or her) personal power; dominates his government, political party and a wide swath of public policy; and asserts his right to make all the big decisions." In projecting himself as a near-messianic figure, disregarding his lack of political experience but ridiculing even his own party and declaring, "I alone can fix it," he promised at his inauguration ceremony to determine not only the course of the United States but also of the world "for many, many years to come" in a "historic movement the likes of which the world has never seen before" (Brown, 2017). The realities that the audience turnout fell far below that of Barack Obama in 2009, and that he failed to impress most Americans—notably the voters who chose his opponent by an excess of three million votes—did not get in the way of his rhetoric. Indeed, that he would never have won but for the vagaries of an anachronistic electoral college system would not enter into his discourse.

Perhaps it was his obvious fragility or the serious nature of the office he holds that caused much of the mockery and teasing from the major media to diminish following the shock of his winning the presidential election. On the other hand, the myth of his strongman image grew from the peripheries into the mainstream: "Donald Trump: Finally Someone with Balls" t-shirts became common at his rallies, and research by the Washington Post revealed that he appeared to appeal to men with "fragile masculinity," those who were secretly insecure about their manhood. Research shows that men often feel pressure to look and behave in stereotypically masculine ways—or risk losing their status as "real men." Socialization of these expectations begins in early childhood and can become unforgiving standards that make some men worry they are falling short. The political process can become a way for fragile men to reaffirm their masculinity, and this became so in the United States in 2016 more than in previous years; by supporting a "tough" politician with aggressive policies, they could reassure themselves and others of their own manliness (Knowles and DiMuccio, 2018). Hence, the apotheosis of the fragile man, awkward, thin-skinned, self-conscious, and unsure of himself, managed to become through his public persona the epitome of manhood for many.

In addition to the lure of his psychological defenses, hypnotist Richard Barker claims hypnotic techniques are one of Donald Trump's most powerful weapons. Mass hypnosis has been around for a very long time, including in politics and religion, but "Donald Trump has mastered it," Barker argues. He uses mass persuasion and suggestion, even though he is "not a very good public speaker," but his magical powers in commanding attention lay almost entirely in his ability to sense what a given audience wants to hear and then to manipulate his speech in such a way to arouse the crowd's emotions. Like a seismograph for crowds, he senses with an agility that no conscious strategy could match, to act as an amplifier of the most secret desires, the least permissible drives, and the sufferings and revolts of those who felt left behind. "America was once great," his frequent narrative goes, and "we need to fight those that are taking our country away from us." By creating expectations, the audience knows what they are going to get, and helping them to visualize brings them into a hypnotic trance. He had been tireless on the campaign trail, and even afterward seemed to crave giving speeches so much that he could not stop even after being elected. He used repetitive phrases—"Lock her up!" or "Build that wall!"—rehearsed his audience, and created message discipline. "He does all the things that a hypnotist would do when you're hypnotizing somebody," the hypnotist described (Kurtz, 2016).

His brash rhetoric was something new, and a stark comparison to most slow-tongued, carefully calibrated politicians. His brutal insult comedy was a spectacle that people paid to see, and the executive chairman of CBS himself admitted the campaign was a "circus" of "bomb-throwing." He said: "It may not be good for America, but it's damn good for CBS⊠. Man, who would have expected the ride we're all having right now?... The money's rolling in, and this is fun" (Bond, 2016). Through insults, chants, entertainment, spectacles of violence, and the assistance of mass media, he was thrusting himself onto the consciousness of thousands, holding audiences under a hypnotic spell, whether they found him refreshing or repulsive.

Before the election almost all of his speeches seemed to center around the following three themes: (a) the corrupt "swamp" of Washington that needed to be drained; (b) the illegal and criminal immigrants entering from Mexico; and (c) how great he is and how he alone can fix it. His rambling events, which sometimes stretched over an hour with only the barest of notes to guide him, was a framework built around the same, simple anchors that created comfort for their predictability. Indeed, people liked what he did and would attend one rally after another to hear him speak. It was not so much what he said that appealed to his audiences, but how he said it, with the familiar rhythm of anecdotes, themes, and phrases he habitually settled into. His heart and soul in the cause of national aggrandizement, he dared to speak the truth and to defy the national authorities as well as "the globalists." His main message was as follows: he is a winner, everyone else is a loser. By supporting him, they are winners, too—and America needs winners (Berenson, 2016).

It was this version of Donald Trump that people saw firsthand: a tireless speaker who rushed from one rally to the next, in states that often felt neglected by the political elites, working himself to exhaustion on their behalf. They do not see the man who owns or operates seventeen different golf courses or properties around the world, including twelve in the United States, two in Dubai, one in Ireland, and two in Scotland, as well as planned courses in Indonesia. He plays only with friends and famous people, including professional golfers, senators, and other political and diplomatic personalities. These are only spotted visits since the White House goes out of its way to bar the press from shadowing him when he goes to his clubs. He golfed so much since taking office on January 20, 2017, that a "Trump Golf Count" website was set up, and as of this writing was seen on his courses or played golf elsewhere over 290 times, nearly 22 percent of his time in office. His cost to the American taxpayer has totaled in the tens of millions of dollars, and the Secret Service has spent at least 550,000 dollars in third-party golf cart rentals and over 500,000 dollars to stay overnight at Donald Trump's properties, including his New Jersey country club (Golf News Net, 2020).

Donald Trump's image as a successful businessman helped carry him to the White House, and a majority of Americans still believe he was successful. Yet, in 2018 the New York Times reported that he inherited 413 million dollars from his father, largely through illegal tax dodges (Barstow et al., 2018). In 2019, the news broke that the "very successful" businessman had lost 1.17 billion dollars between 1985 and 1994, or more money than nearly any other individual American taxpayer—such a massive sum that he was able to avoid paying income taxes for most of those years (Buettner and Craig, 2019). Despite being reminded of these facts in a poll, however, 74 percent of Republicans still clung to the belief that Donald Trump was successful when it came to business. A powerful real estate tycoon feeds people's imagination, as well as offers material for the right-wing propaganda machine, which continued to portray him as a superlative, if not superhuman, character. Many believed that he is the same height and weight as professional baseball player Tim Tebow, and a full two inches taller than Barack Obama, no matter the glaring evidence to the contrary. They also seemed to believe he is as rich as he says he is, that his tax cut was all about the middle class and cost him "a fortune," and that he could not release his tax returns because he is under audit, even though there is no such rule. Even his lack of scruples in losing more than any other taxpayer became a sign of his greatness: "If anything…. it's pretty impressive, all the things that he's done in his life. It's beyond what most of us could ever achieve" (Cummings, 2019).

Donald Trump as his associates see him

To portray Donald Trump as his associates see him, we must take into account a number of factors. We must consider not only the extent of these associates' interactions with him and the reliability of their reports, but also how they compare with one another. In doing so, there is a vast amount of material we could draw from. In fact, there is almost an overabundance of information that has poured out from former colleagues, associates and co-conspirators, as well as by one member of Donald Trump's own family. The sources that have been selected for consideration here include reports and books by five people who provide, within their pages, firsthand accounts of their experiences with the man. The first is Tony Schwartz, a ghostwriter who spent eighteen months shadowing Donald Trump in order to write his memoir. The second is John Bolton, a man who served as Donald Trump's national security advisor for seventeen months. The third is Michael Cohen, who spent twelve years as Donald Trump's lawyer and fixer. The fourth is Bob Woodward, a journalist of presidents who conducted an extraordinary eighteen taped interviews with Donald Trump. The last is Mary Trump, the president's niece, who spent a lot of time around the family. I have personally met with, and interviewed, only three out of those five—Tony Schwartz, Michael Cohen, and Mary Trump—but there is a high degree of consistency between their reports across the board. This, in addition to the consistency also shown when checked against other sources of information, such as investigative reports and sworn testimonies, suffices for an assessment of reasonable validity.

A ghostwriter

In order to protect the public, a personal interview is not always necessary to assess the various effects and influences that a given public persona might have. In many cases, collateral reports produced by others who have interacted with that person are far more valuable. It was for this reason that Tony Schwartz was invited to contribute to The Dangerous Case of Donald Trump (2017), even if he was not to be numbered among the initial twenty-seven mental health experts included in that publication. Schwartz was able to offer what the mental health experts at that time could not: a piece that recounted and reflected on direct personal experiences with Donald Trump. Schwartz spent eighteen months between 1985 and 1987 getting to know Donald Trump better than almost anyone outside the family: he camped out in Donald Trump's office, joined him on his helicopter, tagged along to meetings, and spent weekends with him at both his Manhattan apartment and his Florida estate. Thanks to Schwartz's contribution to The Dangerous Case of Donald Trump, we were able combine expert medical analysis with experiential observation. Bringing those two elements together meant that our assessment could claim reasonable completeness.

In his piece, Schwartz did not pull any punches. His breakthrough book, *The Art of the Deal* (Trump and Schwartz, 1987) earned him forty-eight weeks on the *New York Times* bestseller list. Schwartz's assessment of how it was written is: "I put lipstick on a pig," he told the *New Yorker*. It was because of that book that Schwartz had also decided to speak up during the 2016 presidential campaign. He believed *The Art of the Deal* had caused many Americans' to foster a false conception of Donald Trump's character. Indeed, the book presents Donald Trump as a charmingly brash entrepreneur with an unfailing knack for business: "It pays to trust your instincts" (Trump and Schwartz, 1987), he states at one point, boasting of the "secret" of his success. Schwartz knew, however, that beneath that appealing, if possibly abrasive, façade lay a pathologically impulsive and dangerously self-centered individual. This is an assessment that also finds support in a statement made by Roy Cohn, Donald Trump's personal lawyer, a man who had, in the 1950's, assisted Senator Joseph McCarthy in his vicious crusade against Communism. Cohn, at the end of his life, dying of AIDS, had this to say about Donald Trump: "Donald pisses ice water" (Mayer, 2016).

This coldness and self-centered attitude are particularly evident in Donald Trump's relationships with other people, as observed by Schwartz. Donald Trump spent very little time with his family and appeared to have no close friends. People were disposable in his world, Schwartz claims, because for Donald Trump, "it was all about what you could do for him." In addition to that, Donald Trump had "no attention span," the result of which was "a stunning level of superficial knowledge and plain ignorance." While it drew upon an entirely different set of data, Schwartz's criticism of Donald Trump in 2016 was such that it agrees closely with our assessment as mental health experts: "I genuinely believe," he stated at the time, "that if Trump wins and gets the nuclear codes there is an excellent possibility it will lead to the end of civilization" (Mayer, 2016).

Schwartz's first meeting with Donald Trump was not one that he would have predicted. Its unlikely prompt was an unflattering piece that Schwartz had written for the New Yorker, in which he described Donald Trump as a ham-fisted thug trying to drive out rent-stabilized tenants from his Central Park South building through harassment. After the piece was published, Donald Trump sent Schwartz something closely akin to a fan note. Schwartz was, understandably, shocked: "Trump didn't fit any model of human being I'd ever met. He was obsessed with publicity, and he didn't care what you wrote." This characteristic manifested itself time and time again later, when Schwartz was ghostwriting the memoir. Finding it difficult on occasion to pin down a fidgety and easily-bored Donald Trump, Schwartz started to eavesdrop on his phone calls instead. Rather than being angered by this, and Donald Trump loved the attention. Indeed, according to Schwartz, if Donald Trump "could have had three hundred thousand people listening in, he would have been even happier." All of this ties in with what Schwartz recalls of Donald Trump's habit of "playing people" in these calls: manipulating them by flattering, bullying, and occasionally getting mad, but always in a calculated way. At the end of a call, instead of saying goodbye, Donald Trump's customary sign-off was "You're the greatest!" At one point, Schwartz noted in his journal: "All he is is 'stomp, stomp, stomp'—recognition from outside, bigger, more, a whole series of things that go nowhere in particular" (Mayer, 2016).

Not only did Schwartz's eavesdropping reveal some of the ways in which Donald Trump relates to others, it also exposed a number of inconsistencies. "Lying is second nature to him," Schwartz told the *New Yorker*. "More than anyone else I have ever met, Donald Trump has the ability to convince himself that whatever he is saying at any given moment is true, or sort of true, or at least ought to be true." Indeed, far from being a successful tycoon, he lied strategically and misled the press. Moreover, when his lie was uncovered through reporting by the Village Voice, Donald Trump's conscience was seemingly completely unaffected. When challenged about the facts that had come to light, he would double down, repeat himself, and grow belligerent. While this was the case, Schwartz could not simply portray Donald Trump, in his memoir, as a hateful "one-dimensional blowhard" (Mayer, 2016). As such, when writing the book, he created euphemisms, putting into Donald Trump's mouth phrases such as: "I play to people's fantasies…. People want to believe that something is the biggest and the greatest and the most spectacular. I call it truthful hyperbole" (Trump and Schwartz, 1987).

While he always abhorred Donald Trump's "willingness to run over people, the gaudy, tacky, gigantic obsessions, the absolute lack of interest in anything beyond power and money," Schwartz now greatly regrets the fake charm that he created and ascribed him in the memoir. Having watched Donald Trump pile one hugely expensive project atop the next, like a circus performer spinning plates, Schwartz would go home and say exclaim to his wife: "He's a living black hole!" The countless hours spent with Donald Trump were "draining" and "deadening," and to Schwartz his bid for the presidency seemed merge seamlessly into that continuum. After having spent decades as a tabloid titan, in Schwartz's mind Donald Trump's plan for the future was clear: "the only thing left was running for President. If he could run for emperor of the world, he would" (Mayer, 2016).

A national security adviser

Adding to the portrait of Donald Trump by Tony Schwartz is John Bolton's book, *The Room where It Happened* (2020). Bolton's account is one of someone who actually worked with Donald Trump, and worked not with revulsion but in uncommon agreement. Bolton was of the same mind as Donald Trump on many matters of national and international significance, including on the controversial withdrawal from the Iran nuclear deal. Bolton was widely criticized for choosing to release certain information only in his book, apparently for its sales, rather than to testify before the House of Representatives and possibly contribute to the president's impeachment (Flood, 2020). *The Room Where It Happened* nonetheless provides valuable insights. Most importantly, perhaps, it reveals the degree of alignment between Bolton and Donald Trump, despite some differences regarding policy. What Bolton provides us with, then, is a unique perspective on Trump from someone who was not just a governmental insider who is alarmed at the behavior he has witnessed, but a psychological insider who can use his own resemblance to the president to turn on him.

The same factors that make Bolton such a valuable source, however, also make his writing potentially difficult to interpret. Reading *The Room Where It Happened*, it is important to keep in mind and to balance two things: the author's narcissistic tendency to use the advantage of special insight and information in the his favor, and the inherent competitiveness that prompts the depiction of the opponent in a poor light so that the author might appear in a better one. To provide a fair assessment of Bolton's own reliability would perhaps require a book-length study. Certainly, taking into account all the things already mentioned, Bolton is possibly the least reliable of the associate sources considered in this chapter. Despite this, however, he still provides many compelling and useful insights for this analysis.

Bolton, we must be clear, is no hero and no martyr. Sometimes his agenda was even more extreme than that of the president himself. His experience, though, is extensive and undeniable: former U.S. assistant attorney general for Ronald Reagan; U.S. assistant secretary of state for international organization affairs in the State Department; undersecretary of state for arms control and international security affairs; brief, recess-appointed, ambassador to the United Nations; and, finally, national security advisor to Donald Trump from April 2018 through September 2019. This wealth of experience in and around government is, therefore, an important consideration when trying to understand Bolton's following assessment of Trump: "I don't think he's fit for office. I don't think he has the competence to carry out the job" (Bolton, 2020).

That Bolton perceives Trump to be lacking in competence and clarity of thought is evident throughout his book. He describes his thought process when it comes to matters of governance and policy as being "like an archipelago of dots, leaving the rest of us to discern—or create—policy." By Bolton's account, the possibility of a grand spectacle often lures the president, without consideration of other factors. This tendency, Bolton claims, saw Donald Trump enter into tough negotiations with foreign leaders while in possession of only a minimal understanding of the stakes. The further consequences of this can be seen in his signing of a toothless, vague, agreement with North Korean leader Kim Jong-un in Singapore and in his siding with Russian President Vladimir Putin rather than the U.S. intelligence community. Bolton also claims that, at one point, Donald Trump casually advocated withdrawing the U.S. from NATO for no other reason than to "do something historic" (Bolton, 2020). In this manner, Bolton's account corroborates our standardized mental health assessment from April 2019: that Donald Trump lacks mental capacity, the basic requirement to be considered fit and competent for just about any job, let alone the presidency.

The Room Where It Happened is full of deeply critical and unflattering anecdotes concerning Donald Trump, but the most telling are the ones that are not present: the ones that the White House redacted. When it became apparent, in January 2020, that Bolton had written and was going to publish a book, the White House sent Bolton's lawyer a cease-and-desist letter. This letter demanded that the book not be released without the removal of "voluminous amounts of classified information" and whose publication constituted a "national security risk." Subsequent to the issuing of that letter, William Barr's Justice Department also filed a federal lawsuit requesting that the judge block the release of Bolton's book. The reason behind both of these legal actions soon became clear, as *Vanity Fair* obtained some of the details subject to redaction: they are deeply embarrassing for Donald Trump, illustrating his naked politicization of America's foreign policy. In one of the unredacted passages that was leaked, Donald Trump is depicted begging for China's assistance while the 2019 G20 dinner: "Make sure I win…. Buy a lot of soybeans and wheat and make sure we win" (Sherman, 2020), said the would-be strongman, desperate for re-election, abasing himself before Xi Jinping.

That behavior toward Xi is telling. As a needy supplicant, Trump does not criticize the ruthless leader he finds himself conversing with. Indeed, according to Bolton, when Xi explained why China was building concentration camps for the country's minority Uighur population, Donald Trump actually told Xi that he approved of this brutal violation of human rights. By Bolton's account, Donald Trump actually told Xi to "go ahead, you're doing exactly the right thing." Earlier in the same passage, Bolton also writes that, during a phone call to Xi ahead of their G20 meeting, Donald Trump said, "I miss you," before adding: "this is totally up to you, but the most popular thing I've ever been involved with is making a deal with China…. Making a deal with China would be a very popular thing for me'" (Sherman, 2020). For this reason, people have hypothesized that Donald Trump was particularly eager to praise Xi at the start of the pandemic: "China has been working very hard to contain the Coronavirus. The United States greatly appreciates their efforts and transparency," he said on January 24, 2020 (Ward, 2020). He made this statement at the same time as the Chinese authorities were detaining a doctor who, since December 30, 2019, had been trying to alert them to a virus that by then had spread around the world (Shih, 2020).

In addition to these insights about relations with Xi and China, Bolton's book also confirms many crucial elements of the Ukraine scandal that was central to the impeachment case brought against the president in December 2019. Bolton provides firsthand evidence of the fact that Donald Trump conditioned the provision of 391 million dollars in security aid to Ukraine on its first agreeing to publicly announce investigations into supposed wrongdoing by Democrats, including former vice president, Joseph Biden. In other words, he sought to use taxpayer money as leverage to extract help from another country for a partisan political campaign: a quid pro quo that House Democrats claimed to be an abuse of power. As this proved to be a key issue within the impeachment hearings, and as Bolton clearly possessed evidence relating to the case, his actions at the time are questionable. During the hearings, Republicans dismissed the accusation on the basis that testifying witnesses offered only secondhand evidence, but Bolton was present in the room and could have provided firsthand evidence. An extra layer of complexity is also added by the fact that Bolton would, in his book, later state that he saw Trump's inventions in Justice Department investigation against foreign companies, in order to "give personal favors to dictators he liked— to represent "obstruction of justice as a way of life" (Baker, 2020).

A personal lawyer and fixer

Michael Cohen did not merely work for Donald Trump and, out of all those who have spoken out publicly against the president, he was the closest to him. Reflecting back on their relationship, Cohen claims that he got to know Donald Trump better even than the president's own family. This, he argues, was because he was able to bear "witness to the real man, in strip clubs, shady business meetings, and in the unguarded moments when he revealed who he really was: A cheat, a liar, a fraud, a bully, a racist, a predator, a con man." The value of Cohen's account is twofold: it is told from the perspective of not only an onlooker but also an eager participant, now paying the price as federal inmate number 86067-054. In his book, Disloyal: A Memoir, Cohen (2020) provides a credible account of his own internal tensions: on the one hand, knowing that the president is corrupt and totally unsuited to the job; on the other, supporting Donald Trump due to a feeling of kinship for the man for whom he had stiffed contractors, sued creditors, and ripped off realtors for over a decade. "I care for Donald Trump, even to this day," Cohen admits, "and I had and still have a lot of affection for him." Former insiders of cults or abusive relationships are valuable to anthropologists and psychological professionals alike. Indeed, these individuals provide some of the most intimate insights into what really happens within the destructive subculture or relationship but also place it in context.

Cohen's fate after his split from Trump was similar to that of many defectors from gangs, or escapees of abusive relationships, even if it afforded greater opportunity for grandiose and dramatic statements. "The President of the United States wanted me dead," is how Cohen begins his book. He does, however, then proceed to clarify that the statement is not one that Trump himself would ever issue:

Or, let me say it the way Donald Trump would: He wouldn't mind if I was dead. That was how Trump talked. Like a mob boss, using language carefully calibrated to convey his desires and demands, while at the same time employing deliberate indirection to insulate himself and avoid actually ordering a hit on his former personal attorney (Cohen, 2020).

What Cohen describes here is, to a large degree, congruent with what we have witnessed of Donald Trump in public: he has repeatedly incited his followers to acts of violence against those he opposes or dislikes, or who have criticized him, while avoiding the assumption of responsibility. Cohen himself used to be one of those followers, ensnared by the malevolent charm of a mob "Boss" who gave directions for his dirty work obliquely, always leaving room for deniability. From the twenty-sixth floor of Trump Tower, Donald Trump would summon Cohen to fix messes of his own making: buying the silence of women with whom he had had affairs, or managing disgruntled contractors and any others whom Donald Trump had cheated. If Donald Trump operated in a manner at times akin to a mafia godfather, his performance as a father was less accomplished: his neglected children were starved of his love and were "forever trapped in a cycle of seeking his approval" (Cohen, 2020).

If *Disloyal* contains many such revelations about Donald Trump's behavior and attitude toward those around him, it also brings into stark relief his always contentious relations with Russia. As Cohen recounts, building a hotel in Moscow had been one of Donald Trump's objectives for almost four decades. Accordingly, as his run for the presidency kicked off in December 2015, Cohen reached out and made contact with Vladimir Putin's press spokesman, Dmitry Peskov. The resulting situation had both seen and unseen elements: Donald Trump publicly praised Putin on the campaign trail while Cohen secretly tried to bring Trump Tower Moscow to fruition. All of these actions were, of course, known to Donald Trump, because of his need to be in charge of everything. By Cohen's account, Donald Trump did indeed collude with the Kremlin, but it was not the sophisticated collusion his critics imagined and hypothesized. Instead, Donald Trump's treason, if it can be called that, was of a much more pedestrian, me-first nature. Sharing with Putin a loathing for Hillary Clinton, Donald Trump would willingly accept any Russian help—hacking, spies, trolls, and oligarchs bearing gifts—so long as it benefited him personally. Donald Trump sucks up to Putin largely because he loves money, believing the one-time KGB colonel to be the world's richest man, worth a trillion dollars—much in the way Cohen was infatuated with the former real estate mogul, supposed billionaire, and star.

In trying to answer the question as to why he would risk everything to serve such a gargantuan con man, Cohen helps us to understand the insider's experience of following Donald Trump. Living in the heart of the president's world, Cohen was intoxicated by a fantastical cocktail of power, strength, celebrity, and complete disregard for the rules. Reflecting on his ultimate seduction by power, at one point in his memoir Cohen likens himself to character of Gollum from *The Lord of the Rings*. Moving more clearly from the realm of fantasy, however, he also suggests that he might be viewed as micro version of the situation currently occurring on a macro scale: Donald Trump mesmerizing America's media, and seducing and duping half of its population. Indeed, Cohen is insistent on the fact that the U.S. population, more so than the Russians, facilitated Donald Trump's rise to power and who may yet keep him there. The cocktail Cohen imbibed has, however, caused a hangover of equal strength: the "weird kind of pleasure in harming others in the service of Donald Trump" that he once enjoyed now causes him "eternal shame" (Cohen, 2020).

If Cohen is now open about his own actions and responsibilities, he also makes clear that he was not always working alone. Indeed, he work closely, on occasion, with David Pecker, the then CEO of American Media and publisher of the *National Enquirer*. Most notably, the two men cooperated with one another to smother the stories that emerged concerning Donald Trump's extramarital relationships with Stormy Daniels, an adult actress, and Karen McDougal, a Playboy model. These actions came to be particularly significant for Cohen personally: his own paying off of Daniels was an illegal campaign expense that helped put him in jail. Despite, or perhaps because of, the coverups, corruption, and lying, Cohen admits that Donald Trump has an arsenal of dark gifts. By Cohen's account, the president is in possession of talent, charisma, and pure ruthless ambition, as well as what he perceives to be an innate ability to tap into and exploit voters' deep prejudices and fears. In using these so-called gifts, Donald Trump thinks nothing of the consequence of his actions, living constantly in the present tense, a sort of "shark" that survives only through continuous motion, confident in his own instincts to guide the way. Cohen's own self-destructive descent into a world where this takes place, into "Trumpland", foreshadows that of the nation, according to his "part survivor's memoir, part revenge tragedy" (Harding, 2020).

A presidential journalist

Bob Woodward made his name with Carl Bernstein through *All the President's Men* (1974), where they laid out the history of the Watergate scandal. Woodward might not be the most psychologically-minded interviewer, but his book *Rage* (2020) is extraordinary because of the existence of accompanying tapes, allowing recorded glimpses into intimate conversations. The subject of Rage is Donald Trump and, over the course of eighteen on-the-record, recorded, interviews from December 2019 through August 2020, it presents an incredible account of the president in his own words, as well as in Woodward's. In this respect, the written work is fascinating in its own right, but it is perhaps the recordings that offer us the greatest insights. Listening to the exchanges between the two men, it is possible to gauge the subtle cadences and affective charges that shape the logical progressions of the interviews. At times, Donald Trump appears serious and focused, while simultaneously divulging stunning details about his handling of the coronavirus or a new secret nuclear weapons system. In other interviews, however, he is more frivolous, such as when he gives Woodward a tour of a small office that he calls "the Monica Room" (a reference to the affair between Monica Lewinsky and Bill Clinton). What is clear in all instances is that Trump is clearly trying to impress his interviewer.

Making these interviews still more striking and important is the fact that they are ones that Donald Trump himself requested. Indeed, he went out of his way, and against the explicit advice of his aides, to do so. Donald Trump's aides had prevented him from speaking with Woodward for his earlier book *Fear* (2018); after learning of this, the president then asked Woodward to interview him, seemingly under the conviction that he could charm a more flattering account from the journalist. This impulsive behavior and thought process is captured in intimate detail in the impromptu calls that Woodward would often receive from Donald Trump, commonly after nine or ten o'clock at night. As such, regarding the revelations of Rage, the White House's standard response to unfavorable stories about the president—branding them as "fake news—second-hand or corrupted with other agendas—is untenable. Here, Donald Trump indicts himself with his own voice, over and over, apparently without realizing it.

A wealth of information makes it difficult to decide which of Donald Trump's interviews with Woodward, or which sections of which interviews, should be looked at here. One particularly telling exchange, however, has Trump discussing Covid-19. Speaking with Woodward, the president states clearly the extent to which he recognized the severity of the threat posed by the worst global pandemic in a century. "It goes through air, Bob. That's always tougher than the touch…. It's also more deadly than ⊠ even your strenuous flus," Donald Trump tells Woodward, before continuing with a slightly different emphasis: "You know, people don't realize, we lose 25,000, 30,000 people a year here." He then proceeds to again state that the novel virus causes five times the mortality and calls it "deadly stuff" (Gangel and Herb, 2020). All of this stands in direct contrast to his public dismissal of the seriousness of the virus, his repeated hampering national efforts, and his cavalier disdain for masks: surely contributing factors to the carnage that the virus has caused in the U.S., with millions infected and almost 200,000 dead.

There are other exchanges Woodward documents in *Rage* that seem even more untethered from reality. At one point, for example, Donald Trump claims he has "done more for the Black community than any other president than Abraham Lincoln" (Woodward, 2020). This is a statement that is in no way supported by the manner in which his department of justice has aggressively and perversely criminalized and terrorized people of color (Maxwell and Solomon, 2018). It does not even always accord with Trump's own words. As the protests over the police killing of George Floyd spread across the country and around the world, Woodward tells Donald Trump about how he, as a privileged white person, has only recently grasped the need to understand and address the anger and pain of Black people. Having said that, Woodward then asks Donald Trump whether he has also experienced a similar epiphany. The president is clear in his response: "No. You really drank the Kool-Aid, didn't you? Just listen to you. Wow. No, I don't feel that at all." Somewhat reversing the issue, Donald Trump then proceeds to complain about something else he is not getting: "I have done a tremendous amount for the Black community. And honestly I'm not feeling the love" (Gangel and Herb, 2020). On that point, his feeling, or lack thereof, is a genuine one: only 10 percent of black voters supported Donald Trump.

The same hubris that led Donald Trump to believe that he has done so much for black Americans, amongst whom unemployment is now at 13 percent, also manifested itself in other aspects of his life and dealings. Perhaps most strikingly, it shaped his unhinged relationship with the North Korean dictator, Kim Jong-un. Getting Kim to give up his nuclear weapons, a long-held goal of the U.S., Trump believed he could achieve solely through the use of his own persuasive powers. Part of this attempt at persuasion took place in twenty-seven letters between the president and Kim that Donald Trump reportedly refers to as "love letters." Significantly, he gave Woodward access to these letters; Woodward notes that the tone of the correspondence between the two leaders is indeed akin to that used by "suitors". The actual real-world significance of this, however, appears to be negligible. Donald Trump met with Kim three times—in Singapore, Hanoi, and in the DMZ between North and South Korea—but he has been no more successful than his predecessors in getting North Korea to dismantle, or even to dial back, its nuclear program. Indeed, the tone of the communication between Donald Trump and Kim might well have been carefully engineered by the latter. In his book, Woodward reports that CIA analysts "marveled" at the letters, remarking on how skillfully their author appealed to both "Trump's sense of grandiosity" and his desire to be seen taking "center stage in history" (Woodward, 2020). What is evident from this is that North Korea, like many other nations, has had a rigorous psychological profile of the U.S. president, whereas the U.S. itself is lacking one.

At one point in an interview, Woodward asks Donald Trump a direct question concerning what it was like to meet with Kim at their first summit, held in Singapore. The response that he receives, both in its tone and its focus, provides a great insight into nature of the president's approach to matters of such political gravity: "It was the most cameras I think I've seen, more cameras than any human being in history"—indeed, even more cameras than he had seen at the Academy Awards. He proceeds to brag about how Kim "tells me everything," seemingly impressed by the dictator's brutality. "He killed his uncle and put the body right in the steps where the senators walked out. And the head was cut, sitting on the chest.... Nancy Pelosi said, 'Oh, let's impeach him.' You think that's tough? This is tough" (Woodward, 2020).

The interviews with Donald Trump make Rage a remarkable account, but Woodward did not only interview the president. The journalist also spoke at length with the former secretary of state, Rex Tillerson, and the former director of national intelligence, Dan Coats. Corroborating what many others have said, Coats describes to Woodward Donald Trump's problematic relationship with the truth: "To him a lie is not a lie. It's just what he thinks. He doesn't know the difference between the truth and a lie." Tillerson, in his interview, took objection to the president's choice of staff, stating that he found what he saw as the chummy dealings between Jared Kushner and Israeli Prime Minister Benjamin Netanyahu, "nauseating to watch" and "stomach-churning." The former secretary of defense, James Mattis, also claims an ambivalent and distant relationship with the president: "I never cared much what Trump said.... I didn't get much guidance from him, generally, other than an occasional tweet." Despite this, Woodward also reports that Coats and Mattis had a phone call on May 25, 2019, in which they agreed there might come a time when it would be necessary to publicly state that Donald Trump was dangerous and unfit to be president. This was just the same conclusion that we had arrived at through our mental capacity evaluation just a month earlier, on April 25, 2019. Woodward may well be more prone to direct reporting than to conducting analysis, and yet he, too, draws a conclusion from his interviews. Toward the end of Rage, he writes: "Trump is the wrong man for the job" (Woodward, 2020).

A niece

In terms of trying to gather the most interpretive collateral information, a credible mental health professional's account of their childhood is of great value. Such an account has been provided by Donald Trump's only niece, Dr. Mary Trump. The quality of information that an individual like Dr. Trump is able to provide allows for a more in-depth analysis of the subject's ingrained personality structure. Especially for someone in a position to exert extensive, and especially adverse, influence on society, it gives us key insight into the reasons why their behaviors are so powerful and how they can spread to others. As a general rule, the more biologically-determined mental illnesses such as schizophrenia or depression result in a person posing even less danger to others even than if they had no illness. By contrast, developmental defects can be very dangerous and yet often go undetected, or, worse, they are misrecognized and improperly celebrated - to the detriment of society. As a result, it is important to identify both early childhood events and also enduring later patterns that might indicate the presence of, or predisposition to, personality problems. The availability and reliability of collateral sources of information determine the depth to which we are able to probe in such a process. If the sources are reliable and credible, we may have the ability to ask them not only for facts but also reactions and resources that they might be able to offer. This holds true particularly in cases in which the defects being analyzed cause suffering not to the person who possesses them but to others with whom they come into contact: a condition we call *ego-syntonic* (the symptoms do not bother their bearer), as opposed to *ego-dystonic* (the symptoms bother their bearer). Dr. Trump meets those criteria and, most importantly, she has provided a credible analysis based on intimate household observations. That analysis, delivered toward the end of Donald Trump's first term in office, corroborates and completes our own independent public health analysis, made by some of the nation's foremost mental health experts at the start of the presidency.

When I interviewed Dr. Trump, in order to establish her reliability, or the extent to which she demonstrated critical self-awareness and realistic appraisal, I asked her: "When did you realize it was not you and your father who were 'a mess' (her uncle's portrayal of them) but Donald Trump himself?" She answered with a good degree of insight:

> It took a really long time because you grow up in this atmosphere that seems totally the way it is…. I think getting disinherited was kind of a tipoff, [and] throughout my training as a clinician, I learned a lot about how to look at systems like families and pathologies and developmental issues, et cetera. Distance and training … helped a lot (Lee, 2020b).

She then added further to her credibility by commenting on some of the difficulties she faced when writing the book. "It was not until I started writing the book," Dr. Trump told me, "that I really got in touch with some things that I, honestly, wish I had not had to" (Lee, 2020b). Listening to her, I was satisfied that she was both a valuable and a reliable source.

In her book, *Too Much and Never Enough* (2020), Dr. Trump provides an account of her uncle's childhood. She describes how, as a toddler, Donald Trump was deprived of the most essential ingredient required for healthy emotional growth and life: parental care. According to the book, "Donald's main source of comfort and human connection was taken from him" when he was not yet three years old, following a harrowing incident that occurred in the Trump family's mansion. That incident centers around Donald Trump's mother: there was night in which his twelve-year-old sister, Maryanne, discovered her lying unconscious on the bathroom floor in a pool of blood. The cause of this was severe postpartum complications resulting from the birth of her youngest child, Robert, which would see the mother of five repeatedly hospitalized over the subsequent six months. "Having been abandoned by his mother for at least a year, and having his father fail not only to meet his needs but to make him feel safe or loved, valued or mirrored," Dr. Trump argues that, during that early period, "Donald suffered deprivations that would scar him for life." In her assessment, this situation was "an epic tragedy of parental failure." Donald Trump's mother never truly recovered, and nor did her relationship with her son. His father, strikingly, showed utter indifference, if not annoyance, toward his wife's expressions of discomfort or pain; he would often cut her off, saying "Everything's great. Right, Toots? You just have to think positive" (Trump, 2020).

As a child, Donald Trump, unsurprisingly, came to display the classic early signs of serious problems with aggression and psychopathy. By the time he was thirteen, as Dr. Trump claims, "Donald's misbehavior—fighting, bullying, arguing with teachers—had gone too far." What had started as name-calling and teasing had escalated into physical altercations. His father did not necessarily mind the acting out itself, but the fact that it had now become both intrusive and time-consuming bothered him. At the suggestion of fellow board members, he sent Donald Trump to the New York Military Academy as a way to rid himself of the trouble and leave himself free to attend to what he considered to be more important matters. The future president experienced his father's action as another abandonment, and it became the foundation for his further development into being what Dr. Trump describes as a "petty, pathetic little man—ignorant, incapable, out of his depth, and lost to his own delusional spin." This spin, we learn, is essentially all that Donald Trump has learned: relentless and incongruous puffery. Despite being fundamentally infantile and mentally unstable, Donald Trump styled himself a stable genius, even though all evidence pointed, and continues to point, to the contrary. In doing so, regardless of the outcome, his father would back him up. The result of this, according to Dr. Trump, was that as Donald Trump's "failures mounted despite my grandfather's repeated—and extravagant—interventions, his struggle for legitimacy, which could never be won, turned into a scheme to make sure nobody found out that he's never been legitimate at all." To achieve this, he successfully utilized the media to spread his hype, until finally even the banks fell for it. In this manner, from his adolescence in reform school to his coddling in the Oval Office, Donald Trump can be seen to have essentially been "institutionalized most of his adult life" (Trump, 2020).

For Dr. Trump, her uncle's aforementioned relationship with various banks is, in some way, both emblematic and indicative. Analyzing that relationship, she concludes that the banks' "willingness (and then their need) to foster his increasingly unfounded claims to success hung on the hopes of recouping their losses." But, of course, they would never manage this. Dr. Trump argues that this parallels the manner in which the president has been equally effective in drawing in numerous enablers, opportunists, and supporters until they too have become trapped. "Honest work was never demanded of him," she says, "and no matter how badly he failed, he was rewarded in ways that are almost unfathomable." Viewing the current situation this this critical lens of personal experience, Dr. Trump is now terrified that the U.S. this will devolve into "a macro version of my malignantly dysfunctional family." She argued that, having grown up in a family environment in which a "killer" instinct was revered, Donald Trump views cruelty as "a means to distract both us and himself from the true extent of his failures." The potential consequences of this for the public at large are not positive: "He'll withhold ventilators or steal supplies from states that have not groveled sufficiently," Dr. Trump posits, suggesting that what the president "thinks is justified retaliation is, in this context, mass murder." She is similarly clear when it comes to the reason as to why she decided to write about her uncle: "Donald, following the lead of my grandfather and with the complicity, silence and inaction of his siblings, destroyed my father. I can't let him destroy my country" (Trump, 2020). This is damning: her father, the president's older brother, apparently the most empathic and self-reliant member of the family, died at the age of forty-two of alcoholism, prompted by their abuse.

A PROFILE OF TRUMP SUPPORTERS

A public health issue

As I wrote in the introduction of *The Dangerous Case of Donald Trump,* despite its title, Donald Trump is not the main focus of the book. Rather, to understand his presidency as a national public health issue, we need to understand his followers as well as the state of the nation that gave rise to his presidency. Then, we need to study the larger context that he has influenced by virtue of his position. Coauthor Dr. Thomas Singer calls attention to the link between Trump and the American collective psyche. Trump "mirrors, even amplifies, our collective attention deficit disorder, our sociopathy, and our narcissism" (Singer, 2017)—but this would not serve as a diagnosis as much as a recognition of our own pathology. The ascendancy of an individual with grave impairments does not occur in a vacuum, and we are now at a pivotal point where we can either improve the situation or further impair it. Hence, this chapter is devoted to understanding a part of that larger picture: his followers.

Just as normalizing the president's psychology is dangerous, so too would be attempting to normalize the psychology of his followers. This does not mean that each follower of the president will exhibit abnormal psychology; on the contrary, it is more likely that each person will be quite normal when separated from the president and other followers. A group psyche is not the same as the sum of the psychology of individual members, and the themes and conflicts of groups are not the same as our personal struggles, although they interact. The group psyche is a part that lives inside every one of us as individual carriers and sharers in whatever group dynamics of which we are a part. As with individuals, problems can arise within groups that are recognizable and follow distinct patterns. It is worth noting, for example, the various factors at play for the more or less 40 percent of the population that comprises Trump's enduring "base" to act, think, and believe as it does, and we should not ignore how some of this diverges from healthy, rational, and well-informed ways. When such a large portion of the population deviates from health, it becomes a public health problem that should be dealt with through the language of public health, since individual analysis has no mechanism for dealing with persons who are nevertheless "normal" for conforming to the subculture.

The first observation is that it appears that he can do no wrong in the eyes of his followers. In the words of one of his followers: "President Trump has accomplished more positive things for this nation in less than two years than the last three have accomplished in twenty plus years…. Could you please list one thing the demwit party has done for the black people in America?" (Azpiazu and Ocner, 2018). Later, the assertions become more belligerent: "I am here tonight to tell you—to warn you—that this election is a decision between preserving America as we know it and eliminating *everything* that we love," said Charlie Kirk, a young Trump acolyte opening the Republican National Convention (Wehner, 2020).

During a deadly pandemic, his followers can be seen putting their lives and health in danger, not for the good of the country, the economy, or even themselves and their family. It is simply so that their leader can get a media adrenaline rush from Fox News and other right-wing media coverage of protests heeding his call to "liberate" their various states against social distancing and other public health policies that are meant to protect people (Mitchell, 2020). When Donald Trump would resume his rallies, many would show up not wearing masks or practicing social distancing as they chant: "We! Love! You!" (Karni, 2020). This is an extraordinary demonstration of fealty, one that is not lost on a president who seems acutely aware that his best chance of staying in power—and out of jail—relies on his ability to mobilize his supporters. Unfortunately for both the president and his loyal supporters, many of those most loyal to him will be sick or dead because of these actions. They are literally willing to die for the show of support for their leader.

This fealty shows in the willingness to take a dangerous substance—one that might kill them—if Donald Trump stated it would be good for them, such as when he announced that he was taking hydroxychloroquine to ward off the coronavirus. Convinced that their president would never lead them down a dangerous path, people all over America have been asking for the medicine, despite the growing number of lupus and arthritis patients complaining they were unable to fill their prescriptions amid shortages. It did not matter to Donald Trump's followers that medical experts and his own U.S. Food and Drug Administration warned against the drug's dangerous side effects, or that it could cause lethal heart problems. They dismissed studies showing that hydroxychloroquine does not work against Covid-19. When Donald Trump suggested during a televised news briefing that ingesting disinfectants might help treat the virus, the following eight day period saw an increase in accidental poisoning by 121 percent compared to April of 2019 (Kluger, 2020), and at least one instance proved that someone "drank a product because of the advice he'd received" (O'Laughlin, 2020).

While the dynamics between Donald Trump and his followers are complex, they can be summarized in four stages. First, there is the *narcissistic symbiosis*, wherein similarly-impaired personalities are attracted to one another and unattracted to health. Second, there is *cultic programming*, whereby followership of Donald Trump is systematically coordinated and cultivated through psychological conditioning. Third, there has formed what I will call a *battered nation syndrome*, whereby followers are psychologically abused but too invested to leave. Finally, there is *shared psychosis*, or the natural spread of symptoms that results from prolonged exposure to an impaired person in an influential position.

Narcissistic symbiosis

We have seen how brazen actions—calling Mexicans rapists, bragging about sexual assault, provoking war with Iran, causing tens if not hundreds of thousands more Americans to die, and collapsing the world's greatest economy—have failed to produce a serious dent in the president's popularity. Even a rapidly diminishing vocabulary, wandering off, and forgetting his son's name—all serious signs in a man whose father died of Alzheimer's disease—are nothing compared to Joe Biden's relatively insignificant stumbles (Carr, 2020). Why might this be?

There is a considerable amount that has been written about this magnetism and the political psychology of leaders and followers. The great German sociologist Max Weber (1922) first introduced the concept of charismatic authority, describing it as compelling forcefulness on the part of the leader's personality. Psychoanalyst Dr. Irvine Schiffer (1973) describes how leaders—especially charismatic leaders—are at heart the creation of their followers. Psychiatrists started to focus on the follower dynamic after the mass suicide at Jonestown, a settlement of the People's Temple in Guyana, where followers of the Reverend Jim Jones drank poisoned Kool-Aid (Flavor Aid) at his direction in 1978 (Ulman and Abse, 1983). The realization that leader-follower relationships involve important emotional attachments paved the way for the application of attachment theory: leaders often function for their followers, "like parents ... whose role includes guiding, directing, taking charge, and taking care of others less powerful than they" (Popper and Mayseless, 2003). Former CIA psychiatrist Dr. Jerrold Post (2019) has described how narcissistically wounded individuals are drawn to a narcissistically impaired leader in a charismatic leader-follower relationship like a "lock and key."

According to Post, crucial psychological aspects of the leader, like a key, fit and unlock certain psychological aspects of their followers. A sense of grandiose omnipotence of the leader is especially appealing to his or her needy followers. This is different from "reparative charismatics," or a healthy relationship that is drawn together by a need to heal their nation's wounds. Rather, destructive charismatic leaders make use of their followers' defects, employ absolutist polarizing rhetoric, and draw their followers together against an external enemy. The followers may be psychologically healthy but rendered temporarily needy by societal stress, or developmentally mirror-hungry, secretly yearning to merge with another when an idealized figure appears. In *Narcissism and Politics: Dreams of Glory*, Post notes that: "in times of crisis, individuals regress to a state of delegated omnipotence and demand a leader who will rescue them, take care of them" (Post, 2014).

In The Spellbinders, Ruth Ann Wilner (1984) surveyed the vast literature on charismatic leader-follower relationships, and found that there have four characteristics in common:

1. The leader is perceived by the followers as somehow superhuman.
2. The followers blindly believe the leader's statements.
3. The followers unconditionally comply with the leader's directives for action.
4. The followers give the leader unqualified emotional support.

Clinical work with individuals of narcissistic pathology, studies of individuals who join charismatic religious groups, and psychodynamic observations of group phenomena provide persuasive support for the psychological makeup we observe in individuals who are susceptible to this charismatic relationship—the lock of the follower for the key of the leader. The development of "the wounded self" results in these two personality patterns that are important for charismatic relationships.

Post (2019) illustrates two seemingly juxtaposed manifestations of "the wounded self": "the mirror-hungry personality" and "the ideal-hungry personality." These are the templates for the complementary portions of the charismatic leader-follower relationship. The first is the "mirror hungry" personality. Donald Trump has a mirror-hungry leader personality, which feeds off of the adoration of his followers in the charismatic leader-follower relationship he has established. This personality pattern results from "the injured self" whose grandiose façade feeds off of confirming and admiring responses, to protect against the inner sense of worthlessness and lack of self-esteem. To nourish the famished self, the individual feels compelled to display the self to evoke the attention of others. However, no matter how much positive attention one receives, one is never satisfied, continually seeking new audiences as a source of attention and recognition one craves. This constant need for new attention led the high-profile businessman Donald Trump to seek an increasingly prominent celebrity status, culminating in his hit TV reality game show "the Apprentice" in the 2000's. However, as the attention he received from this show could not satisfy him, he sought a new source of attention by running for president of the United States.

Central to the mirror-hungry leader's ability to elicit admiration is the skill in conveying a sense of grandeur, omnipotence, and strength. Ambitious and charismatic individuals who can convey this sense of grandiose omnipotence are drawn to the spotlight. There, they attract individuals seeking idealized sources of strength, by offering a feeling of conviction and certainty to those who are consumed by doubt and uncertainty. This was evident in Donald Trump's support from rural areas and the working class, where his motto to "make America great again" had a strong resonance. Despite a lack of any concrete policy, his extravagant claim that, "I'll be the best jobs president God ever created," appealed especially to those who were struggling and felt abandoned by previous administrations.

Mirror-hungry leaders are drawn to large crowds, where the roar of admiration becomes intoxicating. It was evident during Donald Trump's campaign how much he thrived on followers shouting his name at large rallies. This is why even after the election ended, he continued to hold giant rallies across the country; after more than three hundred rallies in 2016 alone, he held nearly one hundred more during the first three years of his presidency (Kruse, 2020). He continues to need these expressions of admiration from his followers as compensation for his deep-seated insecurity and self-doubt.

In the spotlight, they offer a feeling of conviction and certainty to those who are consumed by doubt and uncertainty. Ideal-hungry follower personalities from rural areas and the working class especially, found greater resonance with the grand-sounding motto: "make American great again." Despite a lack of any concrete policy, the extravagant claim that, "I'll be the best jobs president God ever created," appealed especially to those who were struggling and felt abandoned by the political class.

These rallies have been vital for his supporters as well. There is a quality of mutual intoxication and dependence on both sides, whereby Donald Trump reassures his followers by filling their void, who in turn reassure him of his self-worth. In the words of the infamous pipe-bomber Cesar Sayoc: "the first thing you [hear] entering Trump rally is we are not going to take it anymore, the forgotten ones.... It was fun, it became like a new found drug" (Karimi, 2019). Donald Trump was able to tap into the existing rhetoric of the white supremacist alt-right in the United States, which is a form of idealizing the self by denigrating others—be they foreigners, Latinos, Muslims, and many other groups—to help ward off deep feelings of inferiority. These are "ideal hungry" individuals who view themselves as worthwhile only as long as they can relate to individuals whom they can admire for their prestige, power, unlimited success, beauty, or brilliance. The hypnotic lure of the charismatic leader is compelling for the ideal-hungry follower. The wounded follower feels incomplete by oneself and enduringly seeks to attach to an ideal other. Thus, there is a powerful, almost chemical attraction when the mirror-hungry charismatic leader and the ideal-hungry charismatic follower meet. Donald Trump thrives on the adoring mirroring response of his followers, and he provides them with a sense of completeness and security, like lock and key, in a psychological symbiosis.

This does not mean that all those who voted for Donald Trump are narcissistically wounded individuals. The phenomenon of the charismatic leader-follower relationship is likely too complex to lend itself to a single overarching psychological model. However, the enduring psychological power of the Trump phenomenon relies on his appeal to wounded individuals seeking leadership that can act as a heroic rescuer. While elements of these narcissistic transferences are present in all charismatic leader-follower relationships, ones that induce and rely on the regression of followers are particularly dangerous (Post, 2019).

A leader's stance of total certainty is very attractive to wounded followers who are besieged by doubt. For them, preserving grandiose feelings of strength and omniscience does not allow for expressions of weakness. "Splitting", or the separation of unpleasant aspects of oneself that are either projected onto "the other" or otherwise disowned, is central to maintaining the illusion and allows for no uncertainty. The leader, of course, is also trying to ward off his or her doubt through defensive posturing (Kohut, 1985).

There is the "me" and the "not me," good versus evil, strength versus weakness, "winners" versus "losers". This results in the belief that they are the source of the problem, they are evil, and to eliminate them is to eliminate our problems. Psychoanalyst Phyllis Greenacre observed that to be effectively charismatic it is a great asset to possess paranoid conviction. Indeed, the combination of charisma and paranoia led to some of the most fearful excesses of human violence in history (Robins and Post, 1997).

Cultic programming

There is always a villain—and a hero—at a Trump rally, and that is exactly what his audience expects—along with his insults, bravado, and takedowns of liberals and other enemies. The venue may be Council Bluffs, Iowa, Erie, Pennsylvania, or Topeka, Kansas, but the formula is always the same. Donald Trump's supporters remain as enthusiastic as ever, standing for hours in the hot sun or the pouring rain, exploding into thunderous applause when he took the stage. They wave the same signs, they wear the same hats, and chant the same refrains, "Build that wall!" and "Lock her up!" even years after his election. Lines to get into these rallies wind around buildings and twist through alleys for at least a mile (Colvin, 2018). "I think it's amazing what he's doing, I really do," says Tami Gusching, 32, in Fort Wayne, Indiana. "I love the aggression that he has and the power behind him" (Sikich et al., 2018). "I'm just totally, madly in love with him," says Peggy Saar, 64, from Rochester, Minnesota (Colvin, 2018). "It's a love fest!" says Randal Thom, 58, at a rally in Springfield, Missouri, gesturing to a stranger. "I might not know this guy's name, but I know three things about him: He loves the country, he loves the president, and he bleeds the color red" (Rogers, 2018). Who are these people, and why do they support and even adore Donald Trump, despite his having shown himself as attention-seeking, self-important, dishonest, vindictive, entitled, lacking in insight and accountability, and completely devoid of remorse and empathy?

Cult expert Steven Hassan (2019) sees Trump supporters—63 million strong—as a patchwork of diverse yet distinct groups, each with varying levels of allegiance. They range from fervent followers among Christians and the alt-right, who see Donald Trump as a change agent who can forward their agendas, to traditional Republicans who vote the party line, to pro-lifers, National Rifle Association (NRA) members, and the poor and out of work. Some are old, fearful, and angry, and like how Donald Trump's rhetoric renders emotional legitimacy to their feelings. Others are wealthy with "practical" motivations capable of walling off the harms that arise from Donald Trump's tax cuts for the rich and his government deregulations. Donald Trump's campaign was an unrelenting recruiting machine, using the same rhetoric and techniques of cults, according to Hassan. "Our movement is about replacing a failed and corrupted political establishment, with a new government controlled by you, the American people," began a 2016 Trump campaign ad. "The only people brave enough to vote out this corrupt establishment is you, the American people,... and we will take back this country for you, and we will make America great again" (C-SPAN, 2016).

There are hierarchical structures and systems of thought reform that work to generate cultic programming to those who are susceptible. At the top are White House staffers, some of whom are family members, a core group who are in regular contact with Donald Trump. Cults typically employ a coterie of aides who are loyal and subservient to the leader, carrying out directives and instilling doctrine. Each moderating force is replaced until the leader is surrounded by "yes men" and "yes women" who "let Trump be Trump." The psychology behind it can take the form of obsession with loyalty. Donald Trump makes it a point, for example, to test those around him and to keep his inner circle exclusive to loyalists and devoted staff—and family. His former political aide Manigault Newman and his former "fixer" Michael Cohen both describe leaving Donald Trump's orbit like escaping a cult—"the cult of Trumpworld," as the former puts it (D'Antonio, 2018). A "cult leader," is how Lev Parnas, an associate of Donald Trump's personal attorney Rudolph Giuliani, describe Donald Trump (Gregory, 2020). A similar structure can be found among distinct groups of Trump followers:

Eight out of ten white evangelicals voted for Donald Trump (Martinez and Smith, 2016). Of his followers, those who attend church are generally more receptive to minorities than those who do not, but some churches have encouraged tribalistic impulses, especially the New Apostolic Reformation (NAR). Desiring to turn America into a Christian nation and claiming to receive direct revelations from God, its leaders have appropriated Donald Trump, casting him as a figure of deliverance. This is not a rare belief: according to a Fox News poll, nearly half of Republicans believe Donald Trump has been chosen by God to be president (Bump, 2019).

Another segment of his base is the white working class. Donald Trump cultivated this marginalized and disenfranchised, disengaged group of Americans that Hillary Clinton largely ignored, and they were key to his election victory in 2016. He flaunted his wealth in a way that endeared him to them, claiming to have made his fortune with hard work, savvy negotiating skills, and by beating the "establishment" at its own game. During the first presidential debate, Donald Trump bragged that avoiding federal taxes made him smart (Mangan, 2016). He cast himself as an outsider, an underdog who understood working-class malaise and would "drain the swamp" of political elites to bring change for "the forgotten man" and "forgotten woman." He enthralled his audience and spoke their language, playing to their wants and needs. He blamed their situation on "global elites" who have "robbed our working class and stripped our country of its wealth and put that money into the pockets of a handful of large corporations and political entities" (Newburger, 2018). He also gave them a good story—a vision of a new America that he alone could "fix". Of course, his interactions with them are always limited to crowds, and his speaking numbs his listeners to the point where they are willing to believe almost anything he says. He courts and entertains them at one moment and frightens them the next by building up "enemies" who are responsible for all their problems. His words whip up emotions, and somehow he always seems to say what the majority of his audience are already secretly feeling but unable to verbalize. He is acutely tuned into the audience's responses, which energize him. As a result of this reciprocal relationship, his ascendance to power emotionally intoxicate him and his audience alike.

His once-unlikely followers, the Republican Party, are now under his thumb. While Donald Trump had initially promised a more liberal platform, saying he would preserve and defend social security, renegotiate the North American Free Trade Agreement (NAFTA), pull back on Iraq and Afghanistan, and support LGBTQ rights, he reversed himself, pushing a pro-life, pro-gun, anti-immigration, anti-globalist, and climate change-denying agenda. They held their noses and voted the ticket to get a Republican elected, but now the Republican Party is widely seen as the party of Donald Trump, or "Trumpublicans", in large part because of the web of influence the media, religious and populist groups, and large corporations have spun—helping Donald Trump win the presidency. Donald Trump's approval rating with Republicans has never gone below 77 percent, according to Gallup. In July 2020, it was 91 percent, actually up four points since before the coronavirus pandemic (Gallup, 2020), as I projected would happen, from defensive compensation (Lee, 2020a).

Jews make up only about 1.8 percent of the adult population, about 5.9 million people (Brandeis University, 2020), but there is a powerful minority of mostly Orthodox or ultra-Orthodox voters who support Donald Trump. These are largely closed groups who obediently follow what they believe to be traditional Jewish values. The rabbi functions as a guru, interpreting the tradition and directing beliefs, attitudes, and practices. In some groups, women are encouraged not to work but to have as many children as they can, to run the household, and to care for their husbands and family. Children are sometimes homeschooled or sent to parochial schools where they receive both secular and religious education. They are often intolerant of homosexuality, against abortion, and unquestioning of what they are told to believe or do. These characteristics of insular groups can make them susceptible to cultic programming.

Of all the factions in Donald Trump's base, the alt-right is perhaps the most dangerous. They are responsible for the tragedies in Charleston, South Carolina; Charlottesville, Virginia; Pittsburgh, Pennsylvania; El Paso, Texas; and Christchurch, New Zealand. Though the perpetrators seem to have acted alone, they are increasingly connecting using an informal global network, often through the dark web (Ailworth, Wells, and Lovett, 2019). In an online manifesto, the perpetrator who attacked two New Zealand mosques, killing fifty people and injuring fifty others, said he drew inspiration from Donald Trump's rhetoric. White supremacist and nationalistic thinking have existed for centuries in the United States, but Donald Trump's words and deeds—his "America First" sloganeering, his apparent excusing of violence, his racist remarks, and his bullying—have electrified the radical right (Potok, 2017). Arno Michaelis, a founding member of the racist skinhead band the Centurian, who is now an activist and an outspoken critic of white nationalism, describes how hate groups like the Ku Klux Klan actively campaigned for him, organizing and paying for robocalls for Donald Trump. He advises that the president "stop espousing rhetoric that strikes chords with people who are afraid of immigrants" (Bonn, 2019). A person with violent tendencies resonates with others who have the same tendency.

In a 2019 Gallup poll, 43 percent of American households reported owning guns (Saad, 2019)—that is 55 million households with 393 million guns (Karp, 2018). The NRA claims 5.5 million members (Gutowski, 2019). Donald Trump campaigned on a broad pro-gun agenda, which he maintained after the mass shootings at the Marjory Stoneman Douglas High School in Parkland, Florida, which killed seventeen students and teachers, and in Las Vegas, after fifty-eight deaths and hundreds more injuries. The NRA spent more than 30 million dollars in 2016 on behalf of the Trump campaign (Open Secrets, 2016), a staggering sum compared to 2012 when the group spent about 13 million dollars trying to elect Mitt Romney and to unseat President Barack Obama—becoming a decisive factor in Donald Trump's victory. Richard Feldman, a former NRA lobbyist, believed in 2017 that the NRA was at a crest in power, while Republicans controlled the Congress and Donald Trump controlled the White House. At the NRA's leadership forum in Atlanta that year, Donald Trump became the first sitting president since Ronald Reagan to address the Association (Luo, 2017).

QAnon started in 2016, soon after the "Pizzagate" hoax, when it alleged that Hillary Clinton was running a pedophilia ring out of the basement of a pizza parlor. It is a webbed network of conspiracy theories surrounding a person who identified himself as having, "Q Clearance," meaning top-secret security clearance, claiming that there is a secret group working to oust Donald Trump from office. According to conspiracy theory experts, Donald Trump has breathed life into the theme that he is an outsider who Democratic lawmakers are trying to drag down because the change he brings to governing threatens them. Its assertions have also grown more bizarre over time: many now believe that Donald Trump is fighting a satanic "deep state" of global elites involved in pedophilia, human trafficking, and the harvesting of life-extending chemicals from the blood of abused children. "Q" signs are frequent at his rallies, he often "retweets" its messages, and he has now tacitly endorsed QAnon, stating that its followers "love our country" and "like me very much," even after the FBI has identified it as a domestic terrorism threat (Smith and Wong, 2020). When reality requires the president to resort further and further into conspiracy theories to counter the onslaught of unwanted facts, his maladaptive tendencies are bound eventually to support extreme and dangerous distortions. In other words, Q's growth, now international, is a natural consequence of Donald Trump's predisposition for conspiracy theories: his first big step into politics was his alleging that President Barack Obama was not born in the United States, thus making his presidency invalid. "We have a current president who uses conspiracy rhetoric arguably more than any other president in modern history," said political psychologist Dr. Joanne Miller. In 2020, liberal research firm Media Matters tracked fifty QAnon supporters running for Congress, which suggested adherents of a fringe theory were feeling emboldened to come out of the shadows under Donald Trump's leadership (Phillips, 2020).

For Donald Trump and his followers, his rallies provide a place of solidarity and safety (Hassan, 2019). A reporter who attended five rallies in eight days calls them: "the crucible of the Trump revolution, the laboratory where he turns his alternative reality into a potion to be sold to his followers" not as, "We the people," but "We *my* people." Tucked into the love, however, he sensed a menace, as if to say: "I love you people,⊠ because you hate my enemy" (Pilkington, 2018). To the question of what America would be like in 2050 if Clinton had been elected president, retired teacher David Stewart, 66, answered: "Taxes and unemployment would go through the roof, the economy would collapse, there would be riots for food and water." If Donald Trump were not in charge? Retired building foreman Rick Novak, 57, said: "People are going to get killed…. Gang wars. We are going to get gang wars between white and black, whites and Mexicans. We could have our own little Vietnam, right here." As Donald Trump fanned their fears, they expressed their love for him. When he snarled angrily about, "kicking the criminals, the drug dealers and the terrorists the hell out of our country," the gratitude of his people was visceral.

Yet what he creates is far from security. On October 27, 2018, two hours after he posted a rant against "invaders that kill our people," Robert Bowers, 46, entered a synagogue in Pittsburgh, pulled out an AR-15 style assault rifle, and at least three handguns, and killed eleven Jewish worshippers (Pilkington, 2018). As Donald Trump railed against his enemies, Cesar Sayoc, 56, sent sixteen homemade explosives to prominent Democratic politicians and media figures, including former President Obama, former Vice President Joe Biden, and former Secretary of State Clinton, with the belief that Donald Trump's critics were "dangerous, unpatriotic, and evil" (Jacobo, 2019). In March 2019, Donald Trump said in an interview: "I can tell you I have the support of the police, the support of the military, the support of the Bikers for Trump – I have the tough people, but they don't play it tough — until they go to a certain point, and then it would be very bad, very bad" (Wise, 2019). A week later, fifty people died after a shooter attacked two Mosques in New Zealand, explicitly citing "common purpose" with Donald Trump (Al Jazeera, 2019).

"Battered nation syndrome"

If the unwavering support of Donald Trump is because of susceptibility to cultic programming, what explains the passivity of the rest of the nation? Do people still not recognize that Donald Trump is lacking in the emotional maturity, the intelligence, the preparedness, or even the basic sympathy a time of crisis? After more than 19,000 documented lies (Kessler et al, 2020), impeachment, repeated acts of corruption, subversion of justice, and even after the disastrous mishandling of the coronavirus pandemic, his political invincibility, and seemingly uncompromising support can be confusing.

Harper West (2017) described the nation as being in an abusive relationship with Donald Trump, much like the case example she drew from her practice:

> Justin can be harshly critical, calling [Amelia] a "fat loser" and her home-cooked meals "a disaster." But if she asks even reasonable questions, he lashes out at her: "You're always so negative and critical." If she states a fact he disagrees with, he accuses her of making up "fake" stories. Despite Justin's family and financial security, he is joyless and scowls much of the time.

Amelia is mystified how the most minor disagreements seem to escalate into major arguments. I ask if Justin can apologize or admit fault. "Oh, never," she says. "He's very stubborn. It's always my fault. I call him 'Justifying Justin'"….

Justin has lied so frequently that Amelia has become concerned she is "losing her mind" or has a poor memory, aided by the fact that Justin accuses her of these faults. He insists that she forget his mistakes, but brings her mistakes up repeatedly during arguments…. She hesitates to confront him because she has learned that it leads to escalating arguments with no resolution. She is always the one to compromise (West, 2017).

Abusive personalities seek out submissive people who are willing to be controlled and manipulated. In order to hide their feelings of inadequacy, abusive individuals often adopt an aggressive, dominating persona and, in positions of power, surround themselves with a coterie of family and sycophants who avoid questioning them for fear of angry retribution. They rarely admit to weakness or vulnerability because they believe this would subject them to the same kind of abuse and control that they perpetrate on others. Victims of abuse in turn may be blind to these flaws because they replicate an abusive personality they experienced in childhood, and the relationship pattern feels normal, even safe. This may help us to understand why his followers blindly support him and why reporters and Democratic leaders do not oppose him with conviction.

A "battered nation syndrome" can be conceived after the "battered woman syndrome" or "battered man syndrome" that has been described in domestic violence situations, where the "battered" partner comes to form avoidance or numbing of emotions, cognitive difficulties, problems relating to others, and personal image problems (Walker, 2017). The mental health fields have extensive experience with victims who remain loyal to callous and abusive personalities, for the same reasons that politicians and the public seem to display with Donald Trump. Many people stay in abusive relationships because they are ashamed to admit they made a poor choice. With each passing crisis that Donald Trump has mismanaged, his followers seem to be even more fervent in their support, despite the adverse effects they suffer as a result.

As hard as it may be to believe, this kind of die-hard support often appears among those who are embarrassed to admit they made a mistake in voting for him. Shame causes some people to deny and double down on their decisions, rather than admit an error in judgment. Donald Trump also exhibits extremely poor shame tolerance. Abusive personalities, often as the result of childhood attachment traumas, have low self-worth and are overly sensitive to shaming experiences, such as being criticized, making mistakes, or failing in any way. This shows up in an inability to be accountable or to admit an error: Donald Trump's "Sharpiegate" is a relatively benign example; the coronavirus pandemic response a deadly one. Attempts to offload blame can also lead to severe levels of direct violence.

Others in the nation are not blind to his flawed behavior but idolize him for what he has: impunity from criticism. Other bullies desperately wish to spout off opinions and not be challenged or questioned. They roar their approval at rallies when Donald Trump intimidates and dominates others, because they, too, wish to abuse those who are weaker. They see nothing wrong with Donald Trump's lashing out in rage or blame but rather applaud it. In his entitlement, over-confidence, and bloated ego, they see themselves and feel vindicated. Seeing authoritarian, immoral, and unethical behavior in a successful billionaire and president allows them to conclude that these are not faults, but positive attributes.

Abusers intimidate through the degrading of others. Donald Trump uses his size, aggressive handshake, domineering body language, shoe lifts, and even his bright red "power necktie" to intimidate. U.S. Representative Adam Schiff likely knows he is not "shifty," and White House reporters know that the descriptions of them as "fake" or "dishonest" are untrue, but he or she is often too shocked to be able to respond. Abusers rely on subtle putdowns to weaken the victim's confidence, and onlookers steer clear, or shower him with praise, to avoid the same fate.

Members within abusive cults often act against their self-interest, such as by giving away their money, property, children, or rights to a cult leader. In the same way, abused spouses may quit their jobs, relinquish financial security, or give up contact with family and friends at the demand of their abusers. Provoking fear is something abusive personalities do to secure fervent supporters. When fear "hijacks" the human brain, we lose our ability to think rationally and become preoccupied with short-term physical or emotional survival in a way that does not lend itself to thinking comprehensively about complex, long-term problems (Anda et al., 2017). Fear causes us to take cognitive shortcuts, and slogans such as, "Build the wall!" further hinders the consideration of more realistic and nuanced solutions to problems.

Passive reactions to abusive behavior occur because of the ease with which abusers prey on the trust of their victims. Humans are a social species, and most of us enter relationships eager to be liked, engaging in prosocial behaviors. Trust allows us to direct the energy and abilities that we would have been spent warding off enemies, toward building relationships, high-functioning societies, and civilization. Antisocial people, however, play by a different set of rules. If we expect love and trust from them, we will be constantly confused and disappointed when we get back humiliation, emotional abuse, and betrayal.

A desire to keep trying leads victims to stay in abusive relationships and causes many Americans to downplay and hope for more presidential behavior from Donald Trump, despite repeated disappointments. Just as abuse victims have difficulty comprehending that someone who says, "I love you," would cause them harm, Americans find it difficult to believe that a president who has taken an oath to "preserve, protect, and defend" would choose to harm a nation and its sacred institutions, destroy peacebuilding alliances, and subvert the social order. It violates moral standards and our very world view to admit that a leader would work solely for personal gain at the expense of the public.

As with all abusers, without external limits, Donald Trump will likely continue to prey on people's expectations of trust and desire for stability, and our fruitless craving for a capable leader. He will continue to sow distrust and fear, manufacture chaos, and play-act at leadership. Just as abuse victims may need the strength, wisdom, and support of others to help them leave their abuser, the nation needs political leaders, journalists, and intellectuals with the strength of character to confidently call out what they see (Lee, West, and Washington, 2020). Without this, an emotionally battered people can easily succumb to the human tendencies to submit, freeze, and fall into a helpless "battered nation syndrome."

Shared psychosis

I once treated a family around the outskirts of Boston that believed outer-space aliens were invading their neighborhood. The father was a construction worker, the mother a former clerk, and the five children ranged in age from eight to sixteen. They seemed respectable in public, but at home they worried that an alien force had taken over their neighbors, heralding the end of the world. They thought they were the only "sane" ones left and needed to save themselves before the alien invaders besieged them too.

The mother, a domineering personality, chastised the only nonbelieving member, her sixteen-year-old daughter. She had called the emergency room when her parents started barricading doors and sleeping with knives by their beds. Her call was on the earlier side for untreated cases like this. Fear or terror might have escalated into an aggressive attack, as they falsely believed themselves under assault. The mother, identified as the "primary" patient, or the cause of "family psychosis," or *folie à famille*, was taken to the emergency room and then hospitalized. Within a matter of days, both the patient and the entire family dramatically improved.

While there are many medically unjustifiable misconceptions we have about mental pathology, none is perhaps as consequential as the denial that it can be contagious. Just like the novel coronavirus, the transmissibility of mental symptoms should not be taken lightly. Indeed, its contagion could be more efficient than other forms of infection, since it does not require physical exposure but only emotional bonds.

Weakened hosts, an environment that facilitates transmission, and a lack of awareness that it is even possible make individuals highly susceptible. Predisposing personalities, cultic programming, and trapped, prolonged exposure as in the case example above create the optimal conditions for the spread of symptoms. Furthermore, poor mental health contributes to denial, and therefore those who are the most affected are the least likely to admit that anything is wrong.

The transmission of mental symptoms and behavior is especially common in public-sector hospital and prison settings, where untreated symptoms among influential or dominant individuals can become severe and spread among family members, criminal co-conspirators, gangs, and other tight-knit groups (Guivarch et al, 2018). Infectious disease specialist Gary Slutkin of Cure Violence has long advocated that violence be considered an infectious disease whose spread we can interrupt. Research has established evidence for the contagion of international terrorism and suicide. Conceiving violence as a societal disorder requiring public health interventions, population-level, has been very productive, allowing for prevention at a massive scale. It has also helped the world move away from the misleading association of mental illness with dangerousness.

Three conditions are necessary for the spread of mental symptoms:

1.   Severe pathology in an influential figure

The transmission of mental symptoms has been given different names: induced delusional disorder, shared psychosis, *folie à deux, trois, quatre,...,* or *millions*—depending on the number affected—or mass hysteria when affecting a whole population. All describe the same phenomenon, but none are satisfactory. The latest, *induced delusional disorder,* focuses on the most commonly transmitted symptom, delusions, but does not cover other possible symptoms, such as mood. Shared psychosis captures the syndrome-like severity, but is a misnomer because it often does not involve actual psychosis. *Folie à deux,* or "madness in two," is perhaps the most preferred but a foreign phrase. Finally, "mass hysteria" describes well the frenzied quality that arises from the sharing of symptoms among crowds, but often does not actually involve symptoms of "hysteria", or histrionics. The important feature is that mental symptoms are not confined to the person; they take hold and spread across interpersonal boundaries, just as they initially take over one portion, and then eventually the whole of the mind of an individual.

Severe psychopathology in an influential figure, therefore, transmits to others or a group, until the exposed persons or groups come to feel, think, and behave as if they had the same disorder as the primary person. Unlike normal social dynamics, where enthusiasm, common purpose, or even outrage can be "infectious" but individuals retain their uniqueness, the spread of pathology is especially efficient and deleterious, taking over the personalities of those involved.

Shared psychosis at the societal level has been documented since the Middle Ages and scientifically studied in detail in the mid-twentieth century following the downfall of Nazism. A country or a group, seemingly "seized" by irrational fears of persecution, may attack other, relatively powerless groups. Often dramatic and yet easy to miss, it can absorb persons of otherwise sound mind when they have prolonged exposure to a severely impaired individual, usually of influence or authority, who goes untreated. While the sixteen-year-old in the above case example managed not to succumb, she underwent castigation and shunning. Above all, denial among those affected will likely be vehement to the degree that the symptoms are severe (we see this among Trump supporters who avoid consideration of the possibility by calling any such insinuation, "Trump Derangement Syndrome" or "TDS", thereby deflecting the issue onto the inquirer) (Zorn, 2018).

Transmission happens more readily in vulnerable persons, but those who succumb are not necessarily of unsound mind to start. Delusions of persecution or general paranoia are the most common to transmit, but even bizarre beliefs, such as the primary person being of divine origin, are not rare. Exposure to actual delusions is unlike exposure to strategic lies or simple misinformation; they are more infectious because the primary person is genuinely convinced of them and the emotional pressures for others also to believe them is stronger. For example, when an influential figure holds the paranoid belief that a serious viral pandemic is a "hoax", orchestrated by one's enemies to bring down one's presidency, it can be more emotionally persuasive than any reality and is difficult to correct.

2. Group members with high emotional investment

Another condition for the spread of mental disease is emotional investment. Folie à deux describes shared madness within a pair, but here we will focus on folie à groupe, or the spread of mental symptoms in a group. The group can be a household (folie à famille), a prison dormitory or cell-block, a religious or other highly emotionally-bonded group, a community, or a nation. Members may have a high emotional investment in the primary person because of family relations, gang affiliation, similar symptoms to start, blackmail, or other threats—these add to the conditions but are not the symptoms themselves. Symptoms can also compel the conditions that strengthen bonds: causing others to lose their bearings through "gaslighting" (Stout, 2005); the generation of an alternative narrative through an addiction to "tweeting"; orchestration of an alternative belief system through the need to deny reality; intolerance of uncertainty leading to pressures of conformity; and an insatiable need for adulation driving addiction-inducing, hypnotic rallies—all create ideal conditions for transmission. In other words, cultic programming and shared symptoms are a feedback loop.

Induced delusions function like primary delusions: they are both equally resistant to evidence and truth. The cognitive distortions, delusions, and other mental symptoms can emotionally overwhelm normal responses to the same situation. Some individual members may be more vulnerable than others, but with strong emotional bonds and prolonged exposure, fighting submission becomes more difficult. Those who do may experience great pressure, as a result of the primary individual's irrational symptoms, or ostracism by the group, and may eventually give in or give up. Riding the emotional force of pathology, these dynamics can be overwhelming—and because of the disorder that the primary person carries, it might be more aptly called a "transmitted cultural disorder."

3. An environment that fosters contagion

Conditions of isolation, either physically or through filtered information, especially when they "immunize" against alternative viewpoints through phrases such as "fake news" or "the enemy of the people," combined with constant, high levels of exposure to the symptomatic primary individual, is the formula for the generation of shared delusions. The environment is, therefore, extremely important in determining the level of contagion.

Many have remarked on the cult-like quality of the leader-follower arrangement we see with Donald Trump and his supporters. The dynamic alarmed my colleagues in the mental health profession enough to write entire volumes (Lifton, 2019). Existing arrangements of "viral" social media, profit-driven news programs that rely on ratings, and rallies that reinforce herd mentality and conformity, all contribute to an unconscious spread of symptoms.

How is the recognition of shared psychosis, or folie à groupe, helpful? We know from the scientific literature that, when contact with the inducing individual is removed, the shared symptoms usually subside just as dramatically as they have appeared. If removal is not possible, we know that reducing exposure can be helpful. We can prevent epidemics from occurring in the first place by screening for mental impairment before individuals take positions of influence. Further, we can take steps to protect ourselves in the future by promoting public mental health and education about mental disease, as well as reducing environmental "toxins" that include propaganda, brainwashing, and filtered information. Knowing that mental compromise can contribute to physical demise, and recognizing the distinct, characteristic patterns of disease, we can better avoid mistaking it for a normal choice or just another ideology that excites people.

A PROFILE OF THE SUPPORTING ENVIRONMENT

The mental state of a society

At the start of *The Spirit Level,* British epidemiologists Richard Wilkinson and Kate Pickett (2009) eloquently describe what they understand to be the overarching problem of our era:

> It is a remarkable paradox that, at the pinnacle of human material and technical achievement, we find ourselves anxiety-ridden, prone to depression, worried about how others see us, unsure of our friendships, driven to consume and with little or no community life. Lacking the relaxed social contact and emotional satisfaction we all need, we seek comfort in over-eating, obsessive shopping and spending, or become prey to excessive alcohol, psychoactive medicines and illegal drugs.
>
> How is it that we have created so much mental and emotional suffering despite levels of wealth and comfort unprecedented in human history? Often what we feel is missing is little more than time enjoying the company of friends, yet even that can seem beyond us. We talk as if our lives were a constant battle for psychological survival, struggling against stress and emotional exhaustion, but the truth is that the luxury and extravagance of our lives is so great that it threatens the planet (Wilkinson and Pickett, 2009).

What Wilkinson and Pickett are describing is not just a subjective impression. The actual numbers and statistics are just as devastating, if not more so. The United States, for instance, is the country in which the effects in question appear most pronounced, and it has the lowest life expectancy among rich countries. Not only is that the case, but since 2014, the average life expectancy in the country has been going down instead of up, unlike any other rich, developed country (Woolf and Schoomaker, 2019). Moreover, most of the deaths that are contributing to this lowering of the average life expectancy are occurring among people in the prime of their lives, between the 25 and 64. The common causes of death in these cases include opioid addiction, obesity, alcoholic liver disease, and suicide.

These statistics do not fit with the prevailing ethos of the United States. Americans have always been told that material success brings happiness, but the actual results of that mantra look more like social failure in the midst of plenty. Instead, it seems that what matters most for societal mental wellbeing is not overall economic success but, rather, the way in which economies are developed and how they are distributed. Societal forces like income inequality and unstable employment have psychological consequences, and these consequences in turn create ideal conditions for diseases and deaths. As such, what Wilkinson and Pickett imply is that the psychological breakdown of whole societies is the result of choices we make, collectively, about how to organize our social, political, and economic systems. That vital connection, however, seldom materializes within broader political discussions. Indeed, as Wilkinson and Pickett lament, "as soon as anything psychological is mentioned discussion tends to focus almost exclusively on individual remedies and treatments. Political thinking seems to run into the sand" (Wilkinson and Pickett, 2009).

In essence, then, there is an inability or an unwillingness to see the direct link that exists between economic and political policies, on the one hand, and a nation's health and mental health, on the other. It is this inability to perceive the situation as it is that sits, perhaps, at the heart of our general dearth of actual, deeper understanding. This has not always been the case, nor is it a universal phenomenon: in other cultures and time periods, people have been more aware of these influences. When German physician Rudolf Virchow (1848) investigated the typhus epidemic in the region of Upper Silesia, Poland, in the mid-nineteenth century, he came to state the following: "Medicine is a social science, and politics is nothing else but medicine on a large scale." What we can take from that assessment is that tuning into our collective sense of wellbeing and understanding that we have ability to both find problems and devise solutions, is a crucial part of self-awareness. It is that degree of self-awareness that helps us to provide our progress, and our thriving, with meaningful direction.

Accordingly, just as *The Dangerous Case of Donald Trump* was not simply about Donald Trump but, ultimately, the nation's state of mental health that gave rise to his presidency, this profile is also about both ourselves and the nation. In order to present and understand Donald Trump's presidency as a public health issue, we have examined his followers. In doing so, we emphasize that in order to heal from pathology we cannot "normalize" it or pretend that it does not exist. It is equally important to note that pathology is not the person, and hence the aim here is not to stigmatize or to blame individuals. Indeed, pathology is not something that always localizes within the individual; instead, it may exist in the spirit of the nation, which is something common to us all. What this means is that the development and maintenance of national self-awareness must also involve the observation of ourselves. It also means that whatever unhealthy, dependent, and irrational traits we identify in Donald Trump's followers, these cannot be understood as being isolated aberrations. Rather, these traits are a direct consequence of us all, of everyone in society, even those who are not supporters of Donald Trump. It may well also be the case that while those who are most vulnerable may succumb to the most obviously maladaptive behavior, they are at the same time also the least likely to have had a part in creating the unhealthy conditions that led them to that place. In short, we all share responsibility.

To continue to speak collectively, our current prospects do not look good. The greater social context and situation that Donald Trump has influenced and reinforced through his position has brought us to a position that matches disturbingly closely a description by political philosopher Hannah Arendt (1973) in *The Origins of Totalitarianism*:

> Never has our future been more unpredictable, never have we depended so much on political forces that cannot be trusted to follow the rules of common sense and self-interest—forces that look like sheer insanity.... [Humankind is divided] between those who believe in human omnipotence (who think that everything is possible if one knows how to organize masses for it) and those for whom powerlessness has become the major experience of their lives (Arendt, 1973).

Arendt was speaking in reference to the early twentieth century and writing in the aftermath of the Second World War, and yet the situation that she outlines does not sound too foreign to us today. So, we must now ask, how did the U.S. get to this current point? What are some of the national characteristics that have led us to this place?

Until the 1980's, the American experience was similar to other large economies. As recently as 1975, the top 1 percent of the population gained a similar share of the income in the U.S. as they did in countries such as Canada, France, Germany, Italy, Japan, and the United Kingdom. This changed in the subsequent decade. Since 1987 the share of the GDP that went to the top 1 percent in the U.S. exceeded that of all those other countries, year after year. The rate at which this change occurred was remarkable. On average, throughout the 1990's and 2000's, the income share for the top 1 percent in the U.S. kept rising at twice the rate seen in the U.K., and it exceeded that of other advanced economies by an even greater factor. By 2014, the situation in the U.S. was stunning: the top 1 percent of the population had captured 18 percent of income; this represented a significant increase from the figure of 8 percent in 1975 (Alvaredo et al., 2015).

What can be seen if share of the U.S. GDP that is earned by the top 20 percent of the population is equally stark. By 2018, that 20 percent was earning fully 52 percent of all U.S. income (Semega et al., 2019) while the bottom 20 percent, by contrast, earned only earned 3.1 percent. Another factor that, in connection to this, creates wealth inequality is the fact that most low-wage workers cannot save money. These workers also receive no health insurance, sick days, or pension plans from their employers. In simple terms: they cannot get ill, and they have no hope of retiring. What that results in is the creation of significant health care inequality. The poor receive very little in this regard whereas the rich, since they get rich faster, take away in ever larger piece of the pie. As the overwhelming majority of people saw their share of the national income, and the benefits resulting from that, shrink by 1 to 2 percent, the wealthiest 1 percent of people increased their own share of the same by 10 percent. These statistics also describe a decrease in economic mobility with U.S. society. The average wage earned by a worker remained, essentially, the same despite there being a 15 percent increase in their productivity and a corresponding increase in corporate profits of 13 percent per year (Greenhouse, 2009).

Presented with these data, there are many vital questions that one might ask. The one to address here, however, is the following: what kind of effect has this economic situation had on average Americans and on national culture? Since human beings are largely symbolic creatures, factors such as income, wealth, and health inequality matter not only for the economic wellbeing of society but also for its psychological wellbeing. The influences of this situation manifest themselves in many ways. Tracing some of them in their groundbreaking study of the psychology of social class, the American sociologists Richard Sennett and Jonathan Cobb focused on the lived experience of manual laborers and their families. What Sennett and Cobb (1972) discovered through their research was the existence of a class-based battle for status and respect. "The terrible thing about class in our society," they claimed, "is that it sets up a contest for dignity" (Sennett and Cobb, 1972), and this is a contest that those on the bottom rung of society must, by definition, lose. Psychologically, the hardest part of being poor, according to Sennett's and Cobb's assessment, is not the material deprivation itself but rather the sense of "injured dignity," or the loss of self-respect and pride in relation to others. Such a hierarchical system of respect, status, and dignity thus necessarily creates an endless process of shaming and self-doubt.

The often undignified nature of the lives American live on the lower rungs of society is powerfully portrayed by Barbara Ehrenreich in Nickel and Dimed. In that book, Ehrenreich describes her first-hand experience of how, even in times of relative prosperity, many Americans live demeaning lives: subsisting on a minimum wage, surviving in run-down motels, being unable to afford good food, and on occasion sleeping in their cars (Ehrenreich, 2001). By her account, the only way by which people in the lowliest occupations can get by is through exceptional mental and muscular effort, sometimes by working two or three jobs at the same time. A different story, however, emerges in J.D. Vance's *Hillbilly Elegy* (2017), more than a decade after Ehrenreich's work. What Vance describes is a dysfunctional culture of substance abuse, knockdowns, fights, and a pervasive feeling among people that they simply cannot get ahead in life no matter what they do – an attitude that he terms "learned helplessness" (Vance, 2017). It is, again, a bleak account: an entire region of the country gives up without trying, the population bound together by a common feeling of victimhood and a desire to blame others. The sense of demoralization that Vance describes is, alongside depression, a psychological consequence of extreme inequality, and these feelings deepen as the extent of people's poverty grows more extreme.

In the U.S., poverty, and extreme poverty, are serious issues within society. In 2018, Philip Alston, the United Nations special rapporteur on extreme poverty and human rights, published a remarkable report. What Alston revealed was the extent of the poverty that exists within the U.S.: roughly 40 million people live in poverty; almost 18.5 million live in extreme poverty; and nearly 5.3 million spend their daily lives in Third World conditions of absolute poverty. And these people all reside within the borders of the richest nation in the world. Writing in the report, Alston notes:

> Successive administrations, including the current one, have determinedly rejected the idea that economic and social rights are full-fledged human rights, despite their clear recognition not only in key treaties that the United States has ratified, such as the Convention on the Elimination of All Forms of Racial Discrimination, but also in the Universal Declaration of Human Rights, which the United States has long insisted other countries must respect. But denial does not eliminate responsibility, nor does it negate obligations.... In practice, the United States is alone among developed countries in insisting that, while human rights are of fundamental importance, they do not include rights that guard against dying of hunger, dying from a lack of access to affordable health care or growing up in a context of total deprivation (United Nations, 2018).

There are a number of factors that start to explain the somewhat paradoxical situation that Alston describes. Firstly, the constant fight against feelings of shame and humiliation is an important psychological contributor to the extreme conditions in the United States. Americans are raised on the Horatio Alger myth, named after a nineteenth-century U.S. novelist who wrote numerous "rags to riches" stories. What this myth dictates is that anyone can get rich so long as one is smart and works hard; the flipside of that is, of course, that it also implies that if you are not rich then you must be stupid and lazy. Secondly, another factor contributing the unique situation within the U.S. is the fact that the whole economic system of mass production is set up to stimulate people to want to get rich: people are constantly bombarded with advertisements, marketing, and a flood of ever newer consumer goods. Thirdly, the importance of the American Dream and its pervasive influence cannot be underestimated. One of the defining features of the American Dream is the belief that children, the next generation, will have better opportunities and live better lives than their parents. It is, perhaps, a beautiful dream but it is one that is increasingly failing to become a reality. As economists Raj Chetty and colleagues (2017) have shown, while the American Dream was realized for about 90 percent of children born in 1940, it held true only for half of those children born in 1984.

To return to the Horatio Alger myth, it can be clearly shown that the socioeconomic reality in the U.S. simply does not reflect the rags-to-riches fantasy. In fact, the situation is quite the opposite. In recent years, several large studies have found that, contrary to historic perceptions, the U.S. is now less socially and economically mobile than the United Kingdom and much of mainland Europe. In 2006, to answer the question "Do Poor Children Become Poor Adults?" U.S. economist Miles Corak (2006) reviewed more than fifty studies of nine different countries and ranked Canada, Norway, Finland, and Denmark as the most mobile, with the United States and Britain being tied at the other end of the scale. Similarly, Swedish economist Markus Jantti and colleagues (2006) found that just 8 percent of American men at the bottom rose to the top fifth, compared with 12 percent of British men and 14 percent of Danish men. Moreover, according to the Economic Mobility Project of the Pew Charitable Trusts, about 62 percent of Americans raised in the top fifth of incomes stay in the top two-fifths, while 65 percent born in the bottom fifth stay in the bottom two-fifths (DeParle, 2012). This relative lack of mobility is, if anything, getting worse. What an Economic Report to Congress in 2012 found was that increasing income inequality was inexorably leading to lower economic mobility (Lenzner, 2012). The conclusion? Inequality begets inequality.

Inequality in society, and particularly the juxtaposition of extreme wealth against extreme poverty, is obviously not without consequence. This contrast in economic status fuels the feeling that society embraces some people but not all. Indeed, it is interesting to note at this point that the Latin word for 'lower', as in of lower socioeconomic status, is *inferior*, and that in Roman law the lower classes were termed the *humiliores*, or "the humble classes," after the word for 'low', *humilis*. This may seem like a minor, or overly academic, observation, but the implications are significant. When the notion that to be poor is to be inferior and humiliated is embedded within language itself, it becomes very hard to feel any sense of pride or self-worth whilst in such a position. The same applies, in reverse, for the opposite end of spectrum. The Latin word for 'higher', as in higher socioeconomic status, is superior, which is related to the word for pride, *superbia*, from which the English word superb is also derived. The term for the upper classes in Roman law was *honestiores*, or the "honorable classes," after the word *honestus*, or honest, decent, and virtuous. Comparing all of these terms, and the way in which they are still present in our everyday language and mode of thought, offers a clear insight into the nature of society. An unequal society that systematically divides itself into those who are inferior and those who are superior, into "losers" and "winners", results in the creation of a large proportion of the population who feel fundamentally humiliated. Crucially, it is relative and not absolute poverty that results in this sense of humiliation and shame: if everyone were poor, or had the same resources, such feelings would not exist. It is the apparent difference in wealth that is problematic, and when the poor grow poorer and the rich grow richer at an accelerated rate the feelings of shame and humiliation intensify further.

Therefore, there are major psychological consequences to these features of U.S. society that produce a wide gap between aspiration and possible achievement. These become opportunities for the development of widespread and intense feelings of inferiority and humiliation that can even lead to depression and despair. This phenomenon is discussed at length by the economists Anne Case and Angus Deaton in *Deaths of Despair and the Future of Capitalism* (2020). What Case and Deaton show is that deaths from suicide, drug overdoses, and alcoholic liver disease are rampant among less-educated Americans following the loss of a job, community, and dignity. In assessing why this is the case, Case and Deaton blame the policies and politics transforming the U.S. economy into an engine of inequality and suffering. Speaking in no uncertain terms, they argue that the "American economy has shifted away from serving ordinary people and toward serving businesses, their managers, and their owners" (Case and Deaton, 2020).

The observation that Case and Deaton make concerning the levels of mortality and chronic illness in American society is highly relevant. The correlation between income distribution and population health is remarkable when considered on a global level but it is particularly striking in the example of the United States. Despite its being the wealthiest nation on earth, there are such disparities in income within the country that conditions exist that allow for a lower average life expectancy than in other developed countries (Kulkarni et al., 2011). Trends show that the increase in average life expectancy within the U.S. has been slowing down over the last four decades. While in 1980 the average life expectancy in the U.S. was similar to comparable developed countries, since then it has increased by only 4.9 years as opposed the average increase of 7.8 years seen in similar countries (Organisation for Economic Co-operation and Development, 2020). It is within regions with high levels of unemployment that this recent deceleration in the increase of life expectancy has been most marked. This is especially significant given that the level of employment national has been in a long decline. Whereas in the late 1960's all but 5 percent of men of prime working age, 25 to 54, had jobs, in 2010, 20 percent of those in the same age bracket were unemployed. While things improved slightly as the country recovered from the Great Recession, the change was not drastic: in 2018, despite the recovery 14 percent were still not at work. Furthermore, since a fifth of that 14 percent were looking for work, they were not even counted as being "unemployed" (Case and Deaton, 2020). Such a capitalist, materialistic society equates "self-worth" with "net worth," and the suffering is measurable at national scale, in terms of shortened life-years.

A caste system

When a class system diminishes a person's dignity in all of the ways described, where, or what, can they turn to? In the face of this reduction of personal worth and status, for those who are eligible, the United States offers an alternative source of pride and self-esteem: caste. A caste system is a rigidly stratified social framework into which persons are entered as soon as they are born, and determines their position, or caste, determined by immutable characteristics such as skin color or ethnicity. Perhaps the paradigmatic example of such a system is the hereditary social class structure of Hinduism. The traditional Hindu caste system determines occupation, status in a hierarchy, and customary social interaction and exclusion. The United States has a caste system of its own, as psychiatrist Dr. James Gilligan (1996) has described our arrangement of racial stratification. At the top of this hierarchy are the "WASP's", or White Anglo-Saxon Protestants, and at the bottom are Black Americans, with some Hispanic Americans and other minority ethnic groups closely following. As in the Hindu system, to be of lower caste in the U.S. has real ramifications: you can expect to be subject to social and cultural rejection, to be regarded and treated as inferior, to be arrested and publicly humiliated, subject to police profiling and brutality, in ways no white person would be (Bult, 2020).

Suffering humiliation is one thing, but what political scientist Hannah Arendt argues is that even worse than being humiliated is being ignored. Arendt makes this observation in relation to the experience of Black Americans under the eyes of their white co-citizens, both rich and poor. "The institution of slavery," Arendt states, "carries an obscurity even blacker than the obscurity of poverty; the slave, not the poor man, was 'wholly overlooked'" (Arendt, 1963). Many Black American authors have evoked this sense of being ignored, of living in obscurity, when writing about the experience of being Black in America. Notable among these authors are W.E.B. Du Bois, who addresses the issue in *Dusk of Dawn* (1940), and Ralph Ellison, whose novel, *The Invisible Man* (1952), expresses the same point clearly in its very title. Evidently, poverty in the U.S. is not limited to its Black citizens, but one reason why poor white people have not been quick to revolt against their own economic oppression is because, in terms of caste, Black Americans have always been there to occupy a lower rung on the social ladder than even the poorest white citizens. Essentially, as long as there is a group to look down on from your own position, however lowly that might be, you can find a false consolation for your inferiority in relation to others above you. This behavioral trend, and its recent acceleration, has played a role in Donald Trump's election to the presidency. Robin DiAngelo's *White Fragility* (2018) and Carol Anderson's *White Rage* (2017) describe the white ambivalence and backlash against challenges to these assumptions.

What has just been described is, in essence, one of the reasons why America's pattern of racial terrorism keeps repeating itself: namely that the system of white supremacy that spawns this terrorism remains intact. Toxic as its central beliefs are, we cannot understand white supremacy merely as being white individuals' delusion of being inherently superior to Black people. Indeed, there exists an institutionalized white supremacy whose functioning does not rely on individual bigotry. This form of white supremacy is, instead, a universal operating system that relies on deeply entrenched patterns and practices to disadvantage people of color and privilege whites consistently and universally. The multiple lynchings that have taken place during the coronavirus pandemic perfectly illustrate the relentless energy of the engine of institutional white supremacy as it privileges some and destroys the lives of others. Black, brown, and indigenous people have disproportionately been the victims of these lynchings. This is occurring even as the same people are expected to risk their lives in low-wage jobs in order to make life comfortable for everyone else, while also suffering much higher rates of joblessness and poverty.

There is a difference between individual and institutional white supremacism. The difference also manifests in their respective capacity for destruction: the hidden aspects of institutional, systemic, racism have far more destructive potential than overt actions of individuals. One reason for why this is the case is that racism is a system of advantage and hierarchy based on race, not merely prejudicial sentiments or beliefs (Wellman, 1993). Similarly, psychologists Drs. Steven Roberts and Michael Rizzo (2020) also advocate that racism should not be understood solely as individual people "disliking or mistreating others on the basis of race." While such attitudes and behaviors are part of racism, racism itself is a broader, more complex, phenomenon: it is a system of advantage, a racial hierarchy; in other words, it functions structurally as a caste system. On this matter, they write that "just as citizens of capitalistic societies reinforce capitalism, whether they identify as capitalist or not, and whether they want to or not, citizens of racist societies reinforce racism, whether they identify as racist or not, and whether they want to or not" (Roberts and Rizzo, 2020). This distinction between individual actions and instances of racial violence has a particular contemporary relevance. It is important to be aware of, and to think about, the recent high-profile murders of Black American citizens in the hands of police officers, but we need to also understand that these horrific events are the consequences of a larger system.

A crucial element within this larger system is the criminal justice system. The criminal justice system in many respects embodies the attitudes of our society in general. Within this system, racial profiling is a particular issue that refers to the practice by law enforcement of suspecting individuals of wrongdoing based on stereotypes about their race rather than on their observed behavior. The direct result of this practice is that, in the U.S., people of ethnic minorities are far more likely to be arrested than white people. Moreover, once arrested, these individuals are also more likely to be convicted. Once convicted, people from ethnic minorities are likely to face stiffer sentences than white people for the same crimes. In particular, Black men in the U.S. are six times more likely to receive prison sentences than white men, and almost three times more likely to receive them than Hispanic men (U.S. Bureau of Justice Statistics, 2012). Black Americans have also been hit the hardest by the introduction of tougher sentencing laws: they account for 41 percent of the national prison population while comprising only 13 percent of the population (West and Sabol, 2008). This imbalance is also evident in the behavior of the police: nationally, police are three times more likely to stop and search cars of Black drivers than those of white drivers, and about two times more likely to stop and search cars of Hispanic drivers than those of white drivers (Eith and Durose, 2011). In addition to that, Black Americans are arrested for drug use at three times the rate of whites, and for drug sale or manufacture at four times the rate of whites, despite the fact that the level of drug use and dealing is similar between both racial groups (Snyder, 2011).

The difference between the treatment of Black and white Americans within the criminal justice system does not stop there. Black Americans are twice as likely as whites to be imprisoned when convicted for the same robbery charge, and the number of Black Americans on death row has remained constant for thirty years despite the fact the homicide rate among that section of the population has decreased. (Tonry and Melewski, 2008). Despite the fact that both Black and white Americans are numbered equally among homicide victims, four out of five executions that have taken place since the reintroduction of the death penalty have involved cases in which the victims were white (Baldus et al., 1990). Michelle Alexander, in *The New Jim Crow* (2010) astutely notes what this entails or, indeed, implies about society.

She points out that mass incarceration functions as a system of racialized social control: by gathering entire segments of minority communities and branding them as criminals, the system relegates them to permanent second-class status upon their release. The inferiority of this status is very real: stripping former convicts of the right to vote, to serve on juries, to be free of legal and employment discrimination, and denying them access to education and other public benefits. The functioning of the criminal justice system in this way has enabled the practice of what has been termed "slavery by another name" (Blackmon, 2008): namely, the leasing out of mostly Black convicts to work in abysmal conditions for negligible or no income. In this manner, what is meant to be a system to ensure justice becomes, instead, a vehicle that furthers injustice and structural violence that systematically injure individuals and tear communities apart.

While systematic racism is perhaps most visible in the criminal justice system, it also takes place in many other areas of society: housing, education, employment, health care, and the media. The forms of racism that exist within each of these areas combine to reinforce one another, and they often remain unseen until they become manifest in "incidental" events. Such events might include occasions of unwarranted police brutality and marches by white supremacist terrorist groups, like those that occurred in Charlottesville, Virginia. While his response to such happenings has been mute at best, Donald Trump has, on the other hand, called Black Lives Matter protesters "professional anarchists, violent mobs, arsonists, looters, criminals, rioters, Antifa, and … dangerous thugs" (Bidgood and Goodwin, 2020). His dehumanizing rhetoric has also frequently referred to non-white immigrants as being "aliens", "criminals", "animals", "rapists", "killers", "predators", and "invaders" (Fritze, 2019).

If all of those factors are considered, the mental health effects that they have on members of minority groups, and Black Americans in particular, might be more accurately described as being cultural rather than individual. This emphasis is necessary because of the pervasive legacies of slavery and the corresponding legal and tacit systems of racial oppression that exist in the U.S. The notion of legacy of slavery is important, as research shows that trauma is heritable and transgenerational (Dias and Ressler, 2014). For this reason, Black psychologist Dr. Kevin Washington (2019) asserts that post-traumatic stress disorder (PTSD) is a misnomer in relation to Black Americans: the prefix "post-" suggests that the trauma is finished, rather than ongoing. What Washington suggests is that a different term is required. He argues that when an entire group or a culture in the U.S. experiences a continuing trauma, whether it is in the form of police brutality, poor health care services, environmental racism, "food deserts," or the pipeline-to-prison process, it would be more accurate to refer to this trauma as "persistent enslavement systemic trauma," or PEST. This term recognizes the fact that while physical slavery lies in the past, enslavement is something that assumes many forms: mental slavery persists into the present and is, in many ways, more violent than its physical counterpart. This is, to an extent, reflected in the way in which physical actions are performed to achieve mental effects: the primary purpose of the physical brutality is to cause psychic disruption, and by targeting an entire group of people on all levels of existence, to maintain systemic subjugation. While Washington focuses on the Black American experience, he cautions of the potential for contemporary version of slavery with other races and nationalities throughout the world. Native Americans have suffered genocide and are still living through its aftermath, and there are also other people of color—including Hispanic Americans, Middle Eastern Americans, and Asian Americans—who have also been the targets of racial segregation.

Racism, as it exists in the U.S., affords no simple understanding, as has become clear by this point. Despite this, Roberts and Rizzo represent a movement toward such an understanding by identifying seven factors contributing to racism in the U.S.:

1. Categorizing people into distinct groups
2. Factions, which trigger ingroup loyalty and intergroup competition
3. Segregation, which hardens racist perceptions, preferences, and beliefs
4. Hierarchy, which emboldens people to think, feel and behave in racist ways
5. Power, which legislates racism at local and national levels
6. Media, which legitimizes overrepresented and idealized representations of white Americans while marginalizing and minimizing people of color
7. Passivism, such that overlooking or denying the existence of racism encourages others to do the same

In short, according to Roberts and Rizzo, the U.S. systematically constructs racial categories, places people inside those categories, and then actively segregates people on the basis of those categories. In so doing, it privileges and empowers some people over others, reinforces those differences through biased media, and then leaves those disparities and media in place. Of the seven factors that they list, Roberts and Rizzo believe that perhaps the most insidious is that of passivism, or passive racism, which depends on there being apathy toward systems of racial advantage or a denial that those systems even exist. Such apathy can result in no positive change, and in order to correct systemic racism properly, one must do more and become an "antiracist" (Kendi, 2019).

The question of how to do more, how to respond to such continuing trauma, is equally complex. An important tenet of trauma therapy, however, is to validate patients' truths and personal experience of their subjugation. Witness and testimony are vital: when they do not exist, or are not present, people in crisis "become bounded, out of place and out of time" (Davis, 2014). As such, being believed and not having one's experience denied is crucial to anyone who has witnessed unspeakable horrors, or who has had their world turned upside down through direct experience of torture, rape, physical, or sexual abuse. The first step that for a person to be able to move forward out of isolation and shame is the affirmation of the truth of their experience. Without this affirmation, the work of healing cannot progress (Teng, 2017).

This notion of the importance of validating and affirming an individual's experienced truths has also been making regular appearances in discussions regarding another aspect of society that is both related and relevant here. Gender discrimination can happen in a similar manner as systematic racism and is also a serious and ongoing problem. Part of what helps to perpetuate gendered violence and discrimination is the fact that men find themselves able to ward off or negate feelings of shame, disgrace, and dishonor so long as they can claim themselves to be superior to women. The parallel here is with the attitudes of the poorest white people in the U.S., who are able to accept their poverty only because the system enables them to claim themselves superior to people of other skin tones.

This aspect of male identity is deeply rooted in culture. Distinction, difference, and implicit superiority is central to the traditionally received idea of manhood. In the conventional and stereotypical sex roles that patriarchy prescribes, manhood revolves explicitly around the expectation that men distinguish themselves from women. Again, it is useful at this point to examine briefly the history of the word. In Latin, the term for manliness and manhood, *virtus*, means "courage" and derives from *vir,* a word that is used to mean both "man" and "soldier". Our modern English word "virtue" also derives from *virtus,* a linguistic trace that further reflects the lingering contemporary presence of the qualities most valued by the martial culture of Ancient Rome valued. By contrast, the Latin word for "womanly", *muliebris*, meant simply "unmanly" and was used as a derogatory way of addressing men who did not meet the masculine ideal. In other words, the idealized values and characteristics of courage, virtue, manliness, and soldier-hood could all simply be defined as being "not woman." It is this pervasive and deep-rooted cultural indoctrination that acts as one of the primary reasons why the women's liberation and the transgender movements are particularly threatening to what has hitherto been a privilege from birth.

Indoctrination

Tyrants do not arise in a vacuum, and nor does tyranny emerge within the world without announcement. Instead, tyranny is the result of a long period in which elites cultivate an increasingly unbearable, oppressive socioeconomic inequality that benefits only themselves, at least for a while (Mika, 2017). If these oppressive, hierarchical, structures are to be maintained, especially in a nation that at least nominally adheres to democratic principles, then what is necessary is large-scale indoctrination. In his work, *Thought Reform and the Psychology of Totalism*, psychiatrist Dr. Robert Jay Lifton (1961) outlines the first criterion for thought reform as "milieu control." What he understands by this phrase is the control of information and communication available within the social environment so that, ultimately, the mind of an individual is also controlled. While drawing an accurate distinction between education and subtle forms of thought reform can lead one down a slippery slope, a major difference can be found in terms of what is expected of individuals who have undergone the processes. Whereas a thought-reformed person is expected not to question or to examine critically the doctrine they have learned, an educated person, by contrast, is encouraged to do exactly the opposite.

The media are an invaluable tool for indoctrination. Indeed, recognizing the importance of broadcast communication in influencing public opinion and attempting to discourage partisan indoctrination, the Federal Communications Commission (FCC) in 1949 came to adopt the Fairness Doctrine (Houser, 1972), which allowed that the public interest "can only be satisfied by making available ... varying and conflicting views held by responsible elements of the community" (FCC, 1949). Implementing this regulation was always a difficult process but, in 1987, Ronald Reagan used is presidential power to abolish it altogether (Pagano, 1987). The result of Reagan's action was that AM radio was able to take off, and the task of serving the public interest quickly transformed into that of interesting the public. Education and other activities than required more mental effort, such as the development of critical thinking, took a sideline. Riding this wave was Rush Limbaugh, who, through rhetorical charisma, succeeded in labeling the rest of the media as "biased". Having managed that, Limbaugh proceeded to articulate the need for right-wing media, a media which in turn came to call refer to itself as "fair and balanced."

A former media consultant who helped Richard Nixon win the presidency (Sherman, 2017), papered over Ronald Reagan's budding Alzheimer's and shamelessly stoked racial fears to elect George H.W. Bush, Fox News CEO Roger Ailes may have done more than anyone else to pave the way for Donald Trump's presidency. Ailes recognized that, although people like to think they are rational, they are actually driven by emotions—anger, fear, nostalgia, even disgust. Journalist Tim Dickinson notes in "How Roger Ailes Built the Fox News Fear Factory":

> To watch even a day of Fox News—the anger, the bombast, the virulent paranoid streak, the unending appeals to white resentment … is to see a refraction of its founder, one of the most skilled and fearsome operatives in the history of the Republican Party…. Fox News was a new form of political campaign—one that enables the GOP to bypass skeptical reporters and wage an around-the-clock, partisan assault on public opinion. The network, at its core, is a giant soundstage created to mimic the look and feel of a news operation, cleverly camouflaging political propaganda as independent journalism (Dickinson, 2011).

The success of Fox News as a political propaganda machine can be in countless instance. In the documentary film *The Brainwashing of My Dad*, Jen Senko (Senko et al., 2015) vividly depicts her father's right-wing radicalization: beginning as he started listening to particular radio shows during his daily work commute and growing markedly worse when he started watching Fox News. His new fanaticism rocked the very foundation of Senko's family but she discovered that this was not an isolated phenomenon; similar changes were occurring with alarming frequency across America. As a friend of my own once lamented to me: "we were always worried about the effects television would have on our children, when we should have been worried about the effects it would have on our parents!" One of the effects of watching Fox News is not without a dark irony: in 2012, a Fairleigh Dickinson University survey reported that Fox News viewers were less informed about current events than people who did not follow the news at all. This phenomenon became known as the Fox News effect, and the program, like conservative radio, continued to cultivate an audience that thrives on anger, to prove that liberals are evil, and to otherwise deliver all of its reports with an emotional punch (Poundstone, 2016). It is exactly this kind of communication and attitude toward reporting that Donald Trump would later echo.

In *Network Propaganda*, Yochai Benkler, Robert Faris, and Hal Roberts (2018) draw on their different backgrounds in law, sociology, and media studies to show how manipulation, disinformation, and radicalization have transformed American politics. They challenge the conventional wisdom within Washington that holds that there is symmetry between the two polarized political parties. Liberals and conservatives, they argue in Network Propaganda, live in separate bubbles, where they watch different television networks, frequent different web sites, and absorb different realities. These two sides may operate in different spheres but, the book argues, they should not be understood as being equal when it comes to their evaluation of "news" stories, or even in their grounding in reality. Simply put, liberals want facts whereas conservatives want their biases reinforced. Liberals embrace journalism while conservatives prefer propaganda. The authors conclude, on the basis of this, that "the right-wing media ecosystem differs categorically from the rest of the media environment."

The right-wing media ecosystem described in *Network Propaganda* might, indeed, also be described as being systematic psychological manipulation. According to the authors, false stories are launched on a series of extreme web sites, such as InfoWars—the home of infamous conspiracy theorist Alex Jones—"none of which claim to follow the norms or processes of professional journalistic objectivity." Those stories are then transmitted to outlets such as Fox News and the Daily Caller. These secondary outlets, as Benkler and colleagues observe, claim to follow journalistic norms but often fail in their actual implementation. Notably, it is shown that the same pattern is not mirrored on the left wing: there are no significant media web sites on the left that parallel, in their content, the chronic falsity of those on the right. Indeed, the upstream sources with an allegiance to facts serve rather as a consistent check on the dissemination and validation of the most extreme stories if they emerge on the left, in ways that, equally, have no parallels on the right. The dynamic on the right works to a particular end: it "rewards the most popular and widely viewed channels at the very top of the media ecosystem for delivering stories, whether true or false, that protect the team, reinforce its beliefs, attack opponents, and refute any claims that might threaten 'our' team from outsiders" (Toobin, 2018).

To understand how this process of indoctrination works, it is necessary to consider its basic mechanisms. To that end, in *Brainwashing: The Science of Thought Control*, neuroscientist Kathleen Taylor (2006) brings a neuroscientist's perspective to bear on the "extreme influence" techniques that psychiatrists and psychologists have written about for decades. Taylor points out the usefulness of thinking about brainwashing as being a sequence of carefully planned, influential procedures that are specifically designed to alter drastically the way people think and act. The purpose of brainwashing is to alter identity, to rewrite it so that it serves the imposed will of the brainwasher. Some forms of torture, such as sensory deprivation and physical depletion, may hasten the effects of brainwashing, but they are not essential and, in fact, may even render it less effective in the long run. While torture makes obtaining compliance easier, it is, at the same time, far less likely to bring about actual conversion. Taylor thus exposes the vulnerability of our thoughts, beliefs, and behaviors as advertisers, politicians, religious leaders, talk show hosts, telemarketers, and other pundits constantly target us, seeking to capture first our attention and then our beliefs.

While media outlets such as Fox News might perform it most explicitly, even mainstream media are not immune to implicitly effecting thought reform. In Manufacturing Consent (1988), a scathing critique of the idea that the mass media inform the public objectively, media scholar Edward Herman and linguist Noam Chomsky present the notion that mass media also works to influence opinion:

> It is … difficult to see a propaganda system at work where the media are private and formal censorship is absent. This is especially true where the media actively compete, periodically attack and expose corporate and governmental malfeasance, and aggressively portray themselves as spokesmen for free speech and the general community interest. What is not evident (and remains undiscussed in the media) is the limited nature of such critiques… (Herman and Chomsky, 1988).

Herman and Chomsky continue to trace how money and power are able to determine which news is fit to print, to marginalize dissent, and to allow the government and dominant corporate interests to shape messages to the public. They identify five "filters" that contribute to this distortion of the news:

1. Ownership. Media firms are big corporations, often part of huge conglomerates whose end game is profit, to which critical

journalism takes second place.

2. Advertising. The primary income source of the mass media transforms their audience's attention into a product that they sell to advertisers.

3. Sourcing. Journalism cannot be an effective check on power because it relies on access to news sources, which means complicity with governments, corporations, and other powerful institutions that may revoke the privilege at any time.

4. Flak. Powerful institutions might counter inconvenient stories by discrediting or demonizing their authors through flak (a term deriving from the German word for antiaircraft fire).

5. Common enemy. To manufacture consent, you need an enemy—communism, terrorists, or immigrants—to help corral public opinion and to frighten the population into submission.

These filters work both individually and also in interaction with one another, providing each other with a certain degree of reinforcement. To reach the public, the raw material of news must first pass through these filters; when it emerges at the other side, all that remains are the residues deemed acceptable by the powerful structures and parties involved. As these structures determine the premises of discourse, the angle of interpretation, and what is newsworthy in the first place, they have the effect of operating what essentially amounts to a vast propaganda campaign. It is not easy to think about ways to avoid or navigate this issue successfully. The filters that Herman and Chomsky identify are built into the system in such a fundamental way that alternative bases for a different system of news and media are hardly imaginable.

In addition to control of content, there is growing control of process that has become deleterious. Social media, through opaque algorithms that filter information and encourage addiction, researchers have pointed out how social media work to distort reality, to boost conspiracy theories, to move users to more extreme content and positions, and to incentivize the outrageous and offensive. These proprietary algorithms determine what a person sees without information or consent. Media platforms use them without accountability, while political operators can game the arrangement by creating ecosystems of links and platforming one another. They now "hack" the social brain in ways that work like a drug. One of Facebook's founders, Sean Parker, said that Facebook's goal was to "consume as much of your time and conscious attention as possible," and that it did so by giving users "a little dopamine hit every once in a while, because someone liked or commented on a photo or a post or whatever. And that's going to get you to contribute more content, and that's going to get you ... more likes and comments." The point was to create "a social-validation feedback loop... exactly the kind of thing that a hacker like myself would come up with, because you're exploiting a vulnerability in human psychology" (Podur, 2019). The growing sophistication makes the influence on society ominous. In the face of this, it might have been helpful for the mental health professions to mitigate the harmful effects, but instead of using their knowledge to heal, in the societal sphere, they would fall silent.

Silence on the part of professions

The reason that the mind is tyranny's battleground in its pursuit of power is because the most potent weapon of the tyrant is the mind of the oppressed (Biko, 1978). It is for this same reason that journalists and intellectuals are often the first targets of an oppressive society. The extent to which critical voices are silenced is, equally, a good measure of a society's collective mental health, self-reliance, self-awareness, and capacity for change. In the era of Donald Trump, perhaps the most critical silencing of intellectuals has been the move to stifle mental health professionals' input, just at a time when mental health became a critical national concern. The American Psychiatric Association's (APA's, 2017a) modification of an ethical guideline to prevent any comment on a political figure by mental health professionals, at the start of Donald Trump's presidency, might well be in our day the first sign of encroaching tyranny and of the institutional tightening of information control that Herman and Chomsky (1988) speak of.

Before going further into the details and significance of the APA's action, however, let us first turn to the early twentieth century. It was at that point, over a century ago, that neurologist and founder of psychoanalysis Sigmund Freud helped enhance our understanding of the nonrational human mind. One of the reasons why Freud's work was so radical and influential was that it fundamentally challenged one of the assumptions people like to make: that human beings are rational creatures. What Freud worked to show, however, was that lying beneath the surface of our conscious minds are feelings and drives, often sexual and aggressive, that could control our behavior, unless we brought them to conscious awareness. This newfound knowledge proved to be so effective for individual therapy, it was harnessed also for social, political, and commercial engineering (Hassan, 2019). Indeed, it was the belief of reporter and psychological writer Walter Lippmann (1922) that the public needed active guidance, and this was because of the limited time and opportunities available to learn everything necessary to form public opinions. World War I proved a testing ground for new ways of influencing the way the public thought in this regard. During the conflict, the U.S. government, wishing to sway public opinion in favor of the war, called in Freud's nephew, journalist and "father of public relations" Edward Bernays, to help promote the idea that American participation in the war was necessary to make the world "safe for democracy." Witnessing how mass psychology could be controlled like "flipping a switch," Bernays understood that he could also make people buy ideas or products by appealing to their emotions and desires. In doing so, he became the first person to apply psychological principles to propaganda and advertising, and effectively spawned the modern era of consumerism. In Propaganda, Bernays (1928) spelled out the science of shaping and manipulating public opinion, and he termed this science "the engineering of consent."

Unfortunately, his findings would be mobilized to control the masses to the benefit of the few. The ruling class understood that the more deprived and the unhealthier the masses are, the more controllable they would be and decided that it was easier to manipulate them psychologically than to improve actual conditions. The use and misuse of psychological techniques for political or commercial purposes is extensive and has had a net harmful effect on society's grounding mental health. By contrast, there has been little use of these same techniques to be helpful and to contribute to societal betterment. Just as the free press had to yield its position in society to political propaganda and commercial media, which made relentless use of psychological manipulation, so did intellectuals, notably health professionals and mental health professionals, had to yield their field to politicians and the corporate interests behind them. One cannot argue that the public is better off, or better represented, as a result of its having lost both the free press and access to the best available knowledge, or best health care. Knowledge empowers the people, and hence its squelching can never help but the body that is trying to control them.

The divide between intellectuals and politics is not a new phenomenon. Even during the height of intellectualism in America, it was often observed that the "best brains are not attracted to the government service" (Ahmad, 1970). In cases in which the U.S. government temporarily borrows the service of intellectuals, these individuals are not able to function independently. This marks the U.S. as distinct from most other countries, including the U.K., possibly the nation's closest cousin when it comes to the way in which experts, such as mental health professionals, are consulted. In the U.S., when experts are brought in to work for the government, they have assigned jobs to do and they are not free to speculate in an intellectually uninhibited way. At best, if the government desires to have them, intellectuals may function as advisers. When it comes to issues of mental health, then, the problem is clear: a government most in need of consultation is the one least likely to seek it. If one of its own were mentally afflicted in dangerous ways, it would most likely hire experts who would help hide it. Within the context of the current administration it was, therefore, incumbent on the mental health community to meet its independent professional societal responsibility through the only means it had available: public education.

Such a delivery of public education did not, however, fully materialize in the Trump era. It is at this point we must return to the APA. Regarding the general failure of the mental health community to perform its ethical duties to their full extent, it is difficult adequately to assess the enormity of consequences the APA set in motion when, either under governmental pressure or of its own initiative, it decided to collude with power over truth. The specific method it used to do so was by reinterpreting "the Goldwater rule," into a kind of "gag rule" that silenced an entire profession (Glass, 2017). Its new position had little ethical, scientific, or practice-based validity, and a vast majority of professionals who were speaking up were not members under its jurisdiction: only about 6 percent of practicing mental health professionals are APA members, according to the Bureau of Labor Statistics (Grohol, 2019). Hence, what the APA did was to defend and enforce its position through public campaigns and by promoting its guild rule as if it were universal, or worse, some kind of law. Through its vast lobbying clout, it also enlisted the media, starting with the *New York Times*, and soon all the major media fell in line (Kendall, 2020). By doing so, it engineered a public opinion where one had not previously existed: that the public did not wish to hear from mental health professionals about the mental health of the president.

Only, it was untrue: as insiders of the whole affair, many of us know that the situation was more complex (Fingar, 2020). Through frequent contact with the public through an organization of mental health professionals that formed to step in where we believed that the APA had failed in societal leadership, we knew that vast numbers of people not only wished to hear from mental health professionals but were clamoring constantly to hear from us with the question: "Where are the psychiatrists? Where are the psychologists?" (Lee, 2019c). Not only that, the exceptional success of *The Dangerous Case of Donald Trump,* a book by mental health professionals that became an instant and unprecedented *New York Times* bestseller for a multi-authored book of specialized knowledge, was a clear indication of public demand. Countless members of the APA also resigned even from leadership positions because they disagreed with its new rule. Many of those former members of the APA subsequently joined our organization, specifically in opposition to the APA's complicity with the government. It is currently unknown exactly what proportion of psychiatrists within the APA disagree with the new rules, because the APA refused to do a poll or to hold a discussion. A potential indicator, however, is an informal poll that another organization—the American College of Psychiatrists—conducted. The results showed an overwhelming majority of psychiatrists disagreeing with the current version of "the Goldwater rule" (Bosworth, 2018). Among the dissenters was a past president of the APA, Dr. Steve Sharfstein, who holds heroic stature for resisting pressures the organization experienced under the Bush/Cheney administration to endorse and assist in torture. Moreover, despite the pressure that the APA applied on other organizations, the American Psychoanalytic Association (APsaA) issued an explicit memo to its members stating that "the Goldwater rule" did not apply to them and that they were free to comment (Begley, 2017).

Within our organization, the World Mental Health Coalition, there are many who believe that the APA was singularly responsible for blocking important education that may have helped the public to protect itself and possibly to avert losing thousands of lives. Five months into the pandemic, for example, we were able to create a blow-by-blow account of how exactly mental health professionals foretold the president's mismanagement of the coronavirus pandemic, based on his psychological makeup (Lee, 2020c). Our message that the situation was predictable and preventable could not effectively reach the public, because the APA's change of "the Goldwater rule," whose purpose was to protect public health, now protected a public figure at the expense of public health, arguably violating all core tenets of medical ethics. Conscientious, independent professionals, unable to gain any attention from the media, were inhibited from speaking their conscience (Lee et al., 2019). Given this situation, we stated early on that the APA's distortion of ethics to suit the Trump administration would cause more harm than the APA's psychological counterpart, the American Psychological Association, did to change its ethics guideline to facilitate and design government programs for torture (Risen, 2015). This is because any stifling of speech regarding widespread danger to society was bound to cause far more devastating harm than one thousand torture victims, as bad as that had been. Almost 200,000 deaths later from Covid-19 at the time of this writing, this would be hard to argue.

A PROFILE OF DONALD
TRUMP, CONTINUED

A tradition of political personality profiling

A renowned scholar recently contacted me with an inquiry:

> I'd be interested to know the way that this famous study is viewed
> in your field. I read it yesterday for the first time and found it to be
> remarkable, with eerie echoes to the present. Langer's main point
> seems to be Hitler's neurotic insecurity and guilt and the way they
> manifested in Hitler's need to prove his superman status to himself
> and others, to the point of global destruction. It seems far too close to
> the 'stable genius' for any comfort (Personal Communication, 2020).

The "stable genius" found here to be similar in some of his
characteristics to that disturbing historical reference is, of course, Donald
Trump—according to his own description of himself (Diaz, 2018). The
"famous study" the scholar refers to is the "OSS Hitler Psychological
Portrait" by Dr. Walter C. Langer. The sense of there being a disturbing
similarity between the portrait set out in that study and today's president is
one that is commonly experienced. Other responses I have received from
those who have read Langer's study include, amongst many more: "uncanny
in resemblance" and "I thought I was reading about Trump!"

The author of that psychological portrait, Langer, was an American
psychoanalyst. In 1943, the Office of Strategic Services (OSS), the precursor
of the modern Central Intelligence Agency (CIA), commissioned him
to produce a highly confidential, accurate, psychological study of Hitler.
Undertaken at the height of World War II at the special request of General
William J. Donovan, head of the OSS, Langer's psychological analysis

became an important point of reference for Allied leaders. The accuracy of the analysis contained within the study received contemporary validation: it predicted Hitler's suicide in 1945. Later, in 1972 and nearly 30 years after it was first prepared, Langer's work was published as *The Mind of Adolf Hitler* and became a bestseller.

It is reflection on the value and insight of Langer's work that many members of the public have been asking for a similar "profile" of Donald Trump, and hence my small attempt has now been developed into this current book. "If a profile on a dangerous political figure from the outside was useful," people have said to me, "then a profile on a dangerous political figure from the inside is even more urgent and necessary, since we are more vulnerable." Others have argued: "What advantage do we have if the rest of the world, including all our enemies, have a correct perception of our president, while we are the last to know?" This report is a response to such urgings, but it is also finally written in dedication to that person who persisted in his insistence that I proceed, and to whom I owe a tremendous personal debt for his role in my struggles to provide warning about the dangers of Donald Trump.

Langer was, himself, keenly aware of the value of his study, including its perhaps unrealized potential as a pioneering model that could have been utilized in relation to subsequent significant geopolitical events. In a later introduction to the bestselling report, he wrote:

> I may be naïve in diplomatic matters, but I like to believe that if such a study of Hitler had been made years earlier, under less tension, and with more opportunity to gather first-hand information, there might not have been a Munich; a similar study of Stalin might have produced a different Yalta; one of Castro might have prevented the Cuban situation, and one of President Diem might have avoided our deep involvement in Vietnam (Langer, 1972).

If Langer recognized the usefulness of his study, so too did others. Indeed, such recognition led the American Psychiatric Association (APA) to establish a task force that was meant, among other things, "to arrive at proposals with respect to ethical guide-lines for the writing of... psychobiographies and psychiatric profiling" (1976). Creating a team that had just such an objective, the APA at that point clearly did not doubt psychiatrists' ability to know anything and to arrive at conclusions in the absence of a personal examination, as it would later assert to be the case under the Trump administration. In fact, quite the opposite situation and view prevailed. Langer's analysis and the assistance it provided the OSS were considered to be so useful, so valuable, that Dr. Jerrold Post, a distinguished APA life fellow, launched the CIA's Center for the Analysis of Personal and Political Behavior. That center was essentially a profiling division that would in turn see the creation of a new subspecialty within psychiatry: the profiling of political figures. It is for this and other reasons that I asked him to contribute a chapter to the second edition of *The Dangerous Case of Donald Trump* (Lee, 2019b), and he has collaborated with me on the book's release as well as a major, multidisciplinary conference at the National Press Club in March 2019. At this conference, entitled, "The Dangerous State of the World and the Need for Fit Leadership," thirteen leading experts from the fields of psychiatry, law, history, political science, economics, social psychology, journalism, nuclear science, and climate science came together in unprecedented ways on the unprecedented topic to discuss how the president was unfit from each of their perspectives (C-SPAN, 2019).

Such political profiles have now become a tradition of at least seventy years. Known studies alone are multiple. In the 1950's, the CIA commissioned an analysis of the Vietnamese leader and revolutionary Ho Chi Minh based on remote observations. Then, in 1961, the CIA profiled Soviet Premier Nikita Khrushchev in advance of his meeting with President John F. Kennedy in Vienna. According to historian Michael Beschloss, the process of reading up on his Soviet adversary and counterpart got Kennedy hooked on CIA personality profiles, and he reportedly viewed them as "salacious secrets about foreign leaders." Seventeen years later, in 1978, President Jimmy Carter asked the CIA to prepare psychological profiles on Israeli Prime Minister Begin and Egyptian President Sadat in advance of the Camp David talks. Following that summit, Carter expressed pleasure with the dossiers that the CIA had provided: "After spending 13 days with the two principals, I wouldn't change a word," he said, seemingly impressed by their accuracy. As the situation in Libya in the early 1980's caused concern for the Reagan administration, the CIA tried to make sense of the erratic actions of Libyan strongman, Moammar Qaddafi. Similarly, in 1990 on the eve of the Gulf War, another strongman leader, Saddam Hussein, was also the subject of a "comprehensive political psychology profile," which the CIA's Post presented to the House Armed Services Committee. The following year, the Agency also drew up a classified psychological profile of Haitian President Jean-Bertrand Aristide, whom a military coup had just ousted. That same profile would prove instrumental in withdrawing American support for the exiled leader during the Clinton administration, after preparing to restore him to office in 1994. Finally, an even more recent example comes from 2008, when a Pentagon study went as far as to diagnose Russian President Vladimir Putin with "autism". The Office of Net Assessment's Body Leads project asserted that scrutiny of hours of Putin footage had revealed him to have "Asperger's Syndrome, an autistic disorder which affects all of his decisions" (Gilson, 2015).

Many things can be taken from that historical survey of some of the CIA's actions, not the least of which is that the agency has a long history of producing political and psychological profiles of international figures. It is also evident that CIA has often engaged in diagnosing foreign leaders from afar for the benefit of American politicians and diplomats, and, moreover, that the APA has fully cooperated with such diagnoses. Such operations are not, however, unique to the U.S. and its intelligence agencies; in fact, some other countries' unusually deft handling of Donald Trump suggests a successful use of similar techniques. The reason behind my mentioning, here, of such reports is not to assert any similarity between the profile I am producing and those agency-commissioned ones but the opposite: I wish to make a clear distinction between the two on the grounds of their contexts and the realities that they address.

The profile that I am providing here is distinct from those surveyed above in a number of crucial respects. First, rather than a foreign adversary, we instead face a domestic one, and one who has access to all of the nation's levers of power and secrets. Second, rather than the CIA or any other authoritative organization requesting an evaluation that would allow better understanding, we are instead witnessing multiple arms of government, that are supposed to be checks on the president, turning a blind, and thus enabling, eye. Third, rather than being commissioned to work on issues behind the scenes, psychological professionals instead find themselves at a roadblock, unable to advance without authorization, blacked-out from the media, and actively restrained by one of their professional associations. And, finally, rather than feeling reassured that their elected leaders will protect them, the public has instead, as a direct result of Trump's presidency, been experiencing unprecedented rises in stress and anxiety, including retraumatization, without being given explanations as to why. Following the stifling of mental health experts' voices, the presidency's psychological toll on the nation had already become immense, and this only worsened with the disastrous mismanagement of the coronavirus pandemic and subsequent economic devastation. At the time of writing, widespread suicides, homicides, and "deaths of despair" are projected (Well Being Trust, 2020), but only the tip of the iceberg has yet been seen.

The danger that the country currently faces, then, is both intimate and imminent in nature. As such, and in consideration of the tradition of political personality profiling, the psychological study of any such individual who poses a danger to society on that scale is to be viewed as being both relevant and important. To allow psychological profiles only of foreign enemies and not of domestic leaders is to place ourselves in a situation characterized by a twofold danger. If a foreign enemy were to possess a profile of our leader while we ourselves did not, then they might be able to not only work against us from the outside but also to collude with a domestic enemy to destroy the nation from within. With that in mind, it can be seen as a terrible misfortune that the APA has colluded with the Trump administration to enable the silencing of mental health professionals when it comes to discussing matters pertaining to political figures. As a consequence of that decision, the public may have been kept in the dark and rendered completely vulnerable, and the APA should be held accountable for its failure to protect millions of Americans. Institutions such as the APA exist to fulfill a purpose, and they should not use their resources merely to protect themselves and to cover for one another's errors at the expense of the society they are supposed to serve. From the start, "the Goldwater rule," retrieved from obscurity to supposedly serve that purpose, was a political compromise to start more so than an ethical guideline, and, as such, it was bound to be politically abused. It is in defiance of this unethical action, by an organization that is presumed to uphold professional ethics, that I have embarked on this profile, "Trump's Mind, America's Soul."

A profile of the nation

That our nation is sick and on a suicidal path is now no longer deniable. This is the case both literally, in terms of the grossly inadequate steps to contain the coronavirus pandemic, and figuratively, in terms of the country having brought itself to the brink of fatally undermining core democratic institutions. As the coronavirus has continued to claim a thousand lives a day in the U.S., while most other economically-advanced countries have brought deaths down to double or even single digits, the international community might wonder whether we have lost our collective minds. By the end of 2020, the projected number of Covid-19 deaths in the U.S. is projected to exceed 400,000 (Lewis, 2020). Even more ominous, perhaps, is the psychology of the nation that Donald Trump is shaping: how can one man bring about such a wretched, plague-ridden, and pariah status out of a nation the world once envied, however inaccurately, as a shining example of democracy and economic flourishing? Human beings are adaptable, and when we elevate a mind that embraces base impulses and wanton criminality, this rapidly becomes the standard, after which rapid decline is almost automatic. Donald Trump's delusions of grandeur have been allowed to swell through his three-and-a-half years in office to such a degree that defeat or voluntary departure from office, especially in the face of criminal charges, will have become inconceivable for him. Additionally and commensurate to this, his followers have been conditioned to take any defeat of their strongman leader as a "coup", and even to refuse to accept as legitimate proper election results. Given than he has now coopted a number of government institutions, having replaced career officials with loyalists, we can be certain that those inside and outside his administration will be working heavily to distort, to delay, and perhaps even to distract away from any result other than their desired one, using all means possible.

The pressing question is this: how do we improve from here? How do we move away from pathological rule, further descent into chaos and lawlessness, and fracture of society bound for destruction? The first step forward comes through a thorough understanding, through an accurate formulation. To do this, we must: (a) correctly name the problem; and (b) correctly understand the situation. Naming the problem, as simple as it sounds, is something we have not been able to do. Consider how many excuses we have heard about why we need not hear from experts about a mental health problem, how it is not a mental health problem, and how Donald Trump is a "symptom" and not a problem? He is a symptom, certainly, but he is also an important cause and an immediate offending agent that must be removed for there to be healing. It is rather this kind of either-or thinking that makes us incapable of mobilizing all our resources and cooperating, when it is of critical importance. Denying that a mental health problem is a mental health problem is precisely proof of a mental health problem (I know that is a mouthful, but it is the very nature of mental health problems to affect the mind that would otherwise be capable of recognizing what the problem is). Given this characteristic, naming the problem as one of mental health is 99.9 percent of the struggle. Of note, mental health problems are not solely individual but ecological. We need not, and should not preclude societal considerations or coexisting problems of criminality—that we would do better to think of the whole at once for a better understanding—is the very thesis of this book. As such, we are now able to embark on the creation of a psychological formulation of the situation. This formulation is presented below and consists of three key parts: a formulation of Donald Trump, a formulation of his followers, and a formulation of the nation as a whole.

Formulation of Donald Trump

Mr. Donald J. Trump is a 74-year-old married white male with five children from three marriages. He is currently the president of the United States, a role whose public nature is in keeping with that of the many highly visible jobs he has held in the past. We do not have access to his medical records, and so are unable to provide a definitive diagnosis, but are able to refer to information about him from numerous reliable sources, including firsthand reports by those who have observed him directly and longitudinal information over decades. This type of information is far more valuable than a personal interview in evaluating conditions that are of interest to larger society—such as personality disorders, dangerousness, and unfitness. He exhibits numerous worrying behaviors and symptoms that include the following: (a) pathological narcissism; (b) sociopathy; (c) difficulty with impulse control; (d) frequent mood swings; (e) histrionic traits; (f) dependent traits; and (g) declining cognitive function. If there were more room within this profile, the list might extend further. On the basis of the evidence available, a number of full evaluations that do not require a personal interview have already been performed. The result of one of those was an assessment of psychological dangerousness, for which he abundantly met criteria; this would ordinarily warrant further, involuntary, evaluation and would disqualify him from any job until he is proven no longer to be dangerous. Similarly, a mental capacity evaluation, based on highly reliable information presented in the special counsel's report, evidenced a failure to meet any of the required criteria for rational decision-making, which would also disqualify him for almost any job, let alone president. Cause for further concern is a potential neurological asymmetry with apparent right-sided weakness and forward-leaning posture, whether sitting or standing. This asymmetry may also be related to conditions that are contributing to his difficulties with attention and impulse control; all this has been observed within the context of a family history of Alzheimer's Disease. Furthermore, multiple sources, including his own niece, have alluded to an undiagnosed learning disorder, which may have contributed to Trump's behavioral problems as a child and his capacity as an adult.

He has not had any known suicide attempts or psychiatric hospitalizations, but he has consistently struggled to manage on his own, meeting with multiple bankruptcies, criminal charges, and serious public scandals such that he has required extraordinary institutional support throughout his life—in the form of millions of dollars from his father, from multiple banks, and now the federal government. Earlier in his presidency, it was suggested that he, who has the ultimate responsibility for the use of the most dangerous weapons in the history of the world, and who has the sole capability to murder millions of people in an instant, should undergo an evaluation for the multiple, serious psychological, cognitive, and neurological signs he showed. Rather than give him a proper neuropsychiatric workup, however, Dr. Ronny Jackson, now disgraced and removed from his position as White House physician, performed in January 2018 a 10-minute cognitive screen, on which Donald Trump apparently scored 30 out of 30, but this is a test that full-blown Alzheimer patients have been found to score perfectly (Trezpacz et al., 2015), and hospitalized schizophrenia patients to score in the normal range (Gierus et al., 2015), such that Alzheimer research groups have recommended that the test not be used for ruling out dementia. Hence, unfortunately, a much-needed comprehensive exam was skipped.

He has problems with aggression and violence and is now responsible for a mass homicide of hundreds of thousands who, but for his lies, deceptions, and suppression of the Centers for Disease Control and Prevention (CDC) and medical experts, would otherwise be alive. His history of violence stretches back into his childhood, when he attacked a neighboring toddler with rocks, but his more recent violent acts have, since his candidacy for presidency alone, included the following: verbal attacks; boasts of sexual assaults; repeated threats and incitement of violence; traumatization of children by the thousands; the dispatch of federal forces against peaceful protesters; displays of belligerence against enemy and allied nations alike, including the assassination of a high-ranking Iranian general on an official visit in Iraq and the massacre of Kurdish allies; and the stimulation of a renewed nuclear arms race. There are many more but cannot all be listed here. He has no known history of substance abuse, although stimulant misuse cannot be ruled out in light of evidence from multiple witnesses and reports. His medical history includes a history of obesity, heart problems, and elevated cholesterol.

Of all his signs and symptoms, the most concerning is a ballooning of his pathological narcissism that has led to ever greater, delusional levels of grandeur, feelings of omnipotence, and total belief in the impunity of the presidential office: "Article II means I can do whatever I want" (Speaker's Press Office, 2020). This has escalated to the point where he cannot imagine that he could lose a second term unless the election is "rigged" (Liptak, 2020), believes that he deserves "a redo of four years" (Wade, 2020), and declares himself, "the law of the land" (Baker et al., 2020). Rage attacks are common in such a needy personality, for expectations always outpace reality, and eventually everyone falls short. However, when there is an all-encompassing loss, such as the loss of an election, it can trigger a rampage of destruction and reign of terror in revenge against an entire nation that has failed him. It is far easier for someone of his fragile, inflated self-image to consider destroying himself and the world, including its "laughing eyes," than to delegate himself to the status of "loser" and "sucker" (Goldberg, 2020b)—which will feel like psychic death.

On top of his fragile sense of self is a need for power, a lack of empathy, and cruelty, which all make him dangerous. He has felt no remorse or sorrow for the almost 200,000 Americans lost to Covid-19 but rather his inaction and cavalier attitude have facilitated a most insidious, enduring, and most lethal form of genocide, whether intention is conscious or subconscious. Rather, partly out of envy of other human beings for having the human characteristics that he lacks, he shows signs that he derives pleasure from others' suffering and death (Lee, 2020c). Moreover, he delights in putting people in danger, as when he forces his followers into crowded indoor rallies without masks, as he demands that they prove their loyalty to him with their lives. All of these characteristics are associated with a poor prognosis, and their management should begin with containment and limitation of access to both weapons and power.

Formulation of Trump followers

Mr. Donald Trump's followers are of a wide range of population demographics. Despite that, are of a highly varied demographic. Nevertheless, they are more old (53 percent of age 65 and older) than young, more married (55 percent) than unmarried, more white (54 percent) than colored, more men (52 percent) than women, less educated (50 percent of non-college graduates) than more, and lower income (61 percent of less than 30,000-dollar annual income) than higher (Pew Research Center, 2018; Cole, 2019). If considered individually, most of these followers would likely not be diagnosed with mental health problems; in fact, the probability is high that they would be categorized as being of normal health. As a group, however, Trump followers display a mass psychology of irrationality and impairment, much as has been described in works such as that of French medicine-trained crowd psychologist Gustave Le Bon (1896). Moreover, when an individual in possession of serious impairments is in power, many supporters will themselves start to exhibit the same behaviors and symptoms as in the leader, because of their emotional bonds. A likely common manifestation of that phenomena is decreased ability, on the part of the followers, to imagine that there could be anything wrong with them, as well as a violence-proneness against anyone who would suggest this of them or their leader. Hence, any attempt to normalize these maladaptive characteristics would be as erroneous as seeking to normalize the leader's psychopathology, but caution is warranted. Other particularly "contagious" symptoms are delusions and paranoia. The present remarkable situation is that Trump supporters are steadfast in their approval of him, despite the fact that he is, as we have established, not mentally well or fit for duty according to any metric or standardized technique that mental health professionals employ. There is seemingly no degree of demonstrable incompetence, egregious behavior, or destruction of the nation's democratic norms and welfare that can diminish the resolve of Trump supporters to stand by their leader.

That wide display, across society, of characteristics similar to those that Donald Trump himself presents leads to their coalescence into a number of group characteristics that social psychologists have identified. These group characteristics are: (a) authoritarianism, or an outgrowth of largely narcissistic wounds that cause "regression" to an earlier stage of emotional development that agrees with deference to authority, aggression toward outgroups, and a rigidly hierarchical view of the world; (b) social-dominance orientation, or a related trait that emphasizes being dominant, driven, tough-minded, disagreeable, and relatively uncaring in a "might makes right" world that corresponds to an earlier stage of moral development; (c) outgroup prejudices, which can arise from having relatively little experience of the intergroup contact that is necessary to induce empathy and to reduce fear; and (d) relative deprivation, which has resulted from the massive job losses that came with automation and rising inequality (Pettigrew, 2017). Consideration of these group characteristics can go some way toward explaining the collective psychology of Trump supporters. The president's loyalists are more readily found in areas of low mobility, in which largely Republican state legislations have sharply reduced the funding for institutions of higher learning upon which people depend for education and future opportunity. Such legislation helps to create precisely those conditions of stress under which both individuals and groups of people are more likely to "regress" and to yearn for an authority figure. More specifically, they tend to seek authority figures who they believe are capable of easing their pain and solving their problems like a parent, and hence displaying strong, dominant qualities. Much of that pain, and many of the psychological problems center around grievance and envy, with people feeling as though they are being deprived, in relation to both what they expected to have at a certain point in their lives as well as to what groups they erroneously perceive to be "less deserving" seem to possess. These feelings are rooted in socioeconomic realities, especially relative poverty, but once they translate into psychological injury and take maladaptive form, they become ripe for exploitation.

That exploitation is perhaps most strikingly manifest in the Trump era with staged rallies that have been called, "identity festivals," around their focal slogan, "make America great again," which represents a reactionary call to return to an earlier time in the nation's history when America's position in the world was dominant, its presidents and Supreme Court judges were all white males, its immigration policy was more restrictive, and its society was more racially segregated. Deep within the unconscious, however, it is a metaphorical desire to return to the safety of the womb, where one is protected from the world through impenetrable walls—and is one of the reasons why a concrete wall at the U.S.-Mexico border, no matter how ineffective in keeping out real danger, is irresistible. A demagogue who understands and exploits this fantasy is able to stir those who have felt inept, inferior, and abjectly insignificant into reimagining themselves as a powerful, entitled people of destiny. Through the vilification of outgroups such as immigrants, Democrats, the so-called "elite", and the media that was critical of Donald Trump, his supporters and attendees of his rallies can evacuate their feelings of self-loathing, weakness, and humiliation. In purging themselves of those feelings they transfer them onto others; by casting others as the epitome of evil they are then able to refigure themselves as being superior and chosen. Accordingly, Donald Trump, the man who delivers them this intoxicant, is exalted for the brash social dominance he displays, the prejudices he affirms, and for protecting them from the world, which they experience as a very dangerous and threatening place (Allport, 1954).

That exaltation and sense of identification are behind the inseparable bond that leader and followers have come to share, like parent and child. Once the followers identify with their leader, any criticism of scandal concerning his fraudulence, his inanities, or his criminality is experienced as simultaneously posing an existential threat to themselves; their leader is not just protector but country, constitution, and government itself. Criticism therefore activates defensive denial, disavowal, and a willingness to fight to one's death to protect their "protector". As this is essentially an inviolable bond, if a situation were to arise wherein unfavorable facts, science, and incriminating evidence were to mount, the more they will rather unmoor themselves from reality. In doing so, they find and cling ever more closely to the few sources of information that will corroborate their beliefs and adopt unquestioningly their leader's fixed, false beliefs. Their ability to return successfully to previous levels of functioning depends on the swiftness of any intervention, the completeness of the separation from the leader and sources of propaganda, and the support they receive in the aftermath of the trauma.

Formulation of the nation

The United States of America is a 244-year-old democracy with a mixed history of colonialism and slavery that was experiencing increasing vulnerabilities through political corruption, economic inequality, and increasing public alienation for decades, until all of these factors converged to elect and support the presidency of Donald Trump and have now culminated in the tragic national mismanagement of a global pandemic, in the midst of other national crises. The current episode of systemic deterioration can probably be identified as taking root in the mid-1990's. At that time, with Newt Gingrich as speaker of the House, U.S. politics started to turn into a partisan "blood sport," replete with name-calling, conspiracy theories, and strategic obstructionism—foreshadowing the current presidency. Some may date it back to the 1980 Ronald Reagan victory when his campaign struck a deal with Tehran to delay the release of the hostages until after the presidential election, a possibly treasonous act for his own gain of power. Gingrich's "Republican Revolution" was interested not so much in legislating as it was in using the U.S. Congress as an arena to create conflict and drama; in doing so, it broke bipartisan coalitions in order to "win", and plunged Washington into permanent dysfunction (Coppins, 2018). It was that point in the last decade of the twentieth century that marks, perhaps, the juncture at which normal politics ceased and identifiable characteristics of dysfunctional pathology began to appear. From that point on, U.S. politics became increasingly defined by failure to conform to social norms, deceitfulness, failure to plan ahead, aggressiveness, reckless disregard for safety, irresponsibility, and lack of remorse about that behavior. These proclivities resulted in a stolen presidential election that saw the appointment of George W. Bush, similar to the 2016 election in the electoral college arrogating the people's choice, and also a carelessness toward the September 11 terrorist attacks of 2001 that came to foreshadow the carelessness with which Covid-19 would in turn be handled.

The new pathology within U.S. politics interpreted previous global leadership following the fall of Communism as being insufficiently self-interested, and it worked to abuse its powers for greater hegemony, as well as to exploit the grief and confusion of the nation following September 11, 2001, in order to advance its prior policies and objectives of expansion. One particular think tank, Project for the New American Century, planned and focused on the invasion and control of Iraq since the 1990's, for example. In keeping with the renewal of opportunistic policies, other pathological characteristics also appeared: a grandiose sense of self-importance; a preoccupation with global dominance; a sense of entitlement; the exploitation and dehumanization of others; and the assumption of arrogant and haughty behaviors or attitudes. As all this was taking place, the environment continued to be mismanaged, ignoring the signs of global warming that grew more evident, a new worldwide nuclear arms race began, and many progressions toward democracy started to reverse trends. In that manner, disordered behavior manifested not just in individuals but in nations: through unnecessary wars, American attitudes led not only to the destruction of others but also to self-destruction. Bitterness toward partisan politics and the terrible policies it produced began to build in the population, while other liberal democracies marveled at the its lack of representation.

The financial crash of 2008 only deepened the bitterness. A result of the practices and excesses of the banking system, the financial crisis was also largely self-generated. If the crash itself was devastating, doubly infuriating was the fact that the subsequent bailout bill rewarded the same system that had caused the crisis, even as ordinary people continued to suffer from its repercussions. Leading bankers often went entirely without prosecution, most keeping their fortunes and some their jobs, and before long the banks were back in business. Meanwhile, Americans on the middle and lower economic rungs of society had to take on new debt and often lost their jobs, homes, and retirement savings. Unlike the banks, many average Americans never recovered from the crash, and young people who came of age during the Great Recession were the first generation in a long time to find themselves poorer than their parents.

Following the financial crash, and through the long period of recession, inequality in the U.S. worsened, as did social fragmentation, another marker of declining psychological health. Chasms opened between all different social and political groupings: upper and lower classes, Republicans and Democrats, metropolitan and rural people, native-born and immigrants, ordinary Americans and their leaders. The bonds that hold society together began to tear apart, and the reforms of the Obama years, in health care, financial regulation, and green energy, while aspiring to heal those wounds, proved only to be palliative. The long recovery that occurred over the course of the last decade mainly served to enrich corporations and investors, to lull professionals, and to leave the working class even further behind. Moreover, the long-term effects of the economic slump increased polarization and discredited authority, especially that of the government. The result of that, however, was a response that is typical of dysfunctional societies; an abused nation chose to place its trust in another abuser who would only accelerate those problems: Donald Trump.

Continuing what he began in his election campaign, he has, throughout his entire presidency, pitted citizens against one another along lines of race, sex, religion, citizenship, education, region, and political allegiance. As a result of those actions, a third of the country has locked itself in a hall of mirrors that it believes to be reality; a third has driven itself mad with the effort of trying to hold onto the idea of knowable truth; and a third has given up even trying to do anything at all. Having acquired a federal government crippled by years of right-wing ideological assault and steady defunding, Donald Trump has effectively set about finishing the job by destroying the professional civil service, filling it with loyalists who will work only to further his own interests, and forcing them to function as his private operations. The major legislative accomplishment of his administration, one of the largest tax cuts in history, was of equally little benefit to the majority of Americans: it sent hundreds of billions to the wealthy who then subsequently rushed to contribute to Trump's re-election fund.

By early 2020, when the coronavirus pandemic reached the U.S., the nation had already received over three years of Donald Trump's wreckage along these lines. It was for these reasons that, when confronting the challenges of Covid-19, the response of the U.S. was shockingly inadequate. Despite months of advance warning of the virus' arrival, and despite a vast amount of resources at its disposal, the U.S. squandered every opportunity and depleted every means until the nation's economy and world stature have all but collapsed. It acted not like an economically-advanced nation but as one with an ineffective infrastructure and a government either too corrupt or too inept to act as required. The consequences have been stark. The "American carnage" he vowed to stop in his inaugural address was his actual world view, with which he would make reality match, and the U.S. was its unfortunate recipient. The pandemic has not united Americans against a common threat; nor has it acted as a great leveler. Instead, the pandemic and its handling have become a source of indignation: Black, brown, and poor people are suffering and dying in disproportionate numbers; the rich are profiteering during the crisis even as tens of millions of people are laid off and left without employment (Packer, 2020). A report in early August 2020 revealed, 643 Forbes-certified billionaires grew their collective wealth by an estimated 685 billion dollars (Helenowski, 2020), just as the nation itself plummets into a new Great Depression.

Meanwhile, the U.S. now resides in a newly unstable world: unconstrained North Korea, coupled with a more assertive China, could further destabilize Northeast Asia; an Iran that no longer feels bound by the non-proliferation treaty membership is an ever more destabilizing actor in the Middle East; and, in an election year, Russia, China, Saudi Arabia, and Israel all have a stake in swaying the results. We have a president who believes he is manipulating everyone else in his infinite wisdom, but of course the opposite is true. Without stable leadership, and with most major authorities and institutions corroded, the nation is more vulnerable than ever. Even if the cataclysm does not happen, we will no longer be living in the same world, and the damage he has done to our institutions, our identity, and our sense of reality is already a gift to our enemies.This formulation of the nation makes two things strikingly clear. First, we can see that it is possible for societies to become sick, just as individuals do. Second, it is evident that the response to societal sickness must be the same as that given to a sick individual: triage and treat, and keep treating until the nation returns to normal levels of functioning. Given the current situation that our society finds itself in, the provision of care needs to occur with great urgency if the sickness is to be treated with success.

A plan

We see from the above formulations that societal sickness and individual disorder intertwine, especially where an influential public figure is concerned. The distinction should not be between society and individual, or between political office and civilian status, but whether there are patterns and characteristics consistent with pathology, and how best to treat it. A hallmark of mental compromise is that one loses insight, or the ability to recognize that something is wrong. We observe this in clinical settings: the sicker the patients, the more they insist they are well and avoid evaluation and treatment at all cost. Healthy individuals and societies, on the other hand, are quick to examine themselves, and to seek attention or guidance for anything that bothers them, so that they can correct and improve problems before they get out of hand. As they are anxious to resolve any issues so that they can advance, they also do not hesitate to solicit advice from experts. This healthy impulse to monitor and to seek help for oneself diminishes, however, as an individual or society falls into sickness. It is therefore imperative that we take action before insight, or self-awareness, dissipates and is entirely lost. Once that point has been reached and passed, the course of disease accelerates, and the hope for the individual or the society to save itself is nearly gone.

At the societal level, mental health experts are supposed to perform the vital task of facilitating that insight, in addition to also helping to put into context what the general public is seeing in the case of an impaired leader.

When a two-party political system obscures the difference between what is partisan and what is pathological, for example, expertise can help identify the distinction through standardized, neutral methods. Without that differentiation having been made, pathology can infiltrate almost any human institution to exploit its fault lines, to bulldoze rational systems, and to take over. A lay population is more likely to conflate pathology with the wide spectrum of normalcy, since human health accommodates great variation, and without knowing how deeply disturbances can run, it is natural to see things in the frame of the familiar. Mental health experts, on the other hand, have the research-based knowledge and clinical training required to recognize the stereotypical and well-established patterns of pathology. Such experts can then alert the general population as to the existence of these pathologies, and also educate them about their characteristics. This societal role is especially crucial for the most dangerous pathologies, since we mostly assume that others are like us even when they merely take on a "mask of sanity," to borrow the phrase from psychiatrist Dr. Hervey Cleckley's (1941) classic book. In other words, experts can highlight pathology's distinguishing features to help the public to be able to have self-awareness and to protect itself. The aim is not for mental health professionals to overtake the people's decision-making process, but by sharing professional insights and knowledge, to help them make informed and self-benefiting decisions.

Having access to facts and expertise, or the best available knowledge, is critical to a people's ability to govern itself. As such, making themselves available to society is a vital service that independent experts can offer in ways that institutions dependent on government funding, or White House-employed physicians, cannot. The provision of this service should be voluntary but also proactive. We, unlike many other civilized nations, do not have an official, independent advisory system of experts. Instead, experts are called in for limited topics that usually serve politicians' purposes or are "hired" by wealthy and powerful interests that can afford their services. The end result is that expert voices are sometimes misused or stifled precisely in the moment of need. We know from the Trump era that leaders abusing power stifled attempts to remedy the situation, and the American Psychiatric Association, against most of its own membership and against independent professionals, stopped even the truth from getting out.

The public therefore depends on independent experts' sense of conscience and responsibility to society to speak up in times of need. Experts should therefore not feel restricted to waiting until the powers-that-be call them, for this delimits their function merely to being "hired guns." The necessity of such an approach is particularly evident where mental health is concerned, as, because of the nature of mental compromise, the likelihood of experts being called is inversely proportional to need. Moreover, if mental health experts were to present only when authorities request them, then a situation would emerge wherein those without voice or power—increasingly the public—would most likely be left behind. Responsibility to society is one of mental health professionals' primary responsibilities, alongside their responsibility to patients. At times, they may need to provide education about when to consult with experts, or under what circumstances one might expect experts to act on the initiative to warn and to protect the public, and to hold them accountable, just as society does with the rest of professional ethics: patient confidentiality is held to be sacrosanct, but health professionals are also required to break it when necessary to preserve human life. In the case of public figures, further, there is no patient confidentiality but rather the protection of speech under the First Amendment, even before we get to professional societal responsibility.

At this point, we are now in a position to understand how Donald Trump may act in response to the growing pressures of the upcoming election and behave through to the end of his presidency. In that regard, important elements in the equation are the reaction of his followers as well as any action that the nation may choose to take. It is in the hope that those actions, over which we have control, might alter the outcome that is driving this writing. Instead of being pummeled into passive acceptance of the course that unmitigated pathology has dictated so far, we have a choice. In this light, we can review here the likely possibilities for the future in the absence of intervention:

1.   Donald Trump may attempt to destroy the nation and himself. This possibility sits at the top of our list, not only because it is a devastating prospect that we wish to do everything to avoid but also because of the ease with which he could make it a reality. Donald Trump's profound awareness of his incapacity would cause him to do anything to cover up his illegitimacy and to remain in power so that he can prove, above all to himself, that he is not a "loser". This is already being demonstrated by his relentless insistence on reopening the economy, holding "super spreader" rallies, and his continued promulgation of misinformation about the pandemic being almost over, even as it strikes and kills more people than in any other nation. Now, with an election looming, he is on his way to refusing to concede the results, to calling the election a fraud, and to insisting on remaining in office. If all do not work, as the nation reels from disease and destitution and discontent mounts, using his presidential powers to make a dramatic display

of military might, to stoke social unrest, or to stage a terrorist attack will be very tempting, and could set in motion any level of further destruction. We must come to the recognition that he is truly someone who would do anything, no matter how terrible, no matter how destructive, to stay in power.

2.   Donald Trump may isolate himself and hide away. It may seem counterintuitive, but the flip side of extreme violence is cowardice. Donald Trump has shown himself easily frightened, and indeed he once hid in his basement "bunker" when a large crowd of protesters approached the White House. His constant taunting of former vice president and presidential candidate, Joe Biden, that he is hiding, when he is not, may indicate projection and wishful thinking. Hiding away may also include fleeing to another country, should his election defeat and criminal prosecution become more certain. What is important for the public to keep in mind is that this type of cowardice can also easily give way to more impulsive and dangerous acts of retaliation for his perceived humiliation (such as when he attacked peaceful protesters to clear the way for a photo-op, when he was convinced the world was laughing at him for hiding the previous night). He can equally become a danger to the country by leaving it and by giving away the nation's secrets.

3.   Donald Trump may die of natural causes. This is not a small possibility given his age, poor diet and obesity, heart condition, and apparent neurological condition, in the midst of a pandemic that he has worsened and prolonged while taking particularly poor precautions for himself, his staff, and his followers. From the information that we have, it seems the most likely cause of such an eventuality would be either coronavirus infection, a heart attack, a stroke, or any combination of those.

4.   Donald Trump may be assassinated. Although his own suspicion and cowardice keep him protected, if someone had the intent to assassinate him, it would not be difficult because of the ease with which he is manipulated and his own carelessness with communications. An assassination would more likely be from a foreign source than a domestic one, and the assassin would most likely be someone willingly invited rather than an intruder. While his susceptibility to influence currently makes him more valuable alive, and thus affords him a degree of protection, this may change at any time if, for any reason, he were to become a liability rather than an asset.

5.   Donald Trump may descend into "insanity" and/or suicide. His mental fragility is evident by his loose grip on reality, his propensity to grasp at conspiracy theories when under stress, and his inability to deviate from his poor coping mechanisms. Under great strains, further collapse

into psychosis and increasing detachment from reality is not, therefore, a distant possibility. Indeed, as the election nears and his poll numbers drop, it seems already to be happening. If it continues, and he loses touch with reality completely, the dangers may lessen. We could reach a stage where it is difficult for even his most ardent supporters to defend the state of his mental health and, as such, he might finally receive the treatment that he needs. Nevertheless, it is the period leading up to such a psychotic spiral, when he retains enough wherewithal to unleash his fear and paranoia on the world, that will be most dangerous. In this period, we may also include the possibility of suicide. It is hard to imagine a person who has done such great damage to the nation for his personal benefit would be prone to suicide, but a person who hurts others is more, not less, likely to hurt himself. The frightening aspect is that he would probably try to bring down as many people as possible with himself.

6.   Donald Trump may fall under prosecution. This possibility depends less on standard processes and more on the tenacity of individual prosecutors and the demands on the part of the general public. Donald Trump has used his powers to subvert the law many times, such as when he fired a U.S. attorney in New York who was investigating his inner circle. If the public refused to accept his destruction of norms, illegality, and chaos, and continued pressing, then the tide may turn in a manner that allows for his prosecution and sentencing.

7.   Donald Trump may be persuaded to resign. This would be the most ideal solution and yet not the most difficult one to achieve. In fact, because of his irrationality and psychological fragility, he could even be the easiest president to persuade to resign, without any preconditions even being necessary. This tendency can be seen in the ease with which he yielded northern Syria to Turkey, with no tangible gain for the U.S., or his facile signing of a nonbinding agreement with the North Korean leader, just for show. Further increasing the likelihood of this possibility is the fact that he has also, on a number of occasions, displayed considerable impulsivity, often appearing to concur simply with the last person he spoke to, regardless of any promises or commitments he might have made previously. To persuade him to resign from office would, however, require both psychological prowess as well as direct access, and there does not, at the present, appear to be a person with the required skills and inclination in his vicinity (although the hope that this will become a possibility is behind this profile).

Note that a "peaceful transition of power" after losing an election is missing from the above list of possible outcomes. Such a transition could only occur if the last possibility were realized, namely that someone persuaded him to concede. In the absence of successful persuasion, he might instead resort to attempting to stay in power by any number of methods: through challenging the results, instituting martial law or the equivalent in the case of civil demonstrations against his refusal to leave, or invoking any of the vast emergency powers that are vested in the presidency. An alternative to successful persuasion would be swift intervention immediately following election results, but preferably before, along the lines of removing the dangers or removing his influence through the Twenty-Fifth Amendment, urgent impeachment, court-ordered involuntary mental health evaluation, or removal from decision-making and exposure to the public. The more time is allowed to pass with his growing expectations and increasing external pressures and fears, the greater the dangers will grow, which makes the "lame duck" period, were there to be one, the most dangerous of all.

Being now in possession of both this sober synopsis of possible future outcomes as well as our earlier formulations, we are able at this point to devise a plan of action. This plan is grounded in the awareness of the fact that, like almost all mental health problems, a nation's problem is ecological: all of the elements involved are interdependent. What this means, in other words, is that what Donald Trump does is dependent on how his followers respond and also on what the nation chooses to do with him. Similarly, what Trump followers do is dependent on how he directs them and also how the nation engages with them. That network of relations applies to all parties. While this ecological understanding of the situation should be "common sense," clinicians, especially psychiatrists, too often look at individuals as atoms without context. Bio-psycho-social models and ecological frameworks are therefore designed to enable clinicians to break this habit of thinking and approach problems from a different perspective.

Not only clinicians need encouragement to see not only the individual but also the context. The public, likewise, may have the preconceptions that the work of mental health professionals is limited to individual patients only, whereas one of our chief responsibilities is in fact public health. The American Psychiatric Association has actively encouraged this in the Trump era, confusing clinical psychiatry with preventive psychiatry, which is in the domain of public health, but a public figure posing a danger to society is a public health issue, not one of clinical psychiatry. Since I have taught at a law school for fifteen years, I can make an analogy: in the legal profession, there are instances where lawyers personally represent clients, but there are also instances where they might share knowledge to inform the public about general legal matters that affect the nation. Indeed, day after day they come on broadcast programs frequently to comment on current affairs and the importance of a legal viewpoint. Mental health is similar: there are instances where mental health professionals see individual patients, but there are also instances where those of us who consult and advise on policy or intervene at the population level through public health engage in public education. Never do we confuse our role as personal provider with our public health role.

The dimension of prevention through public health is, moreover, becoming ever more important in light of increasing knowledge about all the ways in which social determinants contribute to individual wellbeing. As we now know, more clearly than ever before, that caring for the health of the population in general can help prevent a vast majority of diseases before they even occur, there is no excuse to treating only individuals one at a time and after they have fallen ill. Therefore, while the ecological model might at first seem to make the picture more complex, it affords greater simplicity and new possibilities: since factors contributing to the problem exist on multiple levels simultaneously, we are presented with a variety of different points at which we can intervene to bring about positive change. A consequence of that is that we all have a vital role to play in almost any situation, no matter how small our influence may seem at first.

The effects of reaching an understanding that the nation's problem is ecological can extend further still. If more independent mental health professionals spoke up, and spoke openly, then concepts about which there currently is disagreement can be clarified for the public, and institutional corruption and abuses of power can be exposed, and an ethical consensus can emerge through the engagement of moral agency and autonomy. As a reminder, a public health approach to the current situation does not mean engaging in diagnosing the president and treating him as a private patient. Instead, society is the patient, and professionals have direct responsibility to preserve its safety, health, and wellbeing as well as to serve it through meaningful contributions of their mental health knowledge. What this means is that, if efforts to alert authorities to the dangers faced have not brought about society's protection, they can call on the ultimate authority: the people themselves. What follows here are some specific steps that can be taken in three key phases: intervention at the level of individual, intervention at the level of followers, and intervention at the level of society.

Intervention at the level of individual

Before going into people's interventions, I will do here an intervention of my own, which is to describe two proclivities that are particularly important to look out for in a leader, which are sociopathy and pathological narcissism. We have refrained from diagnoses both here and in The Dangerous Case of Donald Trump (Lee, 2019b), because diagnoses virtually say nothing about matters of public health concern; that is, dangerousness, unfitness, or even criminal responsibility. In other words, no diagnosis in the Diagnostic and Statistical Manual of Mental Disorders (APA, 2013a) ensures any of these outcomes. Nevertheless, the two mentioned major categories predispose to, although do not guarantee, dangerousness, and ethical guidelines encourage professionals to educate the public in general terms. Hence, this information is to answer the public's frequent questions, since the public still thinks in terms of diagnoses and expects diagnoses from mental health professionals (which the American Psychiatric Association has not helped), and education is the intended intervention. Yet, these are still not diagnoses but tendencies, within which exist specific diagnoses (such as antisocial personality disorder or narcissistic personality disorder). Also, diagnosis is an intricate process that happens mostly by exclusion after the review of all medical records, and, until then, a differential diagnosis is important to consider for the following reasons:

When a person repetitively cons others, lies, cheats, and manipulates to get what he wants, does not care whom he hurts as long as he gratifies himself, the indifference to the feelings of others for personal gain may be the sign of a severe disturbance called sociopathy. In humans, the ability to sense the feelings of one another, to care about one another, and to avoid harming others sometimes even at the expense of one's own safety or advantage is called empathy. This basic human characteristic is missing in sociopaths, which leads to an absence of guilt, easy manipulation, and controlling or even hurting others for power or pleasure. Far from being "clever like a fox," they lack an essential part of being human, which is why sociopathy is among the most severe mental disturbances (Dodes, 2017). This disturbance in emotional development can cause failure to conform to social norms; deceitfulness and repeated lying; impulsivity or failure to plan ahead; irritability and aggressiveness; reckless disregard for safety of self or others; consistent irresponsibility; and lack of remorse. Sociopaths make cold-blooded murderers and ruthless rulers, and while they may lack empathy, they can sense the vulnerabilities of others the way predators understand their prey.

Pathological narcissism is present when people have a strong need, in every area of their life, to be treated as if they are special. Other people are simply mirrors, useful only insofar as they reflect back the special view of themselves they so desperately crave. The heart of pathological narcissism may be seen as: entitlement, or acting as if the world and other people owe them and should bend to their will; exploitation, or using the people around them to make themselves feel special, no matter what the emotional or even physical cost to others; and empathy-impairment, or neglecting and ignoring the needs and feelings of others, even of those closest to them, because of their own, all-encompassing and urgent need to feel special (Malkin, 2017). The usual course of unconstrained pathological narcissism is to seek positions of ever greater power and celebrity; to settle for fear is admiration is unavailable, and to seek infamy if celebrity cannot be achieved. Overall, pathological narcissists are predisposed to being dangerous because of the brittleness of their sense of worth. Unable to take responsibility for any errors, mistakes, or failings, they overcompensate by creating a grandiose image of themselves. Any slight or criticism is experienced as a threat to this fragile self-image, and to cope with the resultant hollow and empty feelings, they react with narcissistic rage, which can be brutal and destructive for the perceived source of humiliation (Zinner and Lee, 2020).

These do not determine, but contribute to, concerns based on tendencies (quality measurements) and on dangerousness and unfitness (quantity measurements). Concerns have been great, even before Donald Trump crossed a number of recent alarming thresholds: scaremongering and fomenting violence from the White House (Cassidy, 2020), attacking the electoral process (Rupar, 2020), escalating global instability (Friedman, 2020), and allowing a deadly pandemic to grow exponentially (Lee, 2020c). Given the relatively limited capacity he has, we can expect only a small range of possibilities and, consequently, behavior characterized by considerable predictability. With provocation of or incitement to violence being one of his main maladaptive coping strategies, this means that we are entering a period in which there will be an elevated risk of all forms of war: civil, international, or nuclear. Nothing is off the table, and no stone will be left unturned in his campaign to hold onto power at all cost. The greater our readiness, both psychologically and physically, the more likely we are to emerge unscathed.

The medical standard of care that an individual such as Donald Trump requires is simple. As he is a danger to self and to others, he needs to be contained, to have his access to weapons removed, and to be psychologically evaluated regardless of whether or not he gives consent. The professional evaluation would determine the least restrictive course of management that would ensue, but full containment would not be lifted until he could demonstrate that he is no longer a danger. Such measures are drastic but are sometimes necessary to protect both the patient and the public (and, since patients very commonly express appreciation for the protection once they are better, these measures are fully instituted in the law). It is notable that, before the mid-1960's, all mental health care was involuntary and considered to be necessarily so because of the nature of mental impairment. Currently, we allow for much more leeway in all but the most severe cases where a person is a danger to oneself or others and is refusing treatment. Crucially, there is nothing in mental health law that states that a president is exempt from its prescriptions; in fact, a president is supposed to receive precisely the medical standard of care. In other words, there is no "Office of Legal Counsel memo" equivalent that prevents mental health intervention the way the memo recommends non-prosecution of a sitting president for national security reasons. We might say, however, that "the Goldwater rule" has been similarly abused, in that a guideline has been promoted as an absolute rule so as to facilitate a sitting president being above the law, even at the expense of national security and public safety.

While mental health law dictates that the president is accorded no special privileges, and is denied no needed care, the reality at the current moment is different. For various reasons, including obstruction by the medical community itself, specifically a succession of White House doctors and the American Psychiatric Association, Donald Trump is in a position in which he is least likely to receive the care he needs. Despite that, thousands of mental health professionals have nonetheless come forward and provided broad medical consensus, in a manner without historical precedent, and, responding to relentless public demand, they performed a formalized assessment with the information that made it possible in April 2019. That assessment showed that there was a serious and imminent risk posed to public health and safety because of a lack of mental capacity, and this led to our making the following recommendations:

1.   The President must be removed from access to the nuclear codes. The fate of human civilization should not be dependent on an unstable individual without rational decision-making capacity.
2.   The President's war-making powers should be curtailed. The temptation to draw the nation into a devastating war for reasons other than the good of the nation will be too great for a president who lacks the capacity to lead (Lee et al., 2019).

These still hold as the most significant and necessary interventions. In their absence, we require alternative recommendations based on "softer" treatment principles.

Alternative Intervention at the level of individual

In the absence of concrete limitations, we must not lose courage but turn to the things we can manage, which are considerable. They include:

A.   Behavioral containment
B.   Psychological limit-setting
C.   Care of the self
D.   Grounding in truth
E.   Demand for justice

The underlying principle is this: to set boundaries and to care for ourselves. Now, going through them briefly in turn, behavioral containment refers to removing the individual from a position in which they have access to significant power and the ability to do harm. In our March 2020 "Prescription for Survival," we stated: "we have a Presidency that is incapable of protecting lives but is making a global pandemic deadlier—not just through incompetence and ignorance, but through a dangerous detachment from reality, an inability to care for its citizens, a need to convey false information, and other symptoms." We recommended removal of danger by any means, including any of the following or their combination:

1.   Invocation of the 25th Amendment on the president
2.   A new urgent impeachment of the president, with televised hearings
3.   Immediate voluntary resignation of the president
4.   Emergency court-ordered involuntary mental health evaluation of the president
5.   Complete removal of decision making about this public health emergency from the president *and* suspension of White House press conferences about the coronavirus (World Mental Health Coalition, 2020).

Those recommendations still apply, even and especially as we approach an election: while it is imperative that the people vote in overwhelming numbers and mobilize others to vote, we must recognize that voting alone is insufficient. Even the process of simply beginning to take steps toward containment, especially if they are televised, will help temper the swollen grandiosity that, fostered by four years of flattery from underlings and chants from crowds, has now morphed into grotesque delusions of grandeur capable of great danger. Delusions of impunity that have amplified, as the president discovered that he could violate the norms of civil society and even commit crimes without consequences, may diminish as grounding in reality is reestablished (Herman and Lee, 2017). In any case, the constraints must come from without from other relevant areas for both the president and his enablers also to respect the election process and results. Conversely, if we were to give up prematurely on implementing these procedures, and made it evident that we have surrendered to the course of events, then those same parties would feel further emboldened in their attempt to subvert the elections.

That point then leads to the next treatment principle: psychological limit-setting. Many individuals with Donald Trump's characteristics do not have the ability to set limits for themselves and in fact crave to have limits imposed on their behavior from without, even as they fight against those constraints. This behavior is akin to that of a toddler who may complain and throw temper tantrums when limits are imposed, but who simultaneously gains a sense of comfort and order from those same restrictions. In such a situation, the toddler is testing to see if constraints will come from the authorities, which translate into reassurance that one is receiving care, being held, and even held to account so as to prevent one's going astray or falling apart. For an individual who is no longer a toddler and is disordered in this way, the nation, its people, and its authorities bear some responsibility when behavior gets out of hand. The slower and more tentative the limits, the more out of control the individual will become. "Tiptoeing around" an abusive personality is therefore unproductive, even if it is the first instinctive "survival" response. It is the influence of that response that results in situations wherein the worst abuser is the last to be called out, the pathological liar the last to be called a liar, and the most pernicious white supremacist not even called a racist. Ultimately, this only enables maladaptive behavior.

The issue of limits and their importance is observed in the president's preoccupation with "law and order." Underlying it is his sheer desire to mobilize the forces of the police and federal agents purely in order to satiate his need for violence and power, certainly. However, a more fundamental factor behind that preoccupation is the conviction that the world can only be safe if a strong external force imposes severe limits, as he perceives others' internal life to be as lawless and disorderly as his own. This is one of the key reasons why granting power to developmentally-wounded individuals is very dangerous and often leads to wanton abuses of the power they are given, which ultimately destroys the society or nation within their charge. Accordingly, rather than unbounded indulgence, what is needed instead is to set proper limits early, forcefully, and consistently. This means calling out lies immediately instead of later in private settings or in news articles, strictly adhering to and enforcing norms and standards of behavior—including the law—no matter what the abuser says, and perhaps even to require fitness-for-duty evaluations to candidates before the position is offered, just as all other important jobs that handle life-or-death matters do. Strict limit-setting at an early stage is crucial, as allowing delusions of grandeur, impunity, and omnipotence to balloon for a protracted period before suddenly setting limits without guardrails can be dangerous. The problem of trying to impose limits only at a late stage was demonstrated with the long-delayed but later fast-tracked impeachment in the fall of 2019: extreme retaliation in the form of a massacre and an assassination resulted, just as we predicted (Feinberg, 2019; Porter, 2019), followed by mass firings and exonerations of war criminals. In the absence of concrete boundaries, expert consultations are critical for properly timing and measuring response.

Citizen mobilization is both an important and a highly effective means of limit-setting. It is a monumental task that should place priority on citizens' care for the self, the third treatment principle we listed above. One way this citizen mobilization can occur is through protest marches, which are important, vital, and highly effective (Chenoweth and Stephan, 2011), but does not end there. We may recall that Donald Trump once said, and indeed said only once, "Certainly, if I don't win, I don't win" and that if that were the case then he would "do other things" (Oprysko, 2020). He made that statement within the context of historic Black Lives Matter protests, which demonstrated an astonishing outpouring of civilian dissatisfaction that undoubtedly shocked him. While few at the time made the connection between the protests and his comment, it was a powerful example of how a population can set psychological limits on a president by expressing discontent en masse. The Women's March of 2017 is also not to be underestimated; although prevention and therefore events that have not happened are difficult to see, worldwide protests that engaged over 3 to 5 million in the U.S. alone measurably played a psychological role in tempering his excesses for at least a year.

It is therefore important not to underestimate people's power; indeed, it is the most powerful there is in a society, regardless of form of government. Realizing and cultivating this power, in turn, is the most effective intervention. This entails more than simply mobilizing numbers of people. Effectiveness requires spiritual resolve, resilience, and resourcefulness. These qualities are vital because, as we have seen in the examples of Portland, Chicago, and other cities, the more powerful the movement, the more likely it will be met with force before it succeeds, as it will arouse great fear in unpopular rulers. It is important to interpret the violence that ensues as a sign of weakness, and not to freeze or to surrender but to draw upon the flexibility, creativity, and generativity that come with spiritual grounding. Mohandas Gandhi (1993) likened the rigorous preparation for, and ongoing practice of, nonviolent discipline to the training of a soldier. The advice I regularly give to medical or law students as they go into "battle" with disease or in defense of their clients is: "In an emergency, first check your own pulse." It follows the dicta: "Physician, heal thyself," and "Know thyself." These same imperatives apply to citizens in advance of their mobilization. In other words, in order to achieve greater outward power, the people should, seemingly paradoxically, first tune into themselves and meet their own needs. This involves making sure one is getting enough sleep, eating healthy meals, connecting with friends and family, and limiting news consumption. Balance, personal time, and distance are powerful tools for retaining perspective, knowing when to act and when not to act. Recognizing and attending to one's own state, therefore, is an essential part of everyday responsible practice. Therefore: "Take a break—this is your number one responsibility!"

The importance of this foundation assumes particular significance during the time leading up to the election, when anxiety levels are high. Many are also feeling exhausted in their prolonged efforts, and therefore it is important to remind ourselves that anxiety and exhaustion are normal, shared, and a signal to ourselves to take time for renewal. Pausing to honor the pain we feel for the world, widening our vision, and taking one step at a time, seem counter to the trend of the dramatic, obtrusive, and apparent violence before our eyes, but it is the source of true strength. Hence, it is crucial to set boundaries for spiritual centering: an hour a day, an afternoon a week, and a spontaneous "getaway" once in a while to devote to pure enjoyment while letting nothing intrude. Taking the time to connect back with the universal, through the arts, meditation, or simply time spent with loved ones is essential. Universal human values, such as equality, justice, truth, compassion, and reverence and appreciation for life, mobilize vital strength in times of difficulty. Therefore, these practices, far from being irrelevant, remote, or even selfish, are the crux of our being effective in the world. Having a mentally-impaired leader by nature is demoralizing and draining, for he emits the opposite energy: spiritual dearth, rigidity, fear, paranoia, and violence. Since emotional, psychological, and spiritual pressures are more burdensome than purely physical ones, particularly over prolonged periods of time, it is essential to build up reserves and to keep replenishing them even in the midst of intense battle.

We may "know" this, but it is important to remind one another. It is essential to complement contemplative time with fellowship, community, and like minds gathering to help foster the fourth treatment principle: grounding in truth. Pathology's onslaught of corruption, aggression, and oppression, alongside its constant attempts to subvert reality with unreality, health with sickness, and truth with delusion, can be exhausting. Moreover, to be grounded in truth is particularly important, as a ruler's inability to face reality translates for the population into a deprivation of information, rights, and eventually life. Truth causes the greatest consternation in dangerously impaired leaders. This is because it is a formidable antidote to their power; you reveal that "lying does not make it so." Speaking the truth can be therapeutic in at least two ways: first, it helps you to ground yourself in reality when forces are relentlessly trying to uproot and to topple you; and second, you become part of a life-affirming impulse that coalesces into a powerful collective when everyone does it. Readers may have heard of psychological defense mechanisms such as denial, projection, and reaction formation being used by this presidency, and these can be understood as unconscious actions to divert away from the truth, which is the most intolerable to a disordered leader trying to escape reality. Those three defenses describe a particular sequence of behaviors: the worst perpetrators will be the least willing to admit their wrongdoing (denial), they will solidify that denial by accusing opponents of their own misdeeds (projection), and they will assert themselves to be the opposite of what they truly are (reaction formation): "I am the least racist person in the world!" "There's nobody that has more respect for women than I do!" and so on. Understanding the nature of these dynamics and their progression is a key to scattering their stronghold.

When assaults on reality have induced a "malignant normality," pathology has taken the reins, and things that were unthinkable four years ago have now come to constitute the new normal. And when everyone is lying to you all the time, even if you do not believe the lies, you no longer know what to believe, and your balance is toppled. This hampers you from being able to form opinions, to make judgements, and to take effective action. Donald Trump may condemn opponents of his own guilt; he may never forget those who spoke up against him; and everything he touches, he may destroy—as he has the environment, our alliances, international trade, the judiciary, and even our common sense of decorum. When normality itself becomes extreme, those who speak the truth, or stay with professional standards, come to sound extreme. A moment of decision may come: will one remain with the truth or with mere appearances? The truth may be hard at first and bring on accusations from colleagues or peers, but this is where a stable center can activate a moral compass or the force of conscience that allows one to stand one's ground. This offers courage to those who see the same but are afraid, opens the potential to grow in number, and soon we can mobilize massive strength. This calls for leadership in all and not just followership. The other path leads to a rabbit hole, whereby we must add more and more distortions to justify one's position, to distort reality, and to help the pressures that suppress and oppress.

The American Psychiatric Association is a primary example of an institution that chose a guise of ethics over responsibility, and a pretense of professionalism to ignore a crucial fact: that denial does not make a problem go away. It did great disservice to lead the nation on a course of denial, for it is always easier to prevent than to try to limit losses after a problem has become barely containable. These approaches, while initially self-serving, are maladaptive and, especially in the context of abuse of power, facilitate injustice and harm. In a setting of such rampant corruption, collusion, and concession on the part of powerful institutions, personal grounding helps to maintain the emotional balance that is necessary for moving the needle, especially when no other organized body would. Professions, meanwhile, can create forms of ethical conversation that are impossible between a lonely individual and a distant government (Snyder, 2017). Experts of all fields can aid people in their attempts to ground themselves by functioning as "witnessing professionals" who facilitate reality testing (Lifton, 2017).

At the current moment, people should also feel themselves free to consult with experts, such as mental health professionals who can provide counseling and relief from symptoms such as anxiety or depression. "Trump anxiety disorder" as a syndrome of anxiety and multiple concerns, helplessness and paralysis, and difficulty sleeping deriving directly in relation to the uncertain sociopolitical climate and its events is a condition that nearly every therapist in the country has been dealing with since the start of this presidency (Panning, 2017). Early consultation with mental health professionals can help resolve problems quickly and is itself a sign of strength and resilience, not of weakness.

It is, finally, impossible to understate the importance of being aware of one's own status and potential. Self-knowledge, or autognosis, involves having both the clear and solid insight that true power lies in the people, and that self-knowledge allows for knowledge of the enemy. That is, in proportion that the knowledge of our strength grows, so does the knowledge of the power structure's weakness. Knowledge itself is also power. When there is much gaslighting by an impaired leader who desperately needs to be right in order to bolster his own sense of self and to hold onto a sense of absolute power, then that means much of the population will be put in the wrong. Rather than fix any problems, the leader will make people even to doubt their perception that there is a problem. This is why knowledge and self-knowledge are important, as well as checking that knowledge through access to sound journalism and to evidence-based expertise. One of the ways in which illegitimate power can retain advantage is by blocking or confusing the flow of valid information and sound knowledge. Access to facts and expert insight is precisely the armament for demanding justice, the last treatment principle, and to call out all leaders who are serving themselves rather than those that they supposedly govern. Regardless of the grand showcasing and the parading of authority, illegitimate power is ultimately a weak paper tiger that depends on its façade, and tyrants but buffoons on a soap box if no one obeyed them. Draw the curtain on the Wizard of Oz, and you will find a tiny, weak man; the ability to reality-check, with the support of journalists and experts, allows you to do just that.

Intervention at the level of followers

A wounded psychology is drawn to wounded leaders and attracted to ideas that will make the wounds worse. This is because pathology is drawn to pathology, and the deeper the pathology, the more maladaptive and destructive its choices and course. Because pathology is indistinguishable from normalcy to many in the public sphere, it would do us well to require some kind of screening mechanism for keeping pathology out of politics. This is another method of prevention, since once pathology takes hold of power, it is very difficult to get it out. Empowering followers through true authority and strength is therefore better than listening to what they say in their compromised state; enabling their unhealthy attractions is good for neither them nor anyone else. With true authority—which is the result of some knowledge, skill, or vision—a follower grows in personhood, mutual respect deepens over time, and one gains in independence and power as one absorbs the authority's knowledge, skill, or vision. With false authority— arising from a leader's emotional need for followers—one loses personhood, becomes conformist, and adheres on the basis of fear, growning increasingly dependent and disempowered over time. A population may be predisposed to looking for a parental figure to take care of them in times of distress—or in cases of relative poverty, as in the U.S., which is more psychologically injurious than absolute poverty. One can either exploit the situation or empower this population with education, health care, and employment, to elevate them into making healthy choices.

The tyrant exploits this vulnerability in a society that is already weakened by disorder, blind to it, and unable or unwilling to take corrective measures which would prevent a tyrannical takeover. Once he does, he and his sycophants deepen and widen the disorder, dismantling and changing the society's norms, institutions, and laws to reflect fully their own pathology. By distorting reality and truth, perverting moral values, fortified by magical thinking and contempt for reason, these distortions lead to a kind of absurdist unreality where up is down and black is white, and what one knows to be true may have nothing to do with the officially sanctioned version of the truth. In this manner, the criteria of mental normalcy and pathology are redefined as well, and psychology and psychiatry, like other branches of social science, are coopted to serve the regime. Pathology becomes "normalized", both in the statistical sense and in the standards of mental health, while actual mental health, defined as the capacity for multilevel and multidimensional development, is denigrated and "pathologized". The inherent and violent irrationality, bereft of internal brakes that stem from a conscience, and unchecked by external forces, the tyrant's reign eventually collapses (Mika, 2017). The followers, being both the reason for the power that the tyrant wields, as well as being the tyrant's own creation, become first instruments and then casualties along the way. In order to intervene positively for the followers, it is important to keep in mind that: (a) they are not acting in fully-informed, rational ways, no matter their exceptionally strong insistence; and (b) they are highly dependent followers, not individuated leaders (Donald Trump included!), and therefore guidance and support are necessary. Easily escaping from individual autonomy to group behavior, a positive aspect of this predisposition is that they respond to good leadership.

I am often asked how to engage these followers, which is a chief question for many people. Mental health professionals are indeed frequently confronted with the question: "How do we reason with a Trump supporter?" The quick answer to that query is: "You don't." That Donald Trump's supporters must be convinced and won over, in order from him to be removed from power, is a common misconception that people have. The reality is that the opposite holds true: removing him from power will reduce the followership. In the meantime, people should follow certain general guidelines when engaging with Trump supporters. First, they should not be confronted with facts, for it will only rouse resistance (subconsciously, they already know what is true, which is why they project onto others their own characteristics very accurately; for example, their radically irrational support of the leader can be described as symptomatic of the "Trump Derangement Syndrome" they often accuse of others, or call peaceful protesters "the violent left," even when the FBI reports that the tiny percentage of violence that did occur is from the right-wing Boogaloo Boys). Second, persuasion should not be the goal, for that will only lead to exhaustion: the problem is in their granting an impaired individual power, not in their cognitive system or, most of the time, even their mental health. Third, people should continue to state facts, evidence, and science-based approaches elsewhere, repeatedly and without apology, intimidation, or shame, so that a delusional narrative does not "bulldoze over" the truth through its sheer emotional force, upon which pathology depends.

Rather than facts and arguments, other management principles should be followed with Trump supporters, as follows:

F.   Reduction of exposure to "the leader"
G.   Reduction of cultic programming
H.   Change of circumstances
I.   Emotional support

We begin here with one of the key principles of our professional practice: in all matters of health, we triage before we treat, and the removal of the primary offending agent comes first; it is for this reason that our first principle focuses heavily on Donald Trump. His removal from office and the accompanying reduction of exposure that his supporters have to him will automatically release many from his influence. The reduction of exposure will diminish the natural induction of highly contagious symptoms among the population that comes with having a severely mentally-impaired person in an influential position: violence, paranoia, fixed false beliefs, and loss of connection with reality.

Following that first intervention, the next treatment principle should be employed in order to effect a reduction of cultic programming, programming which can by itself reform thoughts and inculcate fixed false beliefs. Fox News, One America News Network, and other sites that promote right-wing conspiracy theories, as well as social media that filter information to create functional "bubbles", are all forms of programming that work to serve that function. If the level of such programming is also reduced in conjunction with a change of circumstances, as the next principle outlines. By removing people from the circumstances that rendered them vulnerable to predators in the first place, they can be protected from being exploited again. Steps for bringing about such a change might include: reducing relative poverty and enhancing access to education, health care, and social mobility.

Finally, for future healing, especially of the trauma that will inevitably come with the realization that the person they believed to be their "savior" was actually their mental and material abuser, Trump followers will need emotional support from friends, family, and others. Genuine human connection and acceptance will provide them with the strength to abandon cherished beliefs and to help hasten their recovery. One must also be prepared for the instance where some or many cases may take a lifetime to recuperate, or do not recover at all. The difficulty depends on emotional investment, length of time of attachment, and degree of trauma one is likely to experience. Of note, not included here in this assessment are the president's billionaire followers, who are unlikely to reform but instead to look for another "Donald Trump" and to continue to contrive ways of enlisting deprived and emotionally vulnerable populations in order promote an agenda of increasing power and profits. The intervention for this is proper prosecution of white collar crime and the reduction of inequality or imbalances of power.

Intervention at the level of society

The U.S. is unusual among civilized nations in that it does not have a strong "Fifth Estate" of independent experts, to serve as a check on the three branches of government, to supplement the Fourth Estate of the press and the news media. Instead, when decision makers do not find their desired answers through existing channels of evidence, science, and scholarship, they seek other contractors or partisan think tanks to get the perspective they desire. This truncates a chief means of deliberation: one that is based on sound scholarship, with the composure, detachment, and research integrity that come with independence from political considerations. Scholarly disciplines have developed to the point where it is possible to determine the answer to almost any policy question, in almost any area, based on research results alone. This does not mean that scholarship replaces human decision making—indeed, most roles around the world take the form of advisory boards—but it would allow for an important use of the vital resources that are available in a civilized society while serving as neutral ground on which to resolve hyperpartisan issues. Professional and academic standards, as well as the strict monitoring of conflicts of interest, as occurs in scientific research, are designed to help preserve neutrality. The distance and the time for academic rigor that one is afforded, furthermore, would serve as the societal equivalent of "checking one's pulse" before acting in an emergency.

Among matters that have reached emergency proportions because of a lack of expert scholarly input, just like the presidency, is mass inequality. Like the climate crisis and the pandemic, the marginalizing of science and scholarship has allowed society to ignore and to miss alarming warning signs. Now, these matters have reached existential proportions. The level of inequality that existed before the coronavirus pandemic was already crippling, but acting in synergy with other crises, such corruption and incapacity, the scale and severity of inequality has escalated exponentially since the arrival of the virus in the U.S. The price of stocks may have plunged in March 2020, but since then they have been rising in value at record rates, as central banks pledged trillions of dollars in an unprecedented intervention aimed at propping up markets and the economy. That intervention does not, however, help the average worker. In 2016, the wealthiest 10 percent of U.S. households owned 84 percent of all stocks; in the six-month period following March 2020, U.S. billionaire wealth increased by 637 billion dollars, that is, by more than 21percent. While the rich are enjoying remarkable success with that boom, tens of millions of workers remain unemployed during the worst downturn since the Great Depression (Horowitz, 2020).

While the removal of the primary offending agent, Donald Trump, as the emergent and imminent problemin our current "triage", it is only the beginning. Addressing the issue of social inequality is a project that should, indeed, start simultaneously or at least follow closely behind. Inequality is an enormous problem that virtually affects all other areas of our lives. Psychologically, it not only creates social distrust and inept governance, but produces a large population of vulnerable people unable to protect themselves against public health threats, including both a viral and a mental health pandemic. As such, the secondary consequence of rampant inequality is that when crises hit, such as the coronavirus pandemic, the gap between those at each end of the spectrum widens alarmingly further. The same thing that we can currently observe to be taking place will also happen when the nation is met with any of the other growing array of global crises, including those of climate change and of the threat of nuclear war.

What do we mean by mass inequality? In its most global sense, the term can be understood to describe the present situation in which vital areas such as health care, education, and communications are rapidly advancing while the majority of humankind is being increasingly left behind. As that occurs, disparities between people in terms of health, gender, race, economic, and educational status increase, bringing about a cascade of effects that include a diminution of a society's psychological health. In many respects, the consequences of such inequality amount to no less than the difference of life and death, or a "collective suicidal tendency" for humankind, which is the only way we can describe our policies on climate, war, or nuclear weapons, if we only took the time to look. This level of inequality is also called structural violence, and it is the most lethal form of violence (Lee, 2019). The excess deaths alone that result from this type of violence exceed all the deaths resulting from suicides, homicides, and collective violence combined, year after year. As long this deep inequality persists, and structural violence is allowed to continue and persist, we will see high levels of all other forms of violence, since structural violence is also the most potent stimulant of behavioral violence.

The inequality that we can perceive in society is, to an extent, the result of an economic arrangement that has become a squandering mentality. Such a mentality leaves populations impoverished while paradoxically leading them to believe it will in fact make them richer. "Making America where you can get rich again" was a Reagan era claim that accompanied policies that effectively destroyed that ability for the overwhelming majority of people. In a greater extreme, Donald Trump has been mentally defective enough to usurp his followers' reasoning and to offer grand claims to "make American great again," just as he destroyed it. Beyond economic considerations in their own right, higher levels of income inequality within a country correlate strongly with lower levels of good health, among the rich as well as among the poor. In short, greater income inequality can be clearly associated a significant number of negative side-effects, including, among other things, higher levels of mental illness, drug abuse, murder and assault, obesity and obesity☒related death, teenage pregnancy, racism, and incarceration. The Trump phenomenon is an entrenchment in these socioeconomic pathologies: mountains of debt, plutocracy leading to corporate takeover of politics, domination by the military-industrial complex, prejudice, persecution, and loss of direction as a nation. Collectively, they consist of societal pathologies erode America's position of leadership on the world stage. A squandering mentality means that one can only exploit and expend but not grow; leaders of this mentality naturally use their positions to take and to amass ever more power to take. Hence, also numbered among the consequences of significant societal inequality comes to be a higher-than-average death rate—even one of the worst rates in the world—from a pandemic (Worldometer, 2020).

The U.S. currently leads the world in Covid-19 cases and deaths, which was predictable from the universal phenomenon we know: that violence, disease, and death increase in unequal societies. If we look around the world, countries with high inequality also have greater sociopolitical instability in the form of assassinations, coups, and riots. Such countries also generally suffer from inferior institutions, in terms of less efficient governments, as well as a weaker rule of law and a greater prevalence of corruption. Despite its global status, the U.S. has the highest levels of inequality among the advanced economies: it is closer to Mexico, and even to Brazil—one of the most unequal economies—than it is to Denmark or the Netherlands (World Bank, 2020). The situation that prevails in countries with such high levels of inequality is one in which the wealthy are uniquely advantaged and privileged. They have a strong motivation to keep institutions weak in order to minimize redistribution of wealth, while at the same time they also have significant power to influence those same institutions, given their relatively high share of the available resources. The end result of that is a dysfunctional society, such as the one that currently exists in the U.S., in which a mentally-impaired leader becomes almost a necessary ingredient to preserving such an extreme system.

In spite of all that has been said, human beings are, essentially, astonishingly free. Even individuals with severe mental illnesses, who tend to be more rigid, retain remarkable levels of free will. It is for that reason that the presence of "insanity", to use a legal term, seldom leads to an insanity defense, and rightly so. As such, anyone worried about Donald Trump not being properly criminally charged on account of these mental health considerations need not be—he is far from that possibility! Now back to human freedom: this freedom applies equally to the people, who have agency, as the healthy mind is resilient, resourceful, and creative under almost all circumstances. This does not, however, mean that we should neglect this unique asset—on the contrary, we should seek always to maximize and to protect it. We contrast this to the rigidity of a calcified system of predatory capitalism: it cannot adapt to climate change, to a pandemic, and to changes in the population, but rather binds people to it with ever-growing insecurity and instilled fears of losing their livelihoods. Human versatility, on the other hand, is almost infinite and can adjust to an infinite number of situations. The reduction of inequality by itself is not difficult; it does not require large money or effort, and a small amount can bring about massively positive results that ripple into widespread improvement of societal emotional health. It is only the political will that is lacking, or rather freedom from the massive political barriers that "dark money" and relentless special interests have put in place, against the principles and the will of the republic. This is why the reduction of inequality, or structural violence, must be an urgent consideration after the removal of Donald Trump, for the preservation of democracy itself. Meanwhile, we can counteract—not cure—some of these effects through smaller measures:

J. Strengthening unity in diversity
K. Investing in health, including emotional health
L. Investing in education, access to facts, and sharing of expertise
M. Investing in emotional growth, cultural activities, and creativity

The specific ways in which each of these can be implemented are endless, and every gesture adds to the general ecology. A step in the right conceptual direction will be to break out of our compartmentalized, dichotomous thinking: just as both mental impairment and criminality can coexist in Donald Trump, our problems can be both the president and preexisting societal conditions. Indeed, considering them in their complex whole allows us to understand how they interact—for example, far from substituting one for another, mental impairment and criminality make one more dangerous than either alone. An impaired president and societal disrepair work synergistically to bring about more rapid destruction than just one or the other. We can then consider our own actions both as individuals and as members of a greater whole, and practicing both simultaneously will be more productive than either by itself. Finally, mental health would serve a population better if its insights from clinical experience were applied to public mental health and not only be confined to individual treatment; individuals themselves are not isolated but in constant interaction with an ecology.

As we gain perspective and grope toward a unity that integrates greater diversity, we become flexible, resourceful, and effective and better able to find life-affirming solutions for almost any situation. We can break out of rigid rules as we improve in our understanding of principles. Cohesion then becomes easier, as we counteract the conformity that forces fragmentation and division, or the chief manifestations of disease. The more we connect the dots and gain a better grasp of underlying patterns, the more we can also foresee what is coming and prevent problems before they become overwhelming—and we find that even tiny acts matter, if applied in the right places, for an ounce of prevention is indeed worth a pound of cure. This brings us to the purpose of this profile: prevention. The deterioration of this presidency was predictable, and therefore preventable, and prevention is possible where there is knowledge and understanding. Sharing a unified purpose as we recruit and exchange resources across different disciplines and diverse sectors is one of the powerful methods of public health and, as it turns out, an effective way of solving most of society's problems.

AFTERWORD

One of the greatest travesties with regard to the mental health emergency that descended upon our nation has been the silencing of mental health experts. If anything, our era has shown how critical mental health is, in a leader, in a populace, and in systems, and how we must not take it for granted but understand the socioeconomic conditions that support or harm it. One would have thought that the American Psychiatric Association (APA) would lead the way rather than throw a country back to the Dark Ages, when mental health was a topic that could never be discussed, and those who know most about it must hide themselves away. This is what happened when, just as a historic movement of mental health professionals had attained the attention of the people to the extent that it had become the number one topic of national conversation, the APA stepped in with an aggressive campaign to shut down all relevant experts—and succeeded for all the subsequent years. Perhaps it should not have been surprising: my own, singular reason for stepping up to speak out in the first place was my alarm at the APA's alteration of "the Goldwater rule," at the start of the Trump presidency, so that those who kept with the new version of the "rule" would be forced to violate the core tenets of medical ethics. The core tenets I am referring to are that we keep our responsibility to society, which is the second highest, if not commensurate, to our responsibility to patients. They are also to hold human life and our care of that life as paramount: in other words, no other interest should take precedence before human health, safety, and survival. Critically, they include our keeping with the Declaration of Geneva—a universal pledge that all health professionals around the world make, which includes that we speak up in contexts of injustice, and especially not to collude with destructive governments. Finally, there is the principle under which "the Goldwater rule" itself falls: that we participate in activities that improve public health—not harm it in order to protect a nonpatient political figure. Giving priority to a public figure, who is not even a patient, was for me the red flag that presaged tyranny—and, indeed, it was only the first institution to fall in line, later to find company even in the Department of Justice. Some have called this "the original sin" of our era: a gag order that compromised the public's ability to protect itself against all subsequent dangers.

The bottom line, in my view, is that the public has a right to the truth. It has a right to know what is happening, with the greatest clarity possible, and to have critical information at a critical time, especially when it is under threat. The verdict seems simple: the real purpose of "the Goldwater rule" was to keep the truth from coming out, so that those who are awash in federal and pharmaceutical industry funding could keep their profits (Kendall, 2020). But we now see the consequences of trying to cover up a mental health issue: entire segments of the population have signed onto delusional beliefs, the media have successfully participated in gaslighting, and the otherwise healthy experience skyrocketing stress, all the while critical matters of the nation go unaddressed. The role of mental health professionals is to support the education and understanding that are needed for health and safety. Whereas the APA had made its extraordinary choice to leave the public to fend for itself, it had no right to silence independent professionals acting on their own conscience and honest attempt to keep with professional ethics. Even before its blockage of the major media, by creating a fiat, it was requiring that the professionals cede their autonomy and become mere technicians, which is a formula for tyrannical abuse. All arguments for depriving the public of the truth have thus failed me, I have decided to lay it out in this profile, in the best way I know how without holding back anything that I deem critical, for this is what the people expect of us. Society has invested in our knowledge and training, and it is only a matter of course that the people expect mental health experts, who are the guardians of mental health knowledge, to explain mental health phenomena that are overarchingly affecting them. And hence what I do here is all that my medical education has prepared me to do and what I have dedicated my life to doing. If this is not my duty as physician and psychiatrist, I do not know what is.

From the start, I stated that the choice to collude with a destructive regime rather than to uphold ethical principles would likely cause even more harm than an earlier decision by the APA's psychological counterpart, the American Psychological Association, to modify its own ethics guidelines to facilitate and design government programs for torture. This is because any stifling of the dissemination of vital information, in the context of such widespread danger to society, was bound to cause far more devastating harm than 1,000 torture victims, as bad as that was. Now, with 400,000 deaths projected by the end of this year, all because of mental health reasons and not because of the nature of the pandemic itself, I believe that that assessment will be hard to reject. There is a reason why thousands of mental health professionals joined us at the World Mental Health Coalition (WMHC) and chose to step up where the APA has failed in societal leadership. To the present day, we at the WMHC are still calling on the APA to retract its "gag order" and to apologize for misleading the American people and the media.

Before the APA's intervention, the more than fifty Congress members who invited us to meet with them told us that their ability to act depended on our educating the public. The people are empowered for self-government only when they have access to facts and the best available knowledge, including mental health knowledge. Experts, in turn, have a duty to society that far exceeds a mere technical role, which has rather facilitated the relentless psychological manipulation and misinformation that have become the chief means of control and harm. This is a natural consequence of our answering calls only of those with wealth and power, and not acting on our societal obligations. The real duty that experts have is to render their services to the betterment and benefit of humankind. Certainly, that is the minimum that all health professionals have pledged to do since 1948, after another experience of tyranny: Nazism.

REFERENCES

Ahmad, Iqbal (1970). The role of intellectuals in American society. *Peabody Journal of Education*, 47(4), 229-232.

Ailworth, E., Wells, G., and Lovett, I. (2019, August 8). Lost in Life, El Paso Suspect Found a Dark World Online. *Wall Street Journal*. Retrieved from https://www.wsj.com/articles/lost-in-life-el-paso-suspect-found-a-dark-world-online-11565308783.

Al Jazeera (2019, March 16). New Zealand mosque attacks suspect praised Trump in manifesto. *Al Jazeera*. Retrieved from https://www.aljazeera.com/news/2019/03/16/new-zealand-mosque-attacks-suspect-praised-trump-in-manifesto.

Alexander, M. (2010). *New Jim Crow: Mass Incarceration in the Age of Colorblindness*. New York, NY: New Press.

Allport, G. W. (1954). *The Nature of Prejudice*. Boston, MA: Addison-Wesley.

Alvaredo, F., Atkinson, A. B., Piketty, T., Saez, E., and Zucman, G. (2015). *The World Wealth and Income Database*. Paris, France: World Inequality Database. Retrieved from http://www.wid.world/.

American Academy of Psychiatry and the Law (2005). *Ethical Guidelines for the Practice of Forensic Psychiatry*. Bloomfield, CT: American Academy of Psychiatry and the Law. Retrieved from https://www.aapl.org/ethics.htm.

American Medical Association (2016). *AMA Code of Medical Ethics*. Chicago, IL: American Medical Association. Retrieved from https://www.ama-assn.org/sites/ama-assn.org/files/corp/media-browser/principles-of-medical-ethics.pdf.

American Psychiatric Association (1976). *The Psychiatrist as Psychohistorian*. Arlington, VA: American Psychiatric Association.

American Psychiatric Association (2013a). *Diagnostic and Statistical Manual of Mental Disorders* (5th ed.). Washington, DC: American Psychiatric Association.

American Psychiatric Association (2013b). *Principles of Medical Ethics with Annotations Especially Applicable to Psychiatry*. Washington, DC: American Psychiatric Association. Retrieved from https://www.psychiatry.org/psychiatrists/practice/ethics.

American Psychiatric Association (2017a). *APA Reaffirms Support for Goldwater Rule. Washington, DC: American Psychiatric Association.* Retrieved from https://www.psychiatry.org/newsroom/news-releases/apa-reaffirms-support-for-goldwater-rule.

American Psychiatric Association (2017b). *APA's Goldwater Rule Remains a Guiding Principle for Physician Members.* Washington, DC: American Psychiatric Association. Retrieved from https://www.psychiatry.org/newsroom/news-releases/apa-goldwater-rule-remains-a-guiding-principle-for-physician-members.

Anda, R. F., Felitti, V. J., Bremner, J. D., Walker, J. D., Whitfield, C. H., Perry, B. D., Dube, S. R., and Giles, W. H. (2006). The enduring effects of abuse and related adverse experiences in childhood. *European Archives of Psychiatry and Clinical Neuroscience*, 256(3), 174-186.

Anderson, C. (2016). *White Rage: The Unspoken Truth of Our Racial Divide.* New York, NY: Bloomsbury Publishing.

Arendt, H. (1963). *On Revolution.* New York, NY: Viking.

Arendt, H. (1973). *The Origins of Totalitarianism.* Boston, MA: Houghton Mifflin Harcourt.

Associated Press (2017, July 7). 122 adopt 'historic' UN treaty to ban nuclear weapons. *CBC News.* Retrieved from https://www.cbc.ca/news/world/un-treaty-ban-nuclear-weapons-1.4192761.

Associated Press (2019, October 25). More than 5,400 children split at border, according to new count. *NBC News.* Retrieved from https://www.nbcnews.com/news/us-news/more-5-400-children-split-border-according-new-count-n1071791.

Azpiazu, J., and Ocner, M. J. (2018). No, it's not the economy, stupid. Trump supporters fear a black and brown America. *Miami Herald.* Retrieved from https://www.miamiherald.com/opinion/opn-columns-blogs/leonard-pitts-jr/article211963789.html

Baker, P. (2020, June 18). Five takeaways from John Bolton's memoir. *New York Times.* Retrieved from https://www.nytimes.com/2020/06/18/us/politics/john-bolton-memoir-takeaways.html.

Baker, P., and Tackett, M. (2018). Trump Says His 'Nuclear Button' is 'Much Bigger' than North Korea's. *New York Times.* Retrieved from https://www.nytimes.com/2018/01/02/us/politics/trump-tweet-north-korea.html.

Baker, P., Benner, K., and LaFraniere, S. (2020, February 19). As Trump claims to be law of the land, Barr's irritation builds. *New York Times.* Retrieved from https://www.nytimes.com/2020/02/18/us/roger-stone-sentencing.html.

Baldus, D. C., Woodworth, G., and Pulaski, C. A. (1990). *Equal Justice and the Death Penalty: A Legal and Empirical Analysis.* Boston, MA: Northeastern University Press.

Barstow, D., Craig, S., and Buettner, R. (2018, October 2). Trump engaged in suspect tax schemes as he reaped riches from his father.

New York Times. Retrieved from https://www.nytimes.com/
interactive/2018/10/02/us/politics/donald-trump-tax-schemes-fred-
trump.html.

Beckett, L., and Wilson, J. (2019, August 5). 'White power ideology': Why
El Paso is part of a growing global threat. *Guardian.* Retrieved
from https://www.theguardian.com/us-news/2019/aug/04/el-paso-
shooting-white-nationalistsupremacy-violence-christchurch.

Begley, S. (2017, July 25). Psychiatry group tells members they can ignore
'Goldwater rule' and comment on Trump's mental health. *STAT
News.* Retrieved from https://www.statnews.com/2017/07/25/
psychiatry-goldwater-rule-trump/.

Benkler, Y., Faris, R., and Roberts, H. (2018). *Network Propaganda:
Manipulation, Disinformation, and Radicalization in American
Politics.* New York, NY: Oxford University Press.

Berenson, T. (2016, January 13). The 5 essential elements of a Donald
Trump stump speech. *Time.* Retrieved from https://time.
com/4178881/donald-trump-campaign-speeches/.

Bidgood, J., and Goodwin, L. (2020, June 1). Trump vows to crack down
on protesters, ignoring issues of racism and brutality fueling
unrest. *Boston Globe.* Retrieved from https://www.bostonglobe.
com/2020/06/01/nation/trump-vows-crack-down-protesters/.

Bierman, N. (2020, August 24). North Korea was Trump's chief foreign
policy boast, but things got much worse on his watch. *Los
Angeles Times.* Retrieved from https://www.latimes.com/politics/
story/2020-08-24/north-korea-trump-foreign-policy.

Biko, S. (1978). *I Write What I Like.* Oxford, U.K.: Heinemann.

Blackmon, D. A. (2008). *Slavery by Another Name: The Re-Enslavement of
Black Americans from the Civil War to World War II.* New York,
NY: Anchor Books.

Blistein, J. (2016). Donald Trump Hints at Hillary Clinton Assassination.
Rolling Stone. Retrieved from https://www.rollingstone.com/
politics/politics-news/donald-trump-hints-at-hillary-clinton-
assassination-108394/.

Bolton, J. R. (2020). *The Room Where It Happened: A White House
Memoir.* New York, NY: Simon and Schuster.

Bond, P. (2016, February 29). Leslie Moonves on Donald Trump: 'It may
not be good for America, but it's damn good for CBS.' *Hollywood
Reporter.* Retrieved from https://www.hollywoodreporter.com/
news/leslie-moonves-donald-trump-may-871464.

Bonn, T. (2019). Former white supremacist calls on Trump to stop using
fear to motivate people. *Hill.* Retrieved from https://thehill.com/
hilltv/rising/456339-former-white-supremacist-calls-on-trump-
administration-to-stop-using-fear-to.

Borger, J. (2020, May 24). Fumbling the nuclear football: Is Trump
blundering to arms control chaos? *Guardian.* Retrieved from
https://www.theguardian.com/world/2020/may/24/nuclear-
weapons-donald-trump-arms-control-chaos.

Bosworth, T. (2018, February 25). Goldwater rule should be modified, debate audience at the College agree. *MD Edge*. Retrieved from https://www.mdedge.com/psychiatry/article/159384/personality-disorders/goldwater-rule-should-be-modified-debate-audience.

Brandeis University (2020). *American Jewish Population Project*. Waltham, MA: Brandeis University. Retrieved from https://ajpp.brandeis.edu/map.

Breuninger, K. (2019, August 21). "I am the Chosen One," Trump proclaims as he defends trade war with China. *CNBC*. Retrieved from https://www.cnbc.com/2019/08/21/i-am-the-chosen-one-trump-proclaims-as-he-defends-china-trade-war.html.

Britzky, H. (2019, January 5). Everything Trump says he knows 'more about than anybody.' *Axios*. Retrieved from https://www.axios.com/everything-trump-says-he-knows-more-about-than-anybody-b278b592-cff0-47dc-a75f-5767f42bcf1e.html?te=1&nl=frank-bruni&emc=edit_fb_20200311.

Brown, A. (2017, February 7). Donald Trump thinks he's a strong leader. But that's an illusion. *Washington Post*. Retrieved from https://www.washingtonpost.com/news/democracy-post/wp/2017/02/07/donald-trump-thinks-hes-a-strong-leader-but-thats-an-illusion/.

Buettner, R., and Craig, S. (2019, May 8). Decade in the red: Trump tax figures show over $1 billion in business losses. *New York Times*. Retrieved from https://www.nytimes.com/interactive/2019/05/07/us/politics/donald-trump-taxes.html.

Bult, L. (2020, June 30). A timeline of 1,944 black Americans killed by the police. *Vox*. Retrieved from https://www.vox.com/2020/6/30/21306843/black-police-killings.

Bump, P. (2020, April 20). What Trump did about coronavirus in February. *Washington Post*. Retrieved from https://www.washingtonpost.com/politics/2020/04/20/what-trump-did-about-coronavirus-february/.

Bureau of Justice Statistics (2012). *Prisoners in 2011*. Washington, DC: Department of Justice. Retrieved from https://www.bjs.gov/content/pub/pdf/p11.pdf.

Bureau of Labor Statistics (2019). *Occupational Outlook Handbook*. Washington, DC: Bureau of Labor Statistics. Retrieved from https://www.bls.gov/ooh/.

Burns, S. (2016, October 17). Why Trump doubled down on the central park five. *New York Times*. Retrieved from https://www.nytimes.com/2016/10/18/opinion/why-trump-doubled-down-on-the-central-park-five.html.

Carr, H. (2020, October 3). Howie Carr: Media continue to cover up Joe Biden's mental decline. *Boston Herald*. Retrieved from https://www.bostonherald.com/2020/10/03/howie-carr-media-continue-to-cover-up-joe-bidens-mental-decline/.

Carvajal, N. (2020, May 7). Trump Vetoes Iran War Powers resolution. *CNN*. Retrieved from https://edition.cnn.com/2020/05/06/politics/

trump-veto-iran-war-powers/index.html.

Case, A., and Deaton, A. (2020). *Deaths of Despair and the Future of Capitalism.* Princeton, NJ: Princeton University Press.

Cassidy, J. (2020, Septemper 1). Donald Trump's Incitements to Violence Have Crossed an Alarming Threshold. *New Yorker.* Retrieved from https://www.newyorker.com/news/our-columnists/donald-trumps-incitements-to-violence-have-crossed-an-alarming-threshold.

Chenoweth, E., and Stephan, M. J. (2011). *Why Civil Resistance Works: The Strategic Logic of Nonviolent Conflict.* New York, NY: Columbia University Press.

Chetty, R., Grusky, D., Hell, M., Hendren, N., Manduca, R., and Narang, J. (2017). The fading American dream: Trends in absolute income mobility since 1940. *Science,* 356(6336), 398-406.

Cleckley, H. (1941). *The Mask of Sanity.* Saint Louis, MO: Mosby.

Cohen, M. (2020). *Disloyal: A Memoir.* New York, NY: Skyhorse Publishing.

Cole, D. and Subramaniam, T. (2020, September 3). Trump on Covid death toll: 'It is what it is.' *CNN Politics.* Retrieved from https://www.cnn.com/2020/08/04/politics/trump-covid-death-toll-is-what-it-is/index.html.

Cole, M. (2019, December 5). Donald Trump Keeps Navy SEAL's above the Law. *Intercept.* Retrieved from https://theintercept.com/2019/12/05/donald-trump-eddie-gallagher-navy-seals/.

Cole, N. L. (2019, June 29). Meet the people behind Donald Trump's popularity: survey results reveal stark trends in voters and values. *Thought Co.* Retrieved from https://www.thoughtco.com/meet-the-people-behind-donald-trumps-popularity-4068073.

Colvin, J. (2018, October 15). Mixing bravado and insults, Trump rallies delight supporters. *Business Insider.* Retrieved from https://www.businessinsider.com/ap-mixing-bravado-and-insults-trump-rallies-delight-supporters-2018-10.

Cooper, H. (2017, April 5). Trump Gives Military New Freedom. But with That Comes Danger. *New York Times.* Retrieved from https://www.nytimes.com/2017/04/05/us/politics/rules-of-engagement-military-force-mattis.html.

Coppins, M. (2018, November). The man who broke politics: Newt Gingrich turned partisan battles into a bloodsport, wrecked Congress, and paved the way for Trump's rise. Now he's reveling in his achievements. *Atlantic.* Retrieved from https://www.theatlantic.com/magazine/archive/2018/11/newt-gingrich-says-youre-welcome/570832/.

Corak, M. (2006). Do poor children become poor adults? Lessons from a cross-country comparison of generational earnings mobility. *Research on Economic Inequality,* 13(1), 143-188.

Cornfield, M. (2017). Empowering the party-crasher: Donald J. Trump, the first 2016 GOP presidential debate, and the Twitter marketplace for political campaigns. *Journal of Political Marketing*, 16(3-4), 212-243.

Costa, R., and Rucker, P. (2020, September 9). Woodward book: Trump says he knew coronavirus was 'deadly' and worse than the flu while intentionally misleading Americans. *Washington Post*. Retrieved from https://www.washingtonpost.com/politics/ bob-woodward-rage-book-trump/2020/09/09/0368fe3c-efd2- 11ea-b4bc-3a2098fc73d4_story.html?arc404=true&tidr=a_ breakingnews&hpid=hp_no-name_hp-breaking- news%3Apage%2Fbreaking-news-bar&itid=hp_no-name_hp- breaking-news%3Apage%2Fbreaking-news-bar&itid=lk_inline_ manual_4.

Crandall, C. S., Miller, J. M., and White, M. H. (2018). Changing norms following the 2016 US presidential election: The Trump effect on prejudice. *Social Psychological and Personality Science*, 9(2), 186-192.

Croffey, A. (2016, October 14). Why Donald Trump's suits don't fit. *Sydney Morning Herald*. Retrieved from https://www.smh.com. au/lifestyle/fashion/why-donald-trumps-suits-dont-fit-20161014- gs245b.html.

C-SPAN (2016). *Trump Presidential Campaign Ad*. Washington, DC: C-SPAN. Retrieved from https://www.c-span.org/ video/?418167-101/trump-presidential-campaign-ad&start=16.

C-SPAN (2019). *The Dangerous Case of Donald Trump*. Washington, DC: C-SPAN. Retrieved from https://www.c-span.org/ video/?458919-1/the-dangerous-case-donald-trump%20(2).

Cummings, W. (2019, May 15). Most Americans think Trump is a successful businessman. Until they learn about his losses. *USA Today*. Retrieved from https://eu.usatoday.com/story/news/politics/ onpolitics/2019/05/15/trump-business-success-poll/3677609002/.

D'Antonio, M. (2018, August 13). Omarosa is the latest defector from Trump's cult. *CNN*. Retrieved from https://edition.cnn. com/2018/08/13/opinions/omarosa-trump-cult-like-presidency- dantonio/index.html.

Davidson, J. R., Connor, K. M., and Swartz, M. (2006). Mental illness in US Presidents between 1776 and 1974: a review of biographical sources. *Journal of Nervous and Mental Disease*, 194(1), 47-51.

Davis, J. E. (2014). The Catholic schoolgirl and the wet nurse: On the ecology of oppression, trauma and crisis. *Decolonization: Indigeneity, Education, and Society*, 3 (1), 143-58.

DeParle, J. (2012, Jan 5). Harder for Americans to rise from lower rungs. *New York Times*. Retrieved from https://www.nytimes. com/2012/01/05/us/harder-for-americans-to-rise-from-lower-rungs. html?sq=mobility&st=cse&scp=1&pagewanted=all.

Diamond, J. (2016, January 24). Trump: 'I could shoot somebody and I wouldn't lose voters.' *CNN*. Retrieved from https://edition.cnn. com/2016/01/23/politics/donald-trump-shoot-somebody-support/

index.html.

Diamond, J., and Collinson, S. (2016, August 10). Trump: Gun Advocates Could Deal with Clinton. *CNN*. Retrieved from https://www.cnn.com/2016/08/09/politics/donald-trump-hillary-clinton-second-amendment/index.html.

DiAngelo, R. (2018). *White Fragility: Why It's So Hard for White People to Talk About Racism*. Boston, MA: Beacon Press.

Dias, B. G., and Ressler, K. J. (2014). Parental olfactory experience influences behavior and neural structure in subsequent generations. *Nature Neuroscience*, 17(1), 89-96.

Diaz, D. (2018, January 6). Trump: I'm a 'very stable genius'. *CNN*. Retrieved from https://www.cnn.com/2018/01/06/politics/donald-trump-white-house-fitness-very-stable-genius/index.html.

Dickinson, T. (2011, June 9). How Roger Ailes built the Fox News fear factory. *Rolling Stone*. Retrieved from https://www.rollingstone.com/politics/politics-news/how-roger-ailes-built-the-fox-news-fear-factory-244652/.

Dodes, L. (2017). Sociopathy. In B. X. Lee (Ed.), *The Dangerous Case of Donald Trump: 27 Psychiatrists and Mental Health Experts Assess a President*. New York, NY: Macmillan.

Du Bois, W. E. B. (1940). *Dusk of Dawn*. New York, NY: Harcourt Brace and Company.

Ehrenreich, B. (2001). *Nickel and Dimed: On (Not) Getting by in America*. New York, NY: Henry Holt and Company.

Eisenhower, D. D. (1965). *Waging Peace: The White House Years*. New York, NY: Doubleday and Company.

Eith, C., and Durose, M. R. (2011). *Contacts between Police and the Public, 2008*. Washington, D.C.: Department of Justice. Retrieved from https://www.bjs.gov/content/pub/pdf/cpp08.pdf.

Eligon, J. (2018). Hate crimes increase for the third consecutive year, FBI reports. *New York Times*. Retrieved from https://www.nytimes.com/2018/11/13/us/hate-crimes-fbi-2017.html.

Ellison, R. (1952). *The Invisible Man*. New York, NY: Random House.

Fahrenthold, D. A. (2016). Trump recorded having extremely lewd conversation about women in 2005. *Washington Post*. Retrieved from https://www.washingtonpost.com/politics/trump-recorded-having-extremely-lewd-conversation-about-women-in-2005/2016/10/07/3b9ce776-8cb4-11e6-bf8a-3d26847eeed4_story.html.

Federal Communications Commission (1949). *In the Matter of Editorializing by Broadcast Licensees 1949*. Washington, DC: Federal Communications Commission. Retrieved from https://www.scribd.com/document/385901903/In-the-Matter-of-Editorializing-by-Broadcast-Licensees-1949.

Feinberg, A. (2019, October 18). Trump's behavior this week has been so bizarre that psychologists, Republicans and ex-staffers are telling me they're worried. *Independent*. Retrieved from https://

www.independent.co.uk/voices/trump-pelosi-psychologists-syria-erdogan-bizarre-behavior-republicans-a9162396.html.

Feinberg, A., Branton, R., and Martinez-Ebers, V. (2019, March 22). Counties that hosted a 2016 Trump rally saw a 226 percent increase in hate crimes. *Washington Post*. Retrieved from https://www.washingtonpost.com/politics/2019/03/22/trumps-rhetoric-does-inspire-more-hate-crimes/.

Fingar, C. (2020, September 22). The silencing of psychiatry: is the Goldwater rule doing more harm than good ahead of the US 2020 election? *New Statesman*. Retrieved from https://www.newstatesman.com/world/2020/09/silencing-psychiatry-goldwater-rule-doing-more-harm-good-ahead-us-2020-election.

Fisher, M. (2016, August 3). Donald Trump, Perhaps Unwittingly, Exposes Paradox of Nuclear Arms. *New York Times*. Retrieved from https://www.nytimes.com/2016/08/04/world/donald-trump-nuclear-weapons.html.

Flood, A. (2020, June 18). John Bolton's bad reviews don't stop him topping U.S. book charts. *Guardian*. Retrieved from https://www.theguardian.com/books/2020/jun/18/john-bolton-bad-reviews-book-charts-the-room-where-it-happened-trump-presidency.

Friedman, L. and Plumer, B. (2020, April 28). Trump's response to virus reflects a long disregard for science. *New York Times*. Retrieved from https://www.nytimes.com/2020/04/28/climate/trump-coronavirus-climate-science.html.

Friedman, U. (2019, December 16). America is making the world more unstable. *Atlantic*. Retrieved from https://www.theatlantic.com/politics/archive/2019/12/donald-trump-global-instability-cfr-survey/603631/.

Fritze, J. (2019, August 8). Trump used words like 'invasion' and 'killer' to discuss immigrants at rallies 500 times. *USA Today*. Retrieved from https://www.usatoday.com/story/news/politics/elections/2019/08/08/trump-immigrants-rhetoric-criticized-el-paso-dayton-shootings/1936742001/.

Gallup (2020). *President Approval Ratings—Donald Trump*. Washington, DC: Gallup. Retrieved from https://news.gallup.com/poll/203198/presidential-approval-ratings-donald-trump.aspx.

Gamboa, S. (2015, June 16). Donald Trump announces presidential bid by trashing Mexico, Mexicans. *NBC News*. Retrieved from https://www.nbcnews.com/news/latino/donald-trump-announces-presidential-bid-trashing-mexico-mexicans-n376521.

Gandhi, M. (1993). Axioms of non-violence. In R. Iyer (Ed.), *The Essential Writings of Mahatma Gandhi*. New Delhi, India: Oxford University Press.

Gangel, J., and Herb, J. (2020, September 9). 'A magical force': new Trump-Kim letters provide window into their 'special friendship.' *CNN*. Retrieved from https://edition.cnn.com/2020/09/09/politics/kim-jong-un-trump-letters-rage-book/index.html.

Gersen, J. (2017, October 16). How anti-Trump psychiatrists are mobilizing behind the Twenty-Fifth Amendment. *New Yorker.* Retrieved from https://www.newyorker.com/news/news-desk/how-anti-trump-psychiatrists-are-mobilizing-behind-the-twenty-fifth-amendment.

Gierus, J., Mosiołek, A., Koweszko, T., Wnukiewicz, P., Kozyra, O., and Szulc, A. (2015). The Montreal Cognitive Assessment as a preliminary assessment tool in general psychiatry: Validity of MoCA in psychiatric patients. *General Hospital Psychiatry*, 37(5), 476-480.

Gilbert, R. E. (2015). The politics of presidential illness. *Politics and the Life Sciences*, 33(2), 58-76.

Gilligan, J. (1996). *Violence: Our Deadly Epidemic and Its Causes.* New York, NY: G.P. Putnam.

Gilligan, J. (2017). The issue is dangerousness, not mental illness. In B. X. Lee (Ed.), *The Dangerous Case of Donald Trump: 27 Psychiatrists and Mental Health Experts Assess a President.* New York, NY: Macmillan.

Gilson, D. (2015, February 11). The CIA's secret psychological profiles of dictators and world leaders are amazing: psychoanalyzing strongmen, from Castro to Saddam. *Mother Jones.* Retrieved from https://www.motherjones.com/politics/2015/02/cia-psychological-profiles-hitler-castro-putin-saddam/.

Givhan, R. (2015, November 20). Donald Trump thinks he's a fashion critic. Here's what our fashion critic thinks about him. *Washington Post.* Retrieved from https://www.washingtonpost.com/news/arts-and-entertainment/wp/2015/11/20/donald-trump-thinks-hes-a-fashion-critic-heres-what-our-fashion-critic-thinks-about-him/.

Glass, L. L. (2017, July 20). Dealing with American psychiatry's gag rule. *Psychiatric Times.* Retrieved from https://www.psychiatrictimes.com/view/dealing-american-psychiatrys-gag-rule.

Glass, L. L. (2017, July 28). Let psychiatrists talk about Trump's mental state. *Boston Globe.* Retrieved from https://www.bostonglobe.com/opinion/2017/07/28/let-psychiatrists-talk-about-trump-mental-state/hOBqRC8krC3AJBmrcAEEGM/story.html.

Goldberg, M. (2020a, May 11). We're All Casualties of Trump's War on Science. *New York Times.* Retrieved from https://www.nytimes.com/2020/05/11/opinion/coronavirus-trump.html.

Goldberg, J. (2020b, September 3). Trump: Americans who died in war are 'losers' and 'suckers'. *Atlantic.* Retrieved from https://www.theatlantic.com/politics/archive/2020/09/trump-americans-who-died-at-war-are-losers-and-suckers/615997/.

Golf News Net. (2020, September 27). How many times has President Donald Trump played golf while in office? *Golf News Net.* Retrieved from https://thegolfnewsnet.com/golfnewsnetteam/2020/09/27/how-many-times-president-donald-trump-played-golf-in-office-103836/.

Gourguechon, P. L. (2017, June 16). Is Trump mentally fit to be president?
Let's consult the U.S. Army's field manual on leadership. *Los
Angeles Times*. Retrieved from https://www.latimes.com/opinion/
op-ed/la-oe-gourguechon-25th-amendment-leadership-mental-
capacities-checklist-20170616-story.html.

Greenhouse, S. (2009). *The Big Squeeze: Tough Times for the American
Worker*. New York, NY: Anchor.

Gregory, A. (2020, January 17). Trump impeachment: Giuliani associate
Lev Parnas compares president to a cult leader. *Independent*.
Retrieved from https://www.independent.co.uk/news/world/
americas/us-politics/trump-impeachment-trial-parnas-cult-leader-
barr-ukraine-giuliani-a9288001.html.

Grohol, J. M. (2019, April 15). What the media get wrong about the
Goldwater Rule. *Psych. Central*. Retrieved from https://
psychcentral.com/blog/what-the-media-get-wrong-about-the-
goldwater-rule/.

Grohol, J. M. (2019, April 9). Mental health professionals: U.S. statistics
2017. *Psych. Central*. Retrieved from https://psychcentral.com/
blog/mental-health-professionals-us-statistics-2017/.

Guild, B. (2018, May 16). Trump says "We'll see what happens" on North
Korea. *CBS News*. Retrieved from https://www.cbsnews.com/
news/trump-uzbek-president-north-korea-see-what-happens/.

Guivarch, J., Piercecchi-Marti, M. D., and Poinso, F. (2018). Folie à deux
and homicide: Literature review and study of a complex clinical
case. *International Journal of Law and Psychiatry*, 61, 30-39.

Gun Violence Archive (2020). *Mass Shootings in 2019*. Washington,
DC: Gun Violence Archive. Retrieved from https://www.
gunviolencearchive.org/reports/mass-shooting?year=2019.

Gutowski, S. (2019, May 30). NRA membership dues, contributions
rebounded in 2018. *Washington Free Beacon*. Retrieved from
https://freebeacon.com/issues/nra-membership-dues-contributions-
rebounded-in-2018/.

Hafner, J. (2016, February 24). Donald Trump loves the 'poorly
educated'—and they love him. *USA Today*. Retrieved
from https://www.usatoday.com/story/news/politics/
onpolitics/2016/02/24/donald-trump-nevada-poorly-
educated/80860078/.

Harding, L. (2020, September 27). Disloyal: a memoir by Michael
Cohen—disgraced Trump lawyer's kiss and tell. *Guardian*.
Retrieved from https://www.theguardian.com/books/2020/sep/27/
disloyal-a-memoir-by-michael-cohen-review-disgraced-trump-
lawyers-kiss-and-tell.

Hare, R. D. (2003). *The Psychopathy Checklist–Revised*. Toronto, ON:
Multi-Health Systems.

Harvey, F. (2019, September 19). Scientists set out how to halve
greenhouse gas emissions by 2030. *Guardian*. Retrieved from

https://www.theguardian.com/environment/2019/sep/19/power-halve-greenhouse-gas-emissions-2030-climate-scientists.

Hassan, S. (2019). *The Cult of Trump: A Leading Cult Expert Explains How the President Uses Mind Control*. New York, NY: Simon and Schuster.

Helenowski, M. (2020, August 10). Billionaires have made an absolute killing during the pandemic. The number is staggering. *Mother Jones*. Retrieved from https://www.motherjones.com/politics/2020/08/billionaire-coronavirus-wealth-animation-covid-685-billion/.

Herman, E. S., and Chomsky, N. (1988). *Manufacturing Consent: The Political Economy of the Mass Media*. New York, NY: Pantheon Books.

Herman, J. L., and Lee, B. X. (2017). Professions and politics. In B. X. Lee (Ed.), *The Dangerous Case of Donald Trump: 27 Psychiatrists and Mental Health Experts Assess a President*. New York, NY: Macmillan.

Hesse, M. (2016, June 17). The 100 greatest descriptions of Donald Trump's hair ever written. *Chicago Tribune*. Retrieved from https://www.chicagotribune.com/opinion/commentary/ct-donald-trump-hair-20160617-story.html.

Horowitz, C. (1994). Trump's near-death experience. *New York*.

Horowitz, J. (2020, June 17). Inequality in America was huge before the pandemic: The stock market is making it worse. *CNN*. Retrieved from https://www.cnn.com/2020/06/17/investing/stock-market-inequality-coronavirus/index.html.

Houser, T. J. (1972). Fairness doctrine: an historical perspective. *Notre Dame Law Review*, 47, 550.

Hudson, J., and Sonne, P. (2020). Trump administration discussed conducting first US nuclear test in decades. *Washington Post*. Retrieved from https://www.washingtonpost.com/national-security/trump-administration-discussed-conducting-first-us-nuclear-test-in-decades/2020/05/22/a805c904-9c5b-11ea-b60c-3be060a4f8e1_story.html

Hueval, K. V. (2020, September 1). Trump hasn't ended endless wars: Congress must use the War Powers Resolution. *Washington Post*. Retrieved from https://www.washingtonpost.com/opinions/2020/09/01/trump-hasnt-ended-endless-wars-congress-must-use-war-powers-resolution/.

Jacobo, J. (2019, August 6). Cesar Sayoc sentenced to 20 years in prison for mailing pipe bombs to prominent Democrats, CNN. *ABC News*. Retrieved from https://abcnews.go.com/US/cesar-sayoc-sentenced-20-years-prison-mailing-pipe/story?id=64780616.

Jalonick, M. C. and Daly, M. (2016, July 22). Trump says U.S. will be richer, safer if he is president. *Associated Press*. Retrieved from https://apnews.com/d77f1f95ae4a49e89405091b3ca01650/trump-says-us-will-be-safer-richer-if-he-president.

Jantti, M., Bratsberg, B., Roed, K., Raaum, O., Naylor, R., Osterbacka, E., Bjorklund, A., and Eriksson, T. (2006). American exceptionalism in a new light: A comparison of intergenerational earnings mobility in the Nordic countries, the United Kingdom and the United States (Discussion Paper No. 1938). *IZA*. Retrieved from http://ftp.iza.org/dp1938.pdf.

Jhueck, D. (2017). A clinical case for the dangerousness of Donald J. Trump. In B. X. Lee (Ed.), *The Dangerous Case of Donald Trump: 27 Psychiatrists and Mental Health Experts Assess a President*. New York, NY: Macmillan.

Johnson, L. B. (1965). *President Lyndon B. Johnson's Special Message to the Congress, 89th Congress, 1st Session*.

Johnson, R., Persad, G., and Sisti, D. (2014). The Tarasoff rule: The implications of interstate variation and gaps in professional training. *Journal of the American Academy of Psychiatry and the Law*, 42(4), 469-477.

Karimi, F. (2019, April 24). Pipe bomb suspect Cesar Sayoc describes Trump rallies as 'new found drug.' *CNN*. Retrieved from https://edition.cnn.com/2019/04/24/us/cesar-sayoc-letter-trump-rallies/index.html.

Karni, A. (2020, September 9). Trump Resumes the Rallies He Cherishes, but Virus Vexes His Plans. *New York Times*. Retrieved from https://www.nytimes.com/2020/09/09/us/politics/trump-rally-nevada.html.

Karp, A. (2018). Briefing paper: Estimating global civilian-held firearms numbers. *Small Arms Survey*. Retrieved from http://www.smallarmssurvey.org/fileadmin/docs/T-Briefing-Papers/SAS-BP-Civilian-Firearms-Numbers.pdf.

Keillor, G. (2016, June 15). The braggart with the ducktail who would be president. *Chicago Tribune*. Retrieved from https://www.chicagotribune.com/opinion/commentary/ct-trump-orlando-congratulates-himself-keillor-perspec-0615-md-20160615-story.htm.

Kendall, J. (2020, April 25). Muzzled by Psychiatry in a Time of Crisis. *Mad in America*. Retrieved from https://www.madinamerica.com/2020/04/muzzled-psychiatry-time-crisis/.

Kendi, I. X. (2019). *How to be an Antiracist*. New York, NY: One World.

Kessler, G., Rizzo, S., and Kelly, M. (2020, July 13). President Trump has made more than 20,000 false or misleading claims. *Washington Post*. Retrieved from https://www.washingtonpost.com/politics/2020/07/13/president-trump-has-made-more-than-20000-false-or-misleading-claims/.

Kessler, R. C., Aguilar-Gaxiola, S., Alonso, J., Chatterji, S., Lee, S., Ormel, J., Üstün, T. B. and Wang, P. S. (2009). The global burden of mental disorders: an update from the WHO World Mental Health (WMH) surveys. *Epidemiologia e psichiatria sociale*, 18(1), 23-33.

Kluger, J. (2020, May 12). Accidental Poisonings Increased After President Trump's Disinfectant Comments. *Time*. Retrieved from https://time.com/5835244/accidental-poisonings-trump/.

Knowles, E., and DiMuccio, S. (2018, November 29). How Donald Trump appeals to men secretly insecure about their manhood. *Washington Post*. Retrieved from https://www.washingtonpost.com/news/monkey-cage/wp/2018/11/29/how-donald-trump-appeals-to-men-secretly-insecure-about-their-manhood/.

Kobes Du Mez, K. (2020, August 27). The secret to Donald Trump's support among evangelicals: His leadership style aligns with a vision of Christian manhood. *Marketwatch*. Retrieved from https://www.marketwatch.com/story/the-secret-to-donald-trumps-support-among-evangelicals-his-leadership-style-aligns-with-a-vision-of-christian-manhood-11598539487.

Kohut, H. (1985). *Self Psychology and the Humanities: Reflections on a New Psychoanalytic Approach*. New York, NY: W.W. Norton.

Kristensen, H. M., and Korda, M. (2020). *Status of World Nuclear Forces*. Washington, DC: Federation of American Scientists. Retrieved from https://fas.org/issues/nuclear-weapons/status-world-nuclear-forces/.

Kroll, J., and Pouncey, C. (2016). The ethics of APA's Goldwater rule. *Journal of the American Academy of Psychiatry and the Law*, 44(2), 226-235.

Kruse, M. (2019, March 22). Can Trump Survive Mueller? *Politico*. Retrieved from https://www.politico.com/magazine/story/2019/03/22/trump-mueller-report-survive-226101.

Kruse, M. (2020, March 13). What is Trump Without His Crowds? *Politico*. Retrieved from https://www.politico.com/news/magazine/2020/03/13/donald-trump-coronavirus-crowds-129048.

Kulkarni, S. C., Levin-Rector, A., Ezzati, M., and Murray, C. J. L. (2011). Falling behind: life expectancy in U.S. counties from 2000 to 2007 in an international context. *Population Health Metrics*, 9(1), 16.

Kurtz, J. (2016, March 30). Hypnotist: Trump winning with 'Trumpnosis.' *Hill*. Retrieved from https://thehill.com/blogs/in-the-know/274609-hypnotist-trump-winning-with-trumpnosis.

LaMotte, S. (2016, October 14). Is the 'Trump Effect' damaging our psyches? CNN. Retrieved from https://www.cnn.com/2016/10/14/health/trump-effect-damaging-american-psyche/index.html.

Langer, W. C. (1972). *The Mind of Adolf Hitler*. New York, NY: Basic Books.

Le Bon, G. (1896). *The Crowd: A Study of the Popular Mind*. London, U.K.: T. F. Unwin.

Lee, B. X. (2019a). *Violence: An Interdisciplinary Approach to Causes, Consequences, and Cures*. New York, NY: Wiley-Blackwell.

Lee, B. X. (2019b). *The Dangerous Case of Donald Trump: 37 Psychiatrists and Mental Health Experts Assess a President— Updated and Expanded with New Essays*. New York, NY:

Macmillan.

Lee, B. X. (2019c, July 2). American psychiatry's complicity with the state. *Medium*. Retrieved from https://medium.com/@bandyxlee/american-psychiatrys-complicity-with-the-state-8aaf3cee1397.

Lee, B. X. (2020a, March 30). There's a Madman in the White House … And He's Getting Worse. *DC Report*. Retrieved from https://www.dcreport.org/2020/03/30/theres-a-mad-man-in-the-white-house-and-hes-getting-worse/.

Lee, B. X. (2020b, August 13). Mary Trump: 'He understands he is not the person he pretends to be.' *DC Report*. Retrieved from https://www.dcreport.org/2020/08/13/mary-trump-he-understands-he-is-not-the-person-he-pretends-to-be/.

Lee, B. X. (2020c, August 14). The Trump mental health pandemic: A blow-by-blow account of how mental health experts warned that what happened would happen—that a president was likely going to kill (hundreds of) thousands of Americans—but went unheeded. *Medium*. Retrieved from https://medium.com/@bandyxlee/the-trump-mental-health-pandemic-56d4197ab32a.

Lee, B. X., Fisher, E. B., and Glass, L. L. (2019, September 25). A professional association's complicity with tyranny. *Bioethics*. Retrieved from http://www.bioethics.net/2019/09/a-professional-associations-complicity-with-tyranny/.

Lee, B. X., Fisher, E. B., Glass, L. L., Merikangas, J. R., and Gilligan, J. (2019). *Mental Health Analysis of the Special Counsel's Report on the Investigation into Russian Interference in the 2016 Presidential Election*. New York, NY: World Mental Health Coalition. Retrieved from https://www.documentcloud.org/documents/5993879-Report-on-the-Mueller-Report.html.

Lee, B. X., West, H., and Washington, K. (2020, May 7). How to escape our abusive relationship with Trump. *Saint Louis American*. Retrieved from http://www.stlamerican.com/news/political_eye/how-to-escape-our-abusive-relationship-with-trump/article_ea10ede4-9015-11ea-88b1-03c4b0d1689e.html.

Lenzner, R. (2012, March 26). The Great Gatsby curve is a threat to the American Dream. *Forbes*. Retrieved from https://www.forbes.com/sites/robertlenzner/2012/03/26/the-great-gatsby-curve-is-a-threat-to-the-american-dream/#1829812f5a43).

Levine, M. (2020, May 30). 'No Blame?' ABC News finds 54 cases invoking 'Trump' in connection with violence, threats, alleged assaults. *ABC News*. Retrieved from https://abcnews.go.com/Politics/blame-abc-news-finds-17-cases-invoking-trump/story?id=58912889.

Lewis, S. (2020, September 5). Coronavirus model projects U.S. deaths will surpass 400,000 by end of year. *CBS News*. Retrieved from https://www.cbsnews.com/news/covid-19-united-states-coronavirus-deaths-projection-400000-by-end-of-year/.

Lifton, R. J. (1961). *Thought Reform and the Psychology of Totalism: A*

Study of 'Brainwashing' in China. New York, NY: W.W. Norton and Company.

Lifton, R. J. (2017). Our Witness to Malignant Normality. In B. X. Lee (Ed.), *The Dangerous Case of Donald Trump: 27 Psychiatrists and Mental Health Experts Assess a President*. New York, NY: Macmillan.

Lifton, R. J. (2019). *Losing Reality: On Cults, Cultism, and the Mindset of Political and Religious Zealotry*. New York, NY New Press.

Lippmann, W. (1922). *Public Opinion*. New York, NY: Harcourt, Brace and Co.

Liptak, K. (2020, August 17). Trump warns of 'rigged election' as he uses conspiracy and fear to counter Biden's convention week. *CNN*. Retrieved from https://www.cnn.com/2020/08/17/politics/donald-trump-campaign-swing/index.html.

Liptak, K. (2020, August 20). Trump embraces QAnon conspiracy because 'they like me.' *CNN Politics*. Retrieved from https://www.cnn.com/2020/08/19/politics/donald-trump-qanon/index.html.

Loeb, V., Lavelle, M., and Feldman, S. (2020, September 1). President Donald Trump's Climate Change Record Has Been a Boon for Oil Companies, and a Threat to the Planet. *Inside Climate News*. Retrieved from https://insideclimatenews.org/news/31082020/candidate-profile-donald-trump-climate-change-election-2020.

Luo, M. (2017, August 11). How the NRA manipulates gun owners and the media. *New Yorker*. Retrieved on: https://www.newyorker.com/news/news-desk/how-the-nra-manipulates-gun-owners-and-the-media.

Lye, H. (2020, May 19). What is Trump's 'super-duper' missile? *Army Technology*. Retrieved from https://www.army-technology.com/features/what-is-trumps-super-duper-missile/.

Malkin, C. (2017). Pathological narcissism and politics: A lethal mix. In B. X. Lee (Ed.), *The Dangerous Case of Donald Trump: 27 Psychiatrists and Mental Health Experts Assess a President*. New York, NY: Macmillan.

Mangan, D. (2016, September 26). Trump brags about not paying taxes: 'That makes me smart.' *CNBC News*. Retrieved from https://www.cnbc.com/2016/09/26/trump-brags-about-not-paying-taxes-that-makes-me-smart.html.

Martinez, J., and Smith, G. A. (2016, November 9). How the faithful voted: A preliminary 2016 analysis. *Pew Research*. Retrieved from https://www.pewresearch.org/fact-tank/2016/11/09/how-the-faithful-voted-a-preliminary-2016-analysis/.

Maxwell, C., and Solomon, D. (2018, November 7). 25 ways Sessions and his justice department criminalized and terrorized communities of color. *Center for American Progress*. Retrieved from https://www.americanprogress.org/issues/race/news/2018/11/07/460631/25-ways-sessions-justice-department-criminalized-terrorized-communities-color/.

Mayer, J. (2016, July 25). Donald Trump's ghostwriter tells all. *New Yorker*. Retrieved from https://www.newyorker.com/magazine/2016/07/25/donald-trumps-ghostwriter-tells-all.

McCarthy, T. (2020, April 11). Trump v. the states: How the president is remaking the government in his image. *Guardian*. Retrieved from https://www.theguardian.com/us-news/2020/apr/11/trump-states-governors-clashes.

Mika, E. (2017). Who Goes Trump? Tyranny as a Triumph of Narcissism. In B. X. Lee (Ed.), *The Dangerous Case of Donald Trump: 27 Psychiatrists and Mental Health Experts Assess a President*. New York, NY: Macmillan.

Milbank, D. (2018, November 28). Does Trump's great gut mean a tiny brain? *Washington Post*. Retrieved from https://www.washingtonpost.com/opinions/why-would-trump-need-brains-when-he-has-a-gut/2018/11/28/75bc6c38-f341-11e8-80d0-f7e1948d55f4_story.html.

Milman, O. (2020, March 31). Seven of Donald Trump's Most Misleading Coronavirus Claims. *Guardian*. Retrieved from https://www.theguardian.com/us-news/2020/mar/28/trump-coronavirus-misleading-claims.

Mitchell, L. (2020, April 23). Trump's followers are demonstrating their loyalty. *European Interest*. Retrieved from https://www.europeaninterest.eu/article/trumps-followers-demonstrating-loyalty/.

Monahan, J., Steadman, H. J., Silver, E., Appelbaum, P. S., Robbins, P. C., Mulvey, E. P., Roth, L. H., Grisso, T. and Banks, S. (2001). *Rethinking Risk Assessment: The MacArthur Study of Mental Disorder and Violence*. New York, NY: Oxford University Press.

Mueller, R. S. (2019b). *Report on the Investigation into Russian Interference in the 2016 Presidential Election*. Washington, DC: U.S. Department of Justice. Retrieved from https://www.justice.gov/storage/report.pdf.

National Rifle Association (2016). *Targeted Candidates, 2016 Cycle*. Washington, DC: Open Secrets. Retrieved from https://www.opensecrets.org/outsidespending/recips.php?cmte=National+Rifle+Assn&cycle=2016.

New York Times Editorial Board (2016, March 14). The Trump campaign gives license to violence. *New York Times*. Retrieved from https://www.nytimes.com/2016/03/15/opinion/the-trump-campaign-gives-license-to-violence.html.

New York Times Editorial Board (2020, September 9). Mr. Trump knew it was deadly and airborne. *New York Times*. Retrieved from https://www.nytimes.com/2020/09/09/opinion/trump-bob-woodward-coronavirus.html.

Newburger, E. 'Secretive Cabals, Fear of Immigrants and the Tea Party: How the Financial Crisis Led to the Rise of Donald Trump.' CNBC. CNBC, September 11, 2018. Retrieved from https://www.

cnbc.com/2018/09/10/how-the-financial-crisis-led-to-the-rise-of-donald-trump.html.

O'Laughlin, F. (2020, April 28). Health officials: Man drank toxic cleaning product after Trump's comments on disinfectants. *WHDH*. Retrieved from https://whdh.com/news/health-officials-man-drank-toxic-cleaning-product-after-trumps-comments-on-disinfectants/.

Oprysko, C. (2020, March 13). 'I don't take responsibility at all': Trump deflects blame for coronavirus testing fumble. *Politico*. Retrieved from https://www.politico.com/news/2020/03/13/trump-coronavirus-testing-128971.

Oprysko, C. (2020, May 18). Trump says he's taking hydroxychloroquine, despite scientists' concerns. *Politico*. Retrieved from https://www.politico.com/news/2020/05/18/trump-says-hes-taking-unproven-anti-malarial-drug-265546.

Oprysko, C. (2020, June 12). Trump says he'll leave office peacefully if he loses in November. *Politico*. Retrieved from https://www.politico.com/news/2020/06/12/trump-says-will-leave-office-peacefully-if-he-loses-315736.

Organisation for Economic Co-operation and Development (2020). *Life Expectancy at Birth*. Paris, France: Organisation for Economic Co-operation and Development. Retrieved from https://doi.org/10.1787/27e0fc9d-en.

Ouimet, M. (2012). A world of homicides: The effect of economic development, income inequality, and excess infant mortality on the homicide rate for 165 countries in 2010. *Homicide Studies*, 16(3), 238-258.

Packer, G. (2020, June). We are living in a failed state: the coronavirus didn't break America. It revealed what was already broken. *Atlantic*. Retrieved from https://www.theatlantic.com/magazine/archive/2020/06/underlying-conditions/610261/.

Pagano, P. (1987, June 21). Reagan's veto kills fairness doctrine bill. *Los Angeles Times*. Retrieved from https://www.latimes.com/archives/la-xpm-1987-06-21-mn-8908-story.html).

Panning, J. C. (2017). Trump anxiety disorder: The Trump effect on the mental health of half the nation and special populations. In B. X. Lee (Ed.), *The Dangerous Case of Donald Trump: 27 Psychiatrists and Mental Health Experts Assess a President*. New York, NY: Macmillan.

Personal Communication (2020). New York, NY.

Peters, J. W. (2020, April 2). Alarm, Denial, Blame: The Pro-Trump Media's Coronavirus Distortion. *New York Times*. Retrieved from https://www.nytimes.com/2020/04/01/us/politics/hannity-limbaugh-trump-coronavirus.html.

Pettigrew, T. F. (2017). Social psychological perspectives on Trump supporters. *Journal of Social and Political Psychology*, 5(1), 107-116.

Pew Research Center (2018, August 9). An investigation of the 2016 electorate, based on validated voters. *Pew Research Center*. Retrieved from https://www.pewresearch.org/politics/2018/08/09/an-examination-of-the-2016-electorate-based-on-validated-voters/.

Phillips, A. (2020, June 13). Why QAnon supporters are winning congressional primaries. *Washington Post*. Retrieved from https://www.washingtonpost.com/politics/2020/06/13/why-qanon-supporters-are-winning-congressional-primaries/.

Pilkington, E. (2018, November 1). Feel the love, feel the hate: My week in the cauldron of Trump's wild rallies. *Guardian*. Retrieved from https://www.theguardian.com/us-news/2018/nov/01/trump-rallies-america-midterms-white-house.

Podur, J. (2019, January 31). Mind control: How social media supercharged the propaganda system. *Salon*. Retrieved from https://www.salon.com/2019/01/31/mind-control-how-social-media-supercharged-the-propaganda-system_partner/.

Popper, M., and Mayseless, O. (2003). Back to basics: Applying a parenting perspective to transformational leadership. *Leadership Quarterly*, 14(1), 41-65.

Porter, T. (2019, December 5). 350 health professionals sign letter to Congress claiming Trump's mental health is deteriorating dangerously amid impeachment proceedings. *Business Insider*. Retrieved from https://www.businessinsider.com/psychiatrists-submit-warning-trumps-mental-health-deteriorating-2019-12.

Post, J. M. (2014). *Narcissism and Politics: Dreams of Glory*. Cambridge, U.K.: Cambridge University Press.

Post, J. M. (2019). The Charismatic Leader-Follower Relationship and Trump's Base. In B. X. Lee (Ed.), *The Dangerous Case of Donald Trump: 37 Psychiatrists and Mental Health Experts Assess a President—Updated and Expanded with New Essays*. New York, NY: Macmillan.

Potok, M. (2017, February 15). The year in hate and extremism. *Southern Poverty Law Center*. Retrieved from https://www.splcenter.org/fighting-hate/intelligence-report/2017/year-hate-and-extremism.

Poundstone, W. (2016, July 21). A rigorous scientific look into the 'Fox News effect.' *Forbes*. Retrieved from https://www.forbes.com/sites/quora/2016/07/21/a-rigorous-scientific-look-into-the-fox-news-effect/#51f47d5f12ab.

Qiu, L., Marsh, B., and Huang, J. (2020). The President vs. the Experts: How Trump played down the coronavirus. *New York Times*. Retrieved from https://www.nytimes.com/interactive/2020/03/18/us/trump-coronavirus-statements-timeline.html.

Regents of the University of California v. Superior Court of Los Angeles County, 3 Cal.3d 529, 91 Cal. Rptr. 57, 476 P.2d 457 (Cal. 1970).

Risen, J. (2015, April 30). American Psychological Association bolstered CIA torture program, report says. *New York Times*. Retrieved from https://www.nytimes.com/2015/05/01/us/report-says-american-psychological-association-collaborated-on-torture-justification.html.

Roberts, R. (2016, April 28). I sat next to Donald Trump at the infamous 2011 White House correspondents' dinner. *Washington Post*. Retrieved from https://www.washingtonpost.com/lifestyle/style/i-sat-next-to-donald-trump-at-the-infamous-2011-white-house-correspondents-dinner/2016/04/27/5cf46b74-0bea-11e6-8ab8-9ad050f76d7d_story.html.

Roberts, S., and Rizzo., M. (2020). The psychology of American racism. *American Psychologist*, in press.

Robins, R. S., and Post, J. M. (1997). *Political Paranoia: The Psychopolitics of Hatred*. New Haven, CT: Yale University Press.

Rogers, K. (2018, October 12). The Trump Rally: A Play in Three Acts. *New York Times*. Retrieved from https://www.nytimes.com/interactive/2018/10/12/us/politics/trump-maga-rally-play.html.

Rogers, K. (2020, March 17). Trump now claims he always knew coronavirus would be a pandemic. *New York Times*. Retrieved from https://www.nytimes.com/2020/03/17/us/politics/trump-coronavirus.html.

Rupar, A. (2020, August 11). How Trump's mail voting sabotage could result in an election night nightmare. *Vox*. Retrieved from https://www.vox.com/2020/8/11/21358960/trump-mail-voting-sabotage-explained.

Saad, L. (2019). *What Percentage of Americans Own Guns?* Washington, DC: Gallup. Retrieved from https://news.gallup.com/poll/264932/percentage-americans-own-guns.aspx.

Saletan, W. (2020, August 9). The Trump pandemic. *Slate*. Retrieved from https://slate.com/news-and-politics/2020/08/trump-coronavirus-deaths-timeline.html.

Schiffer, I. (1973). *Charisma: A Psychoanalytic Look at Mass Society*. Toronto, ON: University of Toronto Press.

Semega, J., Kollar, M., Creamer, J., and Mohanty, A. (2018). *Income and Poverty in the United States*. Washington, DC: U.S. Census Bureau.

Senko, J., Rackoff, A., and Modine, M. (2015). *The Brainwashing of My Dad* [Motion Picture]. United States: Cinco Dedos Peliculas.

Sennett, R., and Cobb, J. (1972). *The Hidden Injuries of Class*. New York, NY: Vintage.

Sherman, G. (2017). *The Loudest Voice in the Room: How the Brilliant, Bombastic Roger Ailes Built Fox News—and Divided a Country*. New York, NY: Random House.

Sherman, G. (2020, June 18). "Make sure I win": John Bolton's unredacted book shows what Trump was really trying to hide. *Vanity Fair*. Retrieved from https://www.vanityfair.com/news/2020/06/boltons-unredacted-book-shows-trump-trying-to-hide#intcid=recommendations_vf-trending-legacy_f9ee6d14-91d2-4d54-9d9e-78dfd7c2542a_popular4-1.

Sheth, S. (2020, April 14). Trump falsely claims that 'when somebody is the president of the United States, the authority is total.' *Business Insider*. Retrieved from https://www.businessinsider.com/coronavirus-trump-claims-president-authority-is-total-2020-4.

Shih, G. (2020, February 6). Chinese doctor who tried to raise alarm on coronavirus in Wuhan dies on 'front line' of medical fight. *Washington Post*. Retrieved from https://www.washingtonpost.com/world/asia_pacific/chinese-doctor-who-tried-to-raise-alarm-on-coronavirus-in-wuhan-dies-from-disease/2020/02/06/8bf305a2-48f9-11ea-8a1f-de1597be6cbc_story.html.

Shpancer, N. (2020, May 2). Emperor's New Words: Trump Insists Word Salad Is Steak. *Psychology Today*. Retrieved from https://www.psychologytoday.com/us/blog/insight-therapy/202005/emperor-s-new-words-trump-insists-word-salad-is-steak.

Sikich, C., Lange, K. and Hays, H. V. (2018, November 5). Instant recap: Trump urges Fort Wayne crowd to 'vote for Mike Braun tomorrow.' *Indy Star*. Retrieved from https://eu.indystar.com/story/news/politics/2018/11/05/donald-trump-fort-wayne-indiana-rally-today-live-updates/1889395002/.

Singer, T. (2017). Trump and the American collective psyche. In B. X. Lee (Ed.), *The Dangerous Case of Donald Trump: 27 Psychiatrists and Mental Health Experts Assess a President*. New York, NY: Macmillan.

Slutkin, G. (2017). Reducing violence as the next great public health achievement. *Nature Human Behaviour*, 1(1), 0025.

Smith, A. (2017, May 19). Trump to Russian diplomats: Firing 'nut job' James Comey took 'great pressure' off me. *Business Insider*. Retrieved from https://www.businessinsider.com/trump-nut-job-james-comey-russia-2017-5?r=US&IR=T.

Smith, D., and Wong, J. C. (2020, August 19). Trump tacitly endorses baseless QAnon conspiracy theory linked to violence. *Guardian*. Retrieved from https://www.theguardian.com/us-news/2020/aug/19/trump-qanon-praise-conspiracy-theory-believers.

Snyder, H. N. (2011). *Arrest in the United States, 1980-2009*. Washington, DC: Department of Justice. Retrieved from https://www.bjs.gov/content/pub/pdf/aus8009.pdf.

Snyder, T. (2017). On Tyranny: Twenty Lessons from the Twentieth Century. New York, NY: Crown/Archetype.

Speaker's Press Office (2020, February 26). *Pelosi Statement on House Brief in Congressional Oversight Supreme Court Cases*. Washington, DC: Congresswoman Nancy Pelosi's Press Office. Retrieved from https://pelosi.house.gov/news/press-releases/pelosi-statement-on-house-brief-in-congressional-oversight-supreme-court-cases.

Sonne, P., Jaffe, G., and Dawsey, J. (2020, January 12). Killing of Soleimani reflects an aggressive national security team not inclined to curb Trump. *Washington Post*. Retrieved from https://www.washingtonpost.com/world/national-security/killing-of-soleimani-reflects-an-aggressive-national-security-team-not-inclined-to-curb-trump/2020/01/12/a83f5346-333c-11ea-898f-eb846b7e9feb_story.html.

Southern Poverty Law Center (2020, March 18). The year in hate and extremism 2019: A report from the Southern Poverty Law Center. *Southern Poverty Law Center*. Retrieved from https://www.splcenter.org/news/2020/03/18/year-hate-and-extremism-2019.

Stone, A. (2018, April 19). The psychiatrist's Goldwater rule in the Trump era. *Lawfare*. Retrieved from https://www.lawfareblog.com/psychiatrists-goldwater-rule-trump-era.

Stout, M. (2005). *The Sociopath Next Door: The Ruthless Versus the Rest of Us*. New York, NY: Broadway Books.

Sullivan, K. (2018, November 28). Washington Post: Trump says his 'gut' can tell him more than 'anybody else's brain can ever tell me. *CNN*. Retrieved from https://www.cnn.com/2018/11/27/politics/washington-post-trump-gut/index.html.

Sullivan, M. (2020, April 13). What it really means when Trump calls a story 'fake news.' *Washington Post*. Retrieved from https://www.washingtonpost.com/lifestyle/media/what-it-really-means-when-trump-calls-a-story-fake-news/2020/04/13/56fbe2c0-7d8c-11ea-9040-68981f488eed_story.html.

Tarasoff v. Regents of the University of California, 17 Cal.3d 425, 131 Cal. Rptr. 14, 551 P.2d 334 (Cal. 1976).

Taylor, K. (2006). *Brainwashing: The Science of Thought Control*. New York, NY: Oxford University Press.

Teng, B. (2017). Trauma, time, truth, and Trump. In B. X. Lee (Ed.), *The Dangerous Case of Donald Trump: 27 Psychiatrists and Mental Health Experts Assess a President*. New York, NY: Macmillan.

Tonry, M., and Melewski, M. (2008). The malign effects of drug and crime control policies on black Americans. *Crime and Justice*, 37(1), 1-44.

Toobin, J. (2018, August 28). A new book details the damage done by the right-wing media in 2016. *New Yorker*. Retrieved from https://www.newyorker.com/news/daily-comment/a-new-book-details-the-damage-done-by-the-right-wing-media-in-2016.

Toole, J. F., Link, A. S., and Smith, J. H. (1997). Disability in U.S. presidents report: Recommendations and commentaries by the working group. *Archives of Neurology*, 54(10), 1256-1264.

Trezpacz, P. T., Hochstetler, H., Wang, S., Walker, B., and Saykin, A. J. (2015). Relationship between the Montreal Cognitive Assessment and Mini-Mental State Examination for assessment of mild cognitive impairment in older adults. *BMC Geriatrics*, 15(1), 107.

Trump, D. J., and Schwartz, T. (2009). *Trump: The Art of the Deal*. New York, NY: Ballantine Books.

Trump, M. L. (2020). *Too Much and Never Enough: How My Family Created the World's Most Dangerous Man*. New York, NY: Simon and Schuster.

Turse, N. (2020, April 22). U.S. airstrikes hit all-time high as coronavirus spreads in Somalia. *Intercept*. Retrieved from https://theintercept.com/2020/04/22/coronavirus-somalia-airstrikes/.

Ulman, R. B., and Abse, D. W. (1983). The group psychology of mass madness: Jonestown. *Political Psychology*, 637-661.

United Nations (2018). *Report of the Special Rapporteur on Extreme Poverty and Human Rights on his Mission to the United States of America*. Geneva, Switzerland: United Nations. Retrieved from https://undocs.org/A/HRC/38/33/ADD.1.

Vance, J. D. (2016). *Hillbilly Elegy: A Memoir of a Family and Culture in Crisis*. New York, NY: HarperCollins Books.

Virchow, R. (1848). *Die Medizinische reform*, 2.

Wade, P. (2020, August 17). Trump says he'll seek third term because 'they spied on me.' *Rolling Stone*. Retrieved from https://www.rollingstone.com/politics/politics-news/trump-third-term-because-they-spied-on-him-1045743/.

Waldman, P. (2019, December 4). The world is laughing at Donald Trump. *Washington Post*. Retrieved from https://www.washingtonpost.com/opinions/2019/12/04/world-is-laughing-donald-trump/.

Walker, L. E. A. (2017). *The Battered Woman Syndrome*. New York, NY: Springer Publishing.

Ward, M. (2020, April 15). 15 times Trump praised China as coronavirus was spreading around the world. *Politico*. Retrieved from https://www.politico.com/news/2020/04/15/trump-china-coronavirus-188736.

Washington, K. (2019). Persistent Enslavement Systemic Trauma: The Deleterious Impact of Trump's Rhetoric on Black and Brown People. In B. X. Lee (Ed.), *The Dangerous Case of Donald Trump: 37 Psychiatrists and Mental Health Experts Assess a President—Updated and Expanded with New Essays*. New York, NY: Macmillan.

Weber, M. (1922). Theory of social and economic organization. Chapter: "The nature of charismatic authority and its routinization," translated by A. R. Anderson and T. Parsons.

Wehner, P. (2020, September 4). Why Trump supporters can't admit who he really is. *Atlantic*. Retrieved from https://www.theatlantic.com/ideas/archive/2020/09/predicate-fear/616009/.

Well Being Trust (2020). The Well Being Trust and the Robert Graham Center analysis: the Covid pandemic could lead to 75,000 additional deaths from alcohol and drug misuse and suicide. *Well Being Trust*. Retrieved from https://wellbeingtrust.org/areas-of-focus/policy-and-advocacy/reports/projected-deaths-of-despair-during-covid-19/.

Wellman, D. (1993). *Portraits of White Racism*. Cambridge, U.K.: Cambridge University Press.

West, H. (2017). In relationship with an abusive president. In B. X. Lee (Ed.), *The Dangerous Case of Donald Trump: 27 Psychiatrists* and *Mental Health Experts Assess a President*. New York, NY: Macmillan.

West, H. C., and Sabol, W. J. (2008). *Prisoners in 2007*. Washington, DC: Department of Justice. Retrieved from https://www.bjs.gov/content/pub/pdf/p07.pdf.

Wilkinson, R. G., and Pickett, K. (2009). *The Spirit Level: Why Greater Equality Makes Societies Stronger*. London, U.K.: Bloomsbury Press.

Wilner, A. R. (1984). *The Spellbinders*. New Haven, CT: Yale University Press.

Wise, J. (2019, March 14). Trump suggests that it could get 'very bad' if military, police, biker supporters play 'tough'. *Hill*. Retrieved from https://thehill.com/homenews/administration/434110-trump-suggests-that-things-could-get-very-bad-if-military-police.

Wolfsthal, J. (2020). *Blundering towards Nuclear Chaos*. Washington, DC: Global Zero. Retrieved from https://www.globalzero.org/blundering-toward-nuclear-chaos-2020/.

Woodward, B. (2018). *Fear*. New York, NY: Simon and Schuster.

Woodward, B. (2020). *Rage*. New York, NY: Simon and Schuster.

Woodward, B., and Bernstein, C. (1974). *All the President's Men*. New York, NY: Simon and Schuster.

Woolf, S. H., and Schoomaker, H. (2019). Life expectancy and mortality rates in the United States, 1959-2017. *JAMA*, 322(20), 1996-2016.

World Health Organization (2001). *Mental Health: New Understanding, New Hope*. Geneva, Switzerland: World Health Organization. Retrieved from https://www.who.int/whr/2001/en/whr01_en.pdf?ua=1.

World Health Organization (2008). *Global Burden of Disease, Disease and Injury Regional Estimates*. Geneva, Switzerland: World Health Organization. Retrieved from http://www.who.int/healthinfo/global_burden_disease/GBD_report_2004update_full.pdf.

World Medical Association (1948). *Declaration of Geneva*. Ferney-Voltaire, France: World Medical Association. Retrieved from https://www.wma.net/wp-content/uploads/2018/07/Decl-of-Geneva-v1948-1.pdf.

World Medical Association (2020). *World Medical Association: Declaration of Geneva*. Retrieved from https://www.wma.net/policies-post/wma-declaration-of-geneva/.

World Mental Health Coalition (2020). *Prescription for Survival*. New York, NY: World Mental Health Coalition. Retrieved from https://worldmhc.org/prescription-for-survival/.

Worldometers (2020). *Covid-19 Coronavirus Pandemic*. Retrieved from https://www.worldometers.info/coronavirus/.

Wright, R. (2017, April 14). Trump drops the mother of all bombs on Afghanistan. *New Yorker*. Retrieved from https://www.newyorker.com/news/news-desk/trump-drops-the-mother-of-all-bombs-on-afghanistan.

Zinner, J., and Lee, B. X. (2020, August 12). 'A failure to develop an inner sense of worth or self-esteem.' *DC Report*. Retrieved from https://www.dcreport.org/2020/08/12/a-failure-to-develop-an-inner-sense-of-worth-or-self-esteem/.

Zorn, E. (2018, July 31). 'Trump derangement syndrome' afflicts supporters more than critics of Trump. *Chicago Tribune*. Retrieved on: https://www.chicagotribune.com/columns/eric-zorn/ct-perspec-zorn-trump-derangement-syndrome-20180801-story.html.

ABOUT THE AUTHOR

Bandy X. Lee, M.D., M.Div., is a medical doctor, a forensic psychiatrist, and a world expert on violence. She became known to the public by leading a group of mental health professional colleagues in breaking the silence about the current U.S. president's dangerous mental impairments. She is currently president of the World Mental Health Coalition, which is dedicated to promoting public health and safety.

During medical school, she also obtained a divinity degree to expand her understanding of the human condition. Trained at Yale and Harvard Universities, she was chief resident at Massachusetts General Hospital and a research fellow at the National Institute of Mental Health. As a faculty member of the Law and Psychiatry Division at Yale School of Medicine for seventeen years, she taught at Yale Law School for fifteen of those years, covering the mental health aspects of asylum law, criminal justice, and veterans' legal services. Her clinical work consists of psychiatric services at maximum-security prisons and in state hospitals, in addition to working as an expert witness for the state and federal courts.

She served as Director of Research for the Center for the Study of Violence (Harvard, U. Penn., N.Y.U., and Yale), co-founded Yale's Violence and Health Study Group at the MacMillan Center for International Studies, and has led an academic collaborators project for the World Health Organization's Violence Prevention Alliance, helping to translate scholarship into implementation and to support research in low- and middle-income countries. She has consulted with governments on prison reform and community violence prevention, such as for France, Ireland, Alabama, California, Connecticut, Massachusetts, and New York. She has also played a key role in initiating reforms at Rikers Island, a correctional facility in New York City known for extreme levels of violence.

She created a popular Global Health Studies course at Yale College, "Violence: Causes and Cures," which led to the most comprehensive textbook on the subject to date, Violence: An Interdisciplinary Approach to Causes,

Consequences, and Cures (Wiley-Blackwell, 2019). She published over one hundred peer-reviewed articles and chapters, fifteen edited scholarly books and journal special issues, over two hundred op-eds in outlets such as the Guardian, the New York Times, the Boston Globe, the Independent, and Politico, and the New York Times bestseller, The Dangerous Case of Donald Trump: 37 Psychiatrists and Mental Health Experts Assess a President (Macmillan, 2017 and 2019). The last proceeded from an ethics conference at Yale School of Medicine, which led her to consulting with over fifty members of the U.S. Congress.

The World Mental Health Coalition (worldmhc.org) is a professional organization that assembles mental health experts to collaborate with other disciplines for the betterment of public mental health. It also attempts to step in where the American Psychiatric Association has failed in societal leadership. Her current goals center around educating the public on mental health matters that have national and international consequence, so that it can be empowered to protect itself.

She owes great debt to her maternal grandfather, Dr. Geun-Young Lee, a renowned physician who helped inspire many in reconstructing South Korean society after the war, and to her mother, who continued to practice his philosophy in her beloved United States. Everything that the author has done, especially since this presidency, emanates from and is dedicated to her beloved late mother, Dr. Inmyung Lee, healer, writer, and musician.

Made in the USA
Las Vegas, NV
26 March 2024

87802505R00105